The Crimean Campaign With "The Connaught Rangers," 1854-55-56

The Crimean Campaign With "The Connaught Rangers," 1854-55-56

A Personal Account of a Serving Officer of the Regiment

Nathaniel Steevens

LEONAUR

The Crimean Campaign With "The Connaught Rangers," 1854-55-56
A Personal Account of a Serving Officer of the Regiment
by Nathaniel Steevens

First published under the title
The Crimean Campaign With "The Connaught Rangers," 1854-55-56

Leonaur is an imprint of Oakpast Ltd

Copyright in this form © 2012 Oakpast Ltd

ISBN: 978-0-85706-870-5 (hardcover)
ISBN: 978-0-85706-871-2 (softcover)

http://www.leonaur.com

Publisher's Notes

Contents

To
General Sir Horatio Shirley. K.CB.
Colonel of the 88th Connaught Rangers
In Grateful Remembrance of Happy Years Passed Under His
Command
In The "Rangers" and on the Staff,
This Book is respectfully dedicated
By
The Author.

Preface

I have drawn up the narrative contained in the following pages from my own letters and journal, written during the war with Russia in 1854-5-6, throughout which time throughout which time I was present with the army in the Crimea.

I have also added a few incidents and other details, which may enhance the value of the work.

It contains a simple record of my impressions and observations during the campaign, and was composed without any idea that it would ever see the light in a printed form; but, at the request of several friends, who concur in thinking that a personal account of that eventful period, so memorable in the military annals of our country, may prove generally interesting, I have been induced, with some diffidence, to consent to its publication.

The narrative of the Connaught Rangers at the Battle of Inkermann was originally compiled by me—from my journal, as well as from the statements of officers present with the regiment during the action—for the information of Mr. Kinglake, who introduced the purport of its contents, into the Cabinet Edition of The *Invasion of the Crimea*. I am much indebted to him for the courteous permission, which has enabled me to place before my readers the excellent map, which accompanied his graphic description of that battle.

N. S.

London, May, 1878.

How sleep the Brave, who sink to rest
By all their Country's wishes blest!
When Spring, with dewy fingers cold,
Returns to deck their hallowed mould,
She there shall dress a sweeter sod
Than Fancy's feet have ever trod.

W. Collins (*a. d.* 1746).

CHAPTER 1

April 4th to May 27th, 1854

Before commencing the narrative contained in these pages I will review briefly the causes which led to the war between Great Britain and Russia during the years 1854-5-6.

Nearly forty years had elapsed since England had been engaged in a war in Europe; and, with the exception of occasional campaigns in distant lands, this country had enjoyed the blessings of an uninterrupted peace during that period; meanwhile our commercial relations with other countries had considerably increased, and the prosperity of England appeared to be rapidly progressing.

But in 1853 a threatening cloud was arising in the East which was destined to cast a temporary shade over this country. The Russian emperor, following the traditional policy of his predecessors, had long regarded the acquisition of Constantinople with a covetous eye, and only awaited a favourable opportunity for the accomplishment of his ambitious design.

On the ground of religion the *Czar* soon found an excuse for provoking the hostility of the Porte. Early in 1853 an obscure dispute between some Greek and Latin monks—about the exclusive possession of the "Holy Places" in Palestine—served to afford a plausible pretext for the Emperor Nicholas to demand the control over all members of the Greek Church, residing in the Turkish dominions; a demand which the Turkish Government very naturally rejected; consequently a Russian force took possession of the principalities of Wallachia and Moldavia, but suffered a severe defeat by the Turkish troops under Omar Pasha, at the Battle of Oltenitza in November, 1854.

Russia was now fairly involved in a war with the Porte, and the *Czar* seemed to reckon upon the connivance of England, France, and Prussia for the successful accomplishment of his plans; but, while

11

Prussia and Austria remained aloof, the policy of England was entirely opposed to Russia's ambitious and unjustifiable designs upon Turkey; and France, equally jealous of the desire for territorial aggrandisement by which Russia's motives were actuated, cordially united with Great Britain to restrain the ambition of that country. The Porte having claimed the assistance of England and France, the combined fleets of these two countries entered the Black Sea in January, 1854.

These are, briefly, the causes which led to the war in which England was about to engage; and the martial spirit of the British nation being now fairly roused, vigorous preparations were made for the approaching struggle, the duration and result of which no one could foretell.

In the month of February (1854) intimation was received at the headquarters of the 88th Connaught Rangers—then stationed at Bury, Lancashire—that the regiment was to form part of an expeditionary force about to be despatched to Turkey, and the commanding officer (Lieutenant-Colonel Shirley) was instructed to recruit the regiment up to 1000 strong.

Meanwhile negotiations with Russia—continued during the previous winter—having entirely failed, England and France declared war against that country in March, 1854.

In the middle of March the Connaught Rangers—. then detached at Bury, Burnley, and Ashton-under-Lyne—moved to Fulwood Barracks, Preston, with the view to forming the service and *depôt* companies, preparatory to embarkation. The ranks were rapidly completed to the required strength, receiving a very fine detachment of forty men from the 26th Cameronians, who proved to be a valuable acquisition to the regiment The *depôt*, consisting of two companies, with Captains Holme and Stopford, Lieutenant Dunning, and Ensigns Grace, Copley, and Webb, went to Burnley; and Ensign Maule was appointed Adjutant vice Dunning.

We now anxiously awaited final instructions respecting our future movements; and in April we received sudden orders to embark for the East, and on the 4th of that month we left Preston for Liverpool at 9.30 a.m. by a special train.

The night before we marched from Preston we had about 150 men absent from tattoo: as a precautionary measure the commanding officer caused a party of a sergeant and twelve privates, belonging to the *depôt*, to be told off in waiting to complete our numbers, if necessary; but these absentees all turned up the following morning, and *every man was present when the regiment embarked*, the sergeant and his twelve men returning to the *depôt*, much to their disgust

Before the regiment marched out of barracks at Preston, the colonel formed square and addressed us, saying, "that he never felt prouder in his life, *not a man absent from embarkation*; and that he hoped we should add three or four more *jaw-breaking* names to the engagements placed on our colours, feeling confident that the 'Rangers' of the present day would prove equal to the 'Rangers' of the Peninsular War." The gallant colonel also thanked the men for their excellent conduct, and seemed highly gratified at this evidence of the strong feeling of *esprit de corps* which animated the regiment.

We reached Liverpool about eleven a.m., where we were most enthusiastically received in our progress through the town; the dense crowds cheered us vociferously, and the windows and balconies were filled with ladies waving handkerchiefs; as we marched along the streets an old woman, stepping out of the crowd, knelt down before the colours and blessed them.

The day fortunately was very fine; and we embarked on board the Cunard steamer *Niagara* (Captain Leitch), about noon, 943 souls, besides the crew.[1]

The following officers embarked with the regiment:—

Lieutenant-Colonel Shirley.	Lieutenant Ernst.
Major Jeffreys.	,, Baynes.
Captain and Bt.-Major Mackie.	,, Steevens.
Captain Sawrey	,, Wray.
,, G.V. Maxwell.	,, Grogan.
,, Norton.	,, Riley.
,, Brown.	Ensign and Adjutant Maule.
,, Bayley	Ensign Henning.
,, E. H. Maxwell.	,, Browne.
,, Hon. J. J. Bourke.	,, Beresford.
Lieutenant Burke.	,, Radcliffe.
,, Crosse.	Paymaster Belfield.
,, Corbett.	Quartermaster Moore.
,, Maynard.	Surgeon Moore.
,, Gore.	Assistant-Surgeon Shegog.
,, Mauleverer.	,, ,, Williams.

---

1. Marching-out state, 88th Regiment, April 4th, 1854:—32 Officers, 39 Sergeants, 20 Band, 10 Drummers, &c., 810 R. & F.

A total of 911, besides women allowed to accompany their husbands.

We left Liverpool at three a.m. on the 5th, and at noon we passed Holyhead, the lighthouse signalling, "A prosperous voyage and beat the Russians." The weather was very fine and the sea as calm as a duck-pond.

Our quartermaster (Moore), who had served in many campaigns in India, observed that many of us, who had been cheering today, would never see "Old England" again—a prediction which, alas! proved too true.

The band played on the deck in the evening, and we saw the last of "Old England" just before sunset. The following morning we were off the Scilly Isles, though out of sight of land; the wind having changed, we had more swell than on the previous day, which tended to raise grave doubts in the minds of many, regarding their merits as good sailors. During the day we spoke the *Duke of Roxburgh*, homeward bound, and signalled to her, "War declared—troops on board."

At noon on the 7th we were 157 miles off Cape Finisterre, and several swallows came on board during the day—a sign of land being near.

One of our sergeants (Jones) died suddenly in the evening; the following day the poor fellow was consigned to his watery grave: a funeral at sea is even a more solemn and impressive scene than it is on land

During the voyage I shared a cabin with my captain, and was very comfortable.

About three a.m. on the 8th we were off Cape Finisterre, but a thick haze prevented the land from being seen. A few whales and sharks came near the vessel, and many sail were in sight as the fog cleared.

Throughout our voyage our days were passed very similarly. Being generally up at seven, many took a stroll on deck to sharpen the appetite for breakfast at nine; after which the deck was again resorted to as the promenade. After lunching at noon, the time was passed, by some, in whist, chess, or backgammon; and, by others, in a book, or in endeavouring to make out a sail in, the hazy distance. Besides this, we had the usual routine of military duties on board ship.

The band played on deck every evening, after which the men amused themselves with dancing, singing, or listening to the witty anecdotes of some long-winded Pat-landers.

The so-called "Ladies' Cabin" was frequently the evening resort of a few of us, who wished to be quiet, either to write or (reclining on a velvet couch) read a book.

We passed Cape St Vincent at one p.m. on the 9th: a fine, bold, rocky coast. On this lofty point stood a lighthouse and convent. Later in the day we met a French man-of-war steam brig. We passed her very close, giving three cheers, which the French sailors returned, their captain standing on the paddle-box, waving his cap. It occurred to us as singular that, nearly forty-nine years previously, the British and French fleets had been engaged in a bloody battle near the same spot.[2] The clearness of the day enabled us to have a good view of the coast.

Today being Sunday, we had Divine Service on deck at ten a.m., when our colonel officiated, with a drum as his desk.

During the night we signalled with blue lights to a steamer, supposed to be one of the P. and O. boats, *Melita*.

We passed Gibraltar about ten on the morning of the 10th. The weather was very misty, with a stiff easterly wind. On entering the Straits we spoke the *Manilla* screw steamer.

The coast on each side is mountainous, and very rocky. We saw Tangiers, Tarifa (with its little fort and lighthouse), Algesiras, San Roque, and Ceuta—the latter a Spanish fort on the African side. As we passed Gibraltar we signalled, "*Niagara*—Troops—88." The Rock rises majestically from the sea, with its strongly-fortified town at its foot On the African coast, opposite Gibraltar, Ape Hill rose out of the sea to the height of several thousand feet We passed a great many Spanish and Genoese vessels, some with the lateen sails peculiar to the Mediterranean. The weather now became very hot. and a disagreeable hot wind, called *Sirocco*, blew today. We went within thirty miles of the African coast, which rose up from the sea with lofty and cloud-capped mountains, presenting a very fine and bold appearance; and on the evening of the 11th we passes about four miles from Algiers, and saw the light.

On the 13th we were off Cape Bon, 180 miles from Malta. Here we passed close to a French vessel called the *Etienne*, No. 113 Transport, and gave them three cheers.

In the afternoon we were off the mountainous island of Pantel-laria, with its prettily situated town and cultivated hills, producing olives and grapes. It is said to be volcanic in formation, containing a fathomless lake in the centre. We were sufficiently close to distinguish the houses. The island is about twenty miles long, and at this time contained 5000 inhabitants, and belonged to Sardinia; distant from Malta

---

2. The memorable Battle of Trafalgar, October 21st, 1805.

140 miles. As we progressed we were much struck with the beautiful blue colour of the sea.

At two a.m. on the 14th we entered Malta harbour. It was a beautiful moonlight night, and we anchored in Commercial Creek, having completed our voyage, so far, in nine days and twenty-two hours. We found that many regiments had left for Gallipoli, leaving in garrison the 9th, 62nd, 68th, the "Buffs," and the "Guards." I landed in the afternoon with our adjutant and some others, and explored the "city of palaces," as Valetta is called; but, as it was Good Friday, the shops were unfortunately all closed. Having completed the dirty operation of coaling, we left Malta at midnight for Gallipoli. It blew very fresh during the night, and the sea was rather rough, which considerably thinned our numbers at breakfast next morning.

At noon on Sunday, the 16th, we sighted the Morea, and passed Cape Matapan in the evening. The scenery here was very beautiful, with gigantic snow-capped mountains rising majestically from the sea, and villages picturesquely scattered among them. About nine p.m. we passed Cerigo and Cape St Angelo, where, it was said, a hermit resided who, in former times, used to keep watch for the pirates of these seas against the approach of men-of-war.

This morning we were delayed for half an hour, the engine having become overheated in consequence of coal-dust getting into the machinery, and water was pumped upon it for some time.

On the morning of the 17th we were off Negropont. It was a most beautiful day, the sea quite calm, and we had a fine view of this mountainous island; and as, during the day, we progressed through the Archipelago, we were much struck with the beauty and grandeur of the magnificent scenery, which was much enhanced by the mountains on the different islands being covered with snow. We could observe, however, but few habitations and little cultivation, though numerous windmills covered the tops of some of the hills.

This was the calmest day of our voyage, but it became colder as we now steered northward. We sighted the Island of Mitylene just as the setting sun was lighting up, with a rich glow of crimson, the numerous islands, which seemed as if rising out of a sea of fire. As we could not enter the Dardanelles after dark, we anchored between the Island of Tenedos and the mainland.

Soon after dawn on the 18th we passed the snugly situated town of Tenedos and Besika Bay, and entered the fortified mouth of the Dardanelles. The shore on each side was flat and uninteresting, except where a village gave signs of cultivation, or a fort, bristling with guns, frowned upon us. We saw Turkish troops in the various batteries, and met numerous small vessels, the crews loudly cheering us: even the Turks shouted out "Hurrah!"

The morning was very calm and cloudless, and the clear day enabled us to see the distant mountains of Asia, all covered with snow.

After a delightful steam of three hours we reached Gallipoli, a miserable-looking place, near which several British regiments— under the command of General Sir George Brown—were encamped, and also about 22,000 of the French Army. We were told that when the latter disembarked here, they had boats in abundance, as well as mules and waggons ready for them; whereas some of our regiments could not disembark for want of boats, neither could they obtain mules nor waggons for the transport of baggage, &c. The vessel was soon surrounded by boats from shore, but none of us were allowed to land, of course; fancy one of our men—in the generosity of his heart— offering *a piece of pork* to a *Turk* who came on board! We received the order to proceed to Scutari with three hearty cheers, and left Gallipoli at two p.m. Just as we were getting under way, a Turk alongside managed to get his boat under one of the paddle-wheels; we thought he must have been drowned, when, much to our surprise, he appeared out of the top of the paddle-box, wet and frightened, having scrambled up the wheel.

Lieutenant James Burke, R.E.[3] (brother of one of our officers, Lieutenant J. Burke), came on board here, and accompanied us to Scutari. Off Gallipoli were twelve French men-of-war, among them the *Napoleon*. The narrowest part of the Dardanelles is about a mile across with a fort on each side, *à fleur d'eau*.

Early on the morning of the 19th we arrived at Constantinople, after a delightful passage of fourteen days from Liverpool We were very fortunate in having such an excellent commander as Captain Leitch, who did everything he could to make the voyage comfortable, both to officers and men; we afterwards rewarded him with a piece of plate, as a mark of esteem.[4]

About two p.m. we landed at Scutari, and were housed—with the

---

3. Killed at Rustchuk, July 9th, 1854.
4. One considerate act on the part of Captain Leitch deserves to mentioned. He caused a barrel of biscuit to be always open and accessible to all ranks, under charge of a sentry to prevent waste. The men used to help themselves, instead of having the regular ration of biscuit, and this arrangement gave general satisfaction.

33rd, 41st, 47th, 49th, and 77th—in the Turkish barracks, which were situated on a hill overhanging the Bosphorus and the Sea of Marmora, and commanding a fine panoramic view of the picturesque city of Constantinople, and the distant mountainous scenery of Asia Minor. I slept on the floor the first night, and very cold I found it; but my slumbers were sound. The barracks were built of stone—white-washed—and square in form, enclosing a large parade-ground; the building was two stories in height, with a continuous wide and lofty corridor round each storey, on the side overlooking the quadrangle.[5]

Close to the barracks was the Mosque of Suleiman, belonging to a sect of Mahomedans called the "Howling Dervishes;" at certain hours the priest (called *Mufti*) used to appear in the gallery of one of the minarets, or towers, inviting "the faithful" to prayer; presenting a singular effect when several mosques were together.

The town of Scutari, like every other Turkish town which I saw, looked like a place in decay; the inhabitants lazy, indolent, and apathetic, and all attempt at improvement apparently disregarded. I was quartered with my captain (M.) and his other subaltern (G. R. B.) in the barracks; there was a raised platform (called a divan, on which the Turks sit, or recline, and smoke their *chibouques*) at one end of the room, covered with cushions of a very dirty description, and of which we were exceedingly glad to get rid. From our windows we had a very extensive view of the open ground where we afterwards encamped, passing along which were now to be seen bearded Turks, starved-looking mules and various specimens of humanity in every kind of costume. On this spot we had frequent brigade-drills under our Brigadier-General, Colonel Adams, 49th Regiment. Beyond this was the Turkish military hospital—a large red-brick building standing above the Sea of Marmora—with the lofty, snow-covered mountains of Asia Minor skirting the horizon.

On the 22nd I paid my first visit to the other side of the water, in company with a brother officer. What we are accustomed to call Constantinople is divided into three parts; one, called Stamboul, is the purely Turkish portion—containing the mosques of St Sophia and of Sultan Achmet, the Bazaar, and the old *Seraglio*—and is separated from Galata (the Jewish portion) and from Pera (the Frank portion) by an arm of the Bosphorus, called "The Golden Horn." We crossed from Scutari to Stamboul in a *caïque*, or boat peculiar to the country, in

---

5. These barracks were subsequently used as a hospital, well known as the scene of the devoted labours of Miss Florence Nightingale.

the stem of which we reclined on a cushion, and were rapidly pulled across by two Greeks, fine handsome-looking fellows, in *fez*-caps, loose white trousers and shirts, who, after the manner of Mussulman, took off their shoes on entering the boat.

Landing at Stamboul we wended our way to the bazaar (or place where the shops are), gathering, as we went, a motley train of importunate Greeks calling out, "*Terjuman (i.e.* interpreter) Johnny," and offering to act as guides; though always ready to cheat, they are a very necessary evil to those unacquainted with the place.

The picturesque appearance which Stamboul presented, when viewed from a distance, was entirely dispelled when we landed and elbowed our way through its narrow, dirty streets, paved with cobblestones, full of holes, and crowded with horses, mules, Turks, priests, Armenians, &c. &c..

We frequently met a rickety conveyance gaudily painted and bedizened, containing a bundle of bright-coloured clothes, which on closer inspection, proved to be a Turkish lady, with her face covered with *yashmâk*, or veil, which left nothing visible but the eyes; but in some—where the veil was thin—a handsome but pale face might be seen. Turkish porters called *hamal*, carrying enormous bundles on their backs, ran against us at every corner, an occurrence rendered the more frequent through our ignorance of the Turkish mode of saying "By yer leave."

After wending our way through a labyrinth of lanes (for they deserve no other name), we reached the bazaar, consisting of several covered streets at right-angles to each other, all being similarly narrow, dirty, and crowded. Each street is devoted to the sale of one description of article; for instance, in one would be seen nothing but slippers and shoes; in another, shawls or pipes; and so on.

On a platform, in front of each shop, was seated the bearded proprietor, offering to sell his goods, and quite ready to cheat, too; a result which our ignorance of the language rendered inevitable.

After wandering about the place—half-stifled with heat and nearly choked with dust—we crossed over the Golden Horn by the bridge of boats which connected Stamboul with Galata and Pera. To stand on this bridge and to watch the motley crowd which passed along, somewhat reminded me of a theatrical scene: Turks, Greeks, Arabs, men, women, and chidiren thronged along, in their various costumes, some of which made our scarlet coats appear sombre; here a very handsomely dressed Turk on horseback—his horse led by a groom, and followed by his *chibouque-ji*, or pipe-bearer—there a *dervish*, or a Bashi-Bazouk armed to the teeth; and so on in rapid succession.

We found that Galata closely resembled Stamboul in its narrow and ill-paved streets, with the same heat and disagreeable smells, and equally crowded with various obstructions. We were very glad to hurry through this noisome locality and proceed to Pera, inhabited by English, French, and Greeks; containing very good shops of various kinds, several hotels, and also the residences of the different ambassadors.

Almost every Turk that passed us carried a long pipe (called *chibouque*), which, when not in use, was placed inside the back of his coat, with the bowl uppermost.

We ended our day at a Turkish restaurant, where we smoked *chibouques* and *narghilis* (another kind of pipe), drank delicious coffee, and had the infliction of listening to a monotonous song by a Turk, accompanied by a jingling guitar, called *bulgarrha*.

I was told an anecdote today, showing the Turk's opinion of the British soldier. A Turk, while looking on during the disembarkation of one of our regiments, was heard to say; "They are the finest men I ever saw, and hold up their heads well; *but they will all away, they cannot fight like the Turks*"

In the Bosphorus, between Scutari and Pera, stand a tower, called Leander's Tower, which (says tradition) was built by some *sultan* as a refuge for his beautiful daughter, who, it was foretold, would die from the bite of an animal.

She, however, was not safe here, but died from the sting of an asp, conveyed to her, in a bouquet, by her lover. It was a favourite joke of one of our officers to endeavour to force this old story upon us (as a new anecdote) upon each occasion of crossing, quietly saying: "Did you ever hear that interesting story about that tower?" until the question became quite a saying with us.

On the 23rd I crossed over to Pera with two others and went to a Greek fair outside the town abounded in dancers, jugglers, &c., with numerous spectators in every variety of costume; in the midst of all this bustle a Greek funeral was going on, but all around seemed quite indifferent to it.

We dined at the Hotel d'Angleterre (Missèri's), and went to the Opera, where we heard *Rigoletto*; afterwards (with the aid of a Turkish lantern) we blundered over the rough stones and through the dark streets, where we were attacked on all sides by innumerable dogs, which we could only keep off by brandishing our swords.[6] At last we reached Tophana—where the Turkish arsenal is—and crossed thence to Scutari in a *caïque*; reclining on its soft cushion we skimmed along the dark waters of the Bosphorus with our feeble light; all darkness around, save the circle of lamps round the gallery of each minaret

The 7th Fusiliers disembarked on the 22nd, and on the 23rd Sir De Lacy Evans arrived in the *City of London*, and assumed command of the garrison.

The following day the 95th Regiment disembarked, and encamped with the 33rd and 77th Regiments.

In the evening a ball was given at the Austrian Embassy, Pera, to which three officers per regiment, who could speak French and dance, were invited; although I could do a little of both I did not go, having no *dancing-pumps* and little inclination.

On the 25th, the 23rd (Fusiliers) landed, and were encamped with the other regiments. In the afternoon, my friend G. and I repaired to a Turkish bath opposite the barracks, where, for the first time, we underwent the long, parboiling, and somewhat fatiguing process, interspersed with pipes and coffee, the usual accompaniment to every undertaking in Turkey; after this I assisted in marking out the ground for our future encampment.

There now being nine infantry regiments in Scutari, the following brigades were formed, *viz.*:—

The 7th, 23rd, 33rd, under Brigadier-General Sir Colin Campbell.

The 41st, 47th, 49th, under Brigadier-General Adams (49th Regiment).

The 77th, 88th, 95th, under Brigadier-General Pennefather.

General Adams' brigade was nicknamed the *Fleabitten* Brigade, having suffered much in the thickly populated Turkish barracks; that of General Pennefather was called the "Yellow Brigade," the three regiments having yellow facings.

At this time we all thought it would be a very good thing when the troops were moved from this place, as the drunkenness was becoming something beyond conception; but all seemed delayed through the

---

6. The dogs were a perfect plague, infesting in hundreds both Stamboul, Pera, Galata, and Sculari; being the scavengers of these places, and also being held sacred, the Turks never molested them, but when they became too numerous a large number of them was packed off to one of the small islands in the Sea of Marmora with three days' provisions.

commissariat department not yet being properly arranged, and confusion and mismanagement appeared to be the general order of things.

On the morning of the 26th we left the barracks, and encamped about a mile and a half off, in a position quite by ourselves, situated on the side of a hill, whence there was a beautiful view of the entrance to the Bosphorus, together with Stamboul and its many minarets. This was the commencement of our camping life in the East, and our daily occupations presented but little variety. Division- or brigade-drills took place almost every morning, after which the day was passed generally in a visit to Pera, &c., or in exploring the vicinity of the camp.

On the 27th the whole division was formed up to receive the *seraskier-pasha*, or Turkish commander-in-chief. Three battalions of Guards having arrived our line consisted of twelve regiments.

The *seraskier* kept us waiting nearly an hour; meanwhile, with opened ranks, we were standing in the pouring rain, which was driven into our faces, and proved as detrimental to our tempers as it was to our coats; to lessen our discomfort the line was "faced about;" whilst standing at ease in this position a Pat in the front rank remarked to a comrade in the rear rank—

"Shure this is no way to receive a giniral officer, with our backs to him."

At last the stout Turk arrived, and with such an escort too!—a few slovenly-looking soldiers on small, half-starved steeds, accompanied by a few others on foot carrying firelocks. After marching past we returned to camp.

On the morning of the 28th we were, much to our disgust, removed from our beautifully situated camping-ground (to be replaced by the brigade of Guards), and were placed next the 7th (Fusiliers). In front of us was a Turkish cemetery, said to extend nearly three miles, with a thick plantation of cypress-trees, and covered with tombstones having quaint-looking turbans carved on the top of each; the wind blowing through the cypress-trees gave forth a very mournful sound. To our right the Guards were encamped on our former position, and, in the far distance, were to be seen the lofty mountains of Asia Minor, of which Mount Olympus (nearly eighty miles distant) was the most conspicuous, covered with snow.

Being up very early, we generally breakfasted at eight; our dinner-hour was seven p.m., and bedtime about nine; rather different hours to those of a life at home. On the 22nd the bombardment of Odessa took place, and we heard the news today.

Lord Raglan arrived on the 29th, and we were all anxiety to learn our future movements. Every day was busily passed in the purchase of *bât*-ponies, &c., and in making sundry preparations for a campaign. I had not yet invested in pony-flesh, but was on the lookout.

After a drill one morning, our brigadier (Pennefather) made us a speech, saying, "how proud he should feel did an opportunity offer of leading three such fine regiments into the field; that the best-behaved brigade would be the first to start, and it was his cordial wish that we might lead the way." On another occasion he said he should be happy if he only saw a Russian name on our colours.

We had plenty of rain about this time, which tested our tents, and mine proved as leaky as the rest The officers were formed into messes by companies; mine consisted of my captain and his two subalterns. Our daily rations now were one pound of beef and a pound and a half of brown bread.

The women, who accompanied their husbands, were in a pitiable condition now that we were under canvas; it was all very well when they were in barracks, but in camp no provision had been made for them, and numbers of them were living in miserable hovels made of mats, which the rain penetrated as easily as if they were sieves, and the weather was very cold.

Our chaplain having arrived. Divine Service for the brigade took place at eleven a.m. every Sunday.

On the 30th I saw about 500 Bashi-Bazouks—a kind of native cavalry—called *Zeibeks*, pass the camp, headed by a primitive band of three drums, which the musicians (?) played while holding the reins in their mouths; they consisted of men belonging to tribes in the interior and near Smyrna, who came to offer their services to the *Sultan*. Their strength was 2000, and among them some of the greatest villains in the world, who pillaged and burned villages, besides committing every other kind of enormity. They were fine-looking men, armed to the teeth with pistols, carbines, &c., and carrying also a long spear, called *djereed*, which they wielded with great facility; they rode on small, well-trained horses, and showed them off by galloping full-speed, brandishing the spear over their heads, and suddenly pulling up. Their various and brilliant costumes gave them a very picturesque appearance.

In the beginning of May the Light Division was formed under the command of General Sir George Brown, consisting of two brigades, *viz.*—

1st Brigade—7th, 23rd, 33rd Regiments, and the 2nd Battalion Rifle Brigade under Brigadier-General Airey.

2nd Brigade—19th, 77th, 88th Regiments, under Brigadier-General Buller.

We were much amused at the following occurrence, which, it was said, took place while the regiments were in barracks; it appeared that a gallant colonel was quartered in rooms called "the *Sultan's*," and consequently held sacred. One day some *pasha* came to pay his respects; having made his *salaam* at the door, and taken off his shoes according to the Mahomedan custom, he entered the apartment, when—what did he see!—the colonel frying *pork*, the Mussulman's abhorrence.

On the evening of the 4th May a fire broke out in Stamboul, destroying 500 houses. The sea was brilliantly illuminated with the bright light, and the city resounded with the voices of the *muftis* (priests) calling "the faithful" to prayer, bugles blowing, and other signals, together with the howling of innumerable dogs. One noise puzzled us; it proved to be a mode of alarm which the Turkish policemen—called *Zaptis*—adopt, by striking their staves on the ground. This tapping sound, in every direction, had a singular effect.

We observed that the number of dogs had perceptibly diminished since the arrival of the British troops, especially in Scutari, where, if a dog saw a red coat, he was off like a shot; our barrack square used to be full, of them at first, but numbers were killed by the soldiers. In Stamboul the lazy brutes lay sleeping in the streets, not stirring for man or beast; in fact, whenever we rode there our Turkish ponies used to step over them. The weather at this time was very changeable; in the morning it was exceedingly hot, and sometimes in the afternoon it became cold, with violent showers of rain.

The 93rd (Highlanders) and 2nd Battalion R. B. arrived on the 6th from Gallipoli, together with General Sir George Brown and Brigadier-Generals Airey and Buller; we were all very sorry to lose our first brigadier (Pennefather)—a thorough soldier. Troops and stores continued to arrive every day. The commissariat arrangements seemed far from being complete, by all accounts; it was calculated that 20,000 mules were required for the conveyance of the extra infantry ammunition alone, and as yet the department had purchased *fifteen* only. At this time our brigade was frequently marched into the country, and exercised in outlying pickets and patrols. Sometimes we did not return to camp until late in the afternoon, after a hot day's work.

We greatly felt the want of books to read; the few that could be purchased were trashy novels, and very dear.

On the 7th about 200 natives, on foot, with *fez* and turbans on, passed the camp, preceded by a band of one pipe and two drums, which made a hideous noise; they were volunteers for the Turkish army, and, though very ragged, they were fine-looking men.

One day I crossed over to Stamboul with a brother sub. (J. W.), and saw a Turkish infantry regiment embarking for the seat of war. A band of harsh brass instruments played during the embarkation, but as each musician appeared to play no particular tune—in whatever time he pleased—and to enjoy the same freedom in the selection of key, the discord was painfully excruciating.

We were much astonished at seeing one of the Turkish officers enforce his orders by *belabouring* his subordinates *with a stick*—a novel method according to our English ideas of discipline.

We then strolled about the *Sultan's* old *seraglio*, at this time unoccupied, inspecting every corner, until ordered back by the sentries. We afterwards walked through the labyrinth of streets, and saw the large mosque St. Sophia, once a Christian church where St, Chrysostom preached. From one spot we had a very good general view of Constantinople.

Having procured a *caïque* we proceeded along the smooth waters of the Golden Horn; it was beautifully cool on the water, and we enjoyed the change from the hot and dusty streets. The Golden Horn was covered with *caïques* of every description, filled with gaily-dressed Turkish holiday-makers, wending the way to the "Valley of the Sweet Waters" (Turkish, *Tâtli Sû*), a spot where two rivers flow into the Golden Horn, and a great lounge for the Turkish nobs and snobs every Friday—the Mahomedan Sabbath. As we approached the valley the stream narrowed and became very serpentine; the banks on either side were covered with groups of people, mostly women, clad in their brilliant-coloured cloaks (*ferijeh*), their pale faces covered with a *yashmak* (veil) up to the eyes, and their nails stained purple with *henna*; some of them carried bright-coloured parasols—amber, pink, scarlet, &c.

Occasionally we saw groups of women and children singing kind of songs, accompanied by a *tom-tom* (drum) and a twanging guitar (*bulgarrha*). Each turn of the river presented a new scene, which, with the varied cold of the different costumes and the fineness of the day, appeared like a picture in some fairy tale. At length we reached the fashionable promenade, a secluded grassy spot, surrounded by trees, situated on the banks of the narrow stream by which we came. Round and round this shady resort whirled a string of gingerbread-looking gilt carriages, filled with the *belles* (?) of Constantinople; and, on this occasion, the *Sultan's harem* was there; besides which, there were numerous equestrians and pedestrians, foreign and native, in every variety of gay costume. Here the *Sultan* had a kiosk, or summer-house, which he constantly visited.

While we were looking on at this busy scene some officers bowed to the ladies of the *harem* as they passed round, much to the amusement of the thinly-veiled beauties (?), but to the unmistakable indignation of their sable attendants. At last one of the ladies rolled up her handkerchief and threw it into the group of officers as she passed; an immediate scramble for it took place; one of the black fellows rushed in and tried to get it, but was soon pushed off, and the trumpery piece of lace was carried off as a trophy. The Turkish bystanders looked so angry that I was afraid a row would have ensued, but doubtless the presence of numerous English officers prevented it. The *harem* carriages, however, were hurried off.

On the 9th the *Caradoc* arrived, bringing the Duke of Cambridge, who assumed the command of the 1st Division, consisting of the Guards and Highlanders. The Turks seemed much amused at the costume of the latter, and one I saw at Stamboul was followed about by a crowd of bearded and chattering Turks. The Turks always addressed us by the title of "Johnny," or "*Bono* Johnny."

I crossed over to Stamboul with our paymaster, on the 9th, and went to the *At-Bazaar* (horse-market) to purchase a pony. Vocabulary in hand, we bargained away with a turbaned Turk for more than two hours; and, after smoking numerous *chibouques* and drinking an immoderate quantity of coffee, I succeeded in beating him down from 35*l.* to 14*l.*; having bought a headstall, I led the pony through the crowded streets, and brought him across to Scutari in a boat We always found that the purchase of anything from a Turk required the exercise of much patience; for instance, you started your offers to buy, knowing that the bearded shopkeeper sitting on his heels would do his best to cheat you; if he asked fifty *piastres* for anything, I invariably offered half, sometimes less; an indignant look and toss of head was the reply, but after some time he handed the article over with a bland smile.

At our first visit to Stamboul we were amused at the peculiar noise made by the Turks when calling attention to any article for sale; they called out "*Hoosh*," meaning, we supposed, "Here," and, as you passed along, the amount of hissing suggested the resemblance to a flock of geese.

Very conveniently for the garrison, a steamer now ran between Scutari and Galata at different hours, free of charge. Our ponies were picketed near our tents, and, what with the neighing of these "baggagers," the braying of mules, and the howling of dogs, our slumber did not pass undisturbed. One of our captains (G.V. Maxwell) was appointed brigade-major of our brigade at this time.

We were inspected by Lord Raglan on the 16th; the usual military honours having been paid, we returned to our tents dusty as well as ready for breakfast, having paraded at half-past six a.m. The same afternoon I crossed to Stamboul with M., 47th Regiment, once in the 20th Regiment with me; the day was very hot, and we found the heat very oppressive as we threaded our way through Stamboul to the slave bazaar; although they affected to deny the existence of this iniquitous traffic in Turkey, still it was an indisputable fact that you could at this time purchase slaves in Stamboul. The bazaar was a broad street containing shops on each side, which were full of women, principally Nubians, some asleep, others working, and all wearing the *yashmâk*— to hide their we presumed.

The following day, having procured a *firman*, or permit, from the *Sultan*, for which 10*l.* had to be paid, fifty of us belonging to different regiments crossed to see the sights of Stamboul. We first visited the tomb of Sultan Mahmoud, father of the reigning *Sultan* (Abdul Medjid); having taken off our boots, which some replaced with sacred slippers (or else, like myself, walked in socks), we entered a large octagonal room richly gilt and painted, surmounted by a dome, and containing the coffins of Mahmoud, his wife, and children; each coffin was covered in richly embroidered crimson velvet, as well as with handsome shawls; that of the *Sultan* had a *fez* on the top with a diamond aigrette, and in front of each coffin was a reading-desk: holding a copy of the *Koran*, which we were forbidden to touch, though some of us, unobserved, took a sly peep into it

We next visited the 1001 columns, a subterranean chamber like a cathedral crypt, containing rows of pillars. It was discovered at the conquest of Constantinople, and is supposed to have been originally a reservoir; it was at this time occupied by silk-winders. We afterwards proceeded to the *At-Meidân*, or ancient Hippodrome of the Greeks—a large open space, 500 yards long and 40 yards broad, with a lunatic asylum on one side; and the six-minaret mosque of Sultan

Achmed on the other. In the centre stood two obelisks and a pillar, the former—brought from Thebes by Theodosius—were used as the winning-post of the chariot races; the latter—in the form of three serpents entwined—was brought from the temple of Delphi, supported on a tripod sacred to Apollo; this was struck off, at one blow of a battle-axe, by some *sultan* with a long name.

Leaving the *At-Meidân*, we next went to the mosque of St Sophia, once a Christian church. On entering this stupendous building you might almost fancy yourself in St Paul's Cathedral; the marble pillars supporting the dome were very lofty and massive. The only pew (as we should call it) was that appropriated to the *Sultan*: it was placed in a gallery, surrounded by a screen of lattice-work, through which the ladies of the *harem* could see without being seen. In this mosque St Chrysostom once preached, and in various parts of the building were remains of crosses, found at, and retained since, the conquest of Constantinople. I observed hanging from the centre of the dome an ostrich egg, suspended by a string or chain, but I could not ascertain why it was hung there.[7] One of the party horrified the guide by unexpectedly rushing up the winding staircase of one of the minarets, at the top of which he met an astounded priest, and soon made a hasty retreat. I could have spent a longer time in inspecting this interesting building, but it was impossible to do so with a large party.

Outside one of the mosques were kept a great number of pigeons, under the care of a long-bearded Mussulman, who, for a few *piastres*, scattered some grain and gave a shrill whistle, when down came a cloud of pigeons and scrambled in a heap on the ground—a singular sight.

We afterwards visited the *Sultan's* old palace and *seraglio*, not then in use; the rooms were very large, with low ceilings, and were scantily furnished; the walls were gaudily painted, but, altogether, everything looked trumpery and, Turkish-like, falling into decay; the gardens, however, were very prettily and tastefully laid out We were shown a large grating, which, on being opened, disclosed a dark shaft (leading into the Bosphorus), down which, it was said, the refractory wives of

---

7. In Captain Burnaby's *On Horseback through Asia Minor*, vol. 1, we read that when visiting a mosque at Sivas he was struck by seeing a large ostrich egg suspended from the ceiling by a silver chain; and on asking the Turk who showed him over the building why this egg was hung there, he replied: "*Effendi*, the ostrich always looks at the eggs which she lays; if one of them is bad she breaks it. This egg is suspended here as a warning to men, that if they are bad God will break them in the same way as the ostrich does her eggs."

sultans used to be thrown.

Leaving this place I went, with two brother officers to the *Seraski-erât*, or Turkish Horse Guards, ascending a lofty tower there, we had a splendid panoramic view of Constantinople and the surrounding country.[8] We afterwards watched a Turkish regiment at drill, and were astonished at the smartness and precision with which they went through their "manual and platoon exercise;" their band, meanwhile, played discordant tunes which I vainly endeavoured to catch by ear; I tried to get the music from the bandmaster, but, though various pantomimic gestures passed between us, I failed to make myself understood. Although our day of sightseeing was fatiguing, we felt amply repaid for all our walking.

On the night of the 19th a most violent storm rain deluged the camp, washing many out of their tents; fortunately my tent weathered the terrible downpour. Two officers of the 93rd were returning to camp about eight p.m., while the storm was at its height; when on reaching the usually small stream flowing between the barracks and the camp, they found it a swollen torrent; but there was no alternative, cross it they must; in attempting to do so, one of them (McNeish) was carried away, and his body was not found until several days afterwards, and at a long distance from the spot where he tried to cross the other (Clayhills) reached the camp in safety. Several of the women's miserable huts were washed away, and their unfortunate occupants left to the mercy of the rain and wind; some of the women had embarked for England, on board the *Emeu*, but, as she received sudden counter-orders, they returned to the regiment

Lord Raglan having gone to Varna, to hold a council of war with Omar Pasha and Marshal St Arnaud. we were daily in expectation of a move. The army was at this time increased by the arrival of the 55th Regiment, the 17th Lancers, and part of the 8th Hussars, besides artillery; the cavalry were at a place, up the Bosphorus, called Kulali.

Everybody who visits this part of the world is astonished at the enormous loads which a *hamal*, or Turkish porter, can carry on his back, which is well protected by a leather pad; I saw one carrying behind him a barrel of beer, which one of our grenadiers could not raise from the ground. I have often met—in the narrow streets of Stamboul—a *hamal* with a load six feet high (sometimes including a chest of drawers and other household furniture), and so wide as to neces-

---

8. The panorama afterwards exhibited in London was, I believe taken from this tower.

sitate standing in a doorway to let him pass. These men walk down a street shouting "*Sa-oul*," or "*Des-toor*" (take care); and, if you disregard this warning, the next moment may see you nearly through a shop-window, as I was one day, from violent contact with a huge sack.

The *arabas*, or Turkish waggons, are of a very primitive kind, drawn by bullocks; it was very common to meet one of these rickety-looking conveyances, gilt and gaudily painted, full of Turkish women, who scanned us from head to foot

On the 23rd I went to Therapia with G.; we hired a *cäique* at Scutari, and were rowed up the Bosphorus; the day was calm and very hot; the shores on each side were lined with houses of all kinds down to the water's edge; although the country, on either side, was very pretty, still there was a great want of foliage to vary the scene and to relieve the eye. We passed some handsome white marble buildings, the residences of Abbas Pasha and Redschid Pasha. As we approached Therapia, the channel became narrower and the stream more rapid, and the *caïque* had to be towed by some stout Turks ashore, on the lookout for employment

We stopped at a cafe on the way, and had I the usual refreshments, which are always served thus: first a *chibouque* of delicious Turkish tobacco, then a tiny cup of coffee, followed by a sweetmeat called *rahatlakoom* (literally "peace to the throat"), and lastly a glass of water. After lunching at Therapia, we strolled about the place until nearly sunset, when we returned to Scutari. We had a delightful pull down the Bosphorus, the trees and houses being lighted up with the golden rays of the setting sun, and the water as smooth as glass. While at Therapia, H.M.S. *Niger* passed down, bringing intelligence of the unfortunate capture of H.M.S. *Tiger* at Odessa.

On the 24th we had a field-day to celebrate the queen's birthday, and in the evening some regiments had fireworks; the Guards also illuminated their camp, and rockets were fired from some of the ships. In the afternoon we received orders to hold ourselves in readiness to embark for Varna on the 27th, as part of the Light Division; this was afterwards counter-ordered; we were also ordered to leave behind all superfluous articles, so as to march as light as possible; my compressed kit could have been packed in a carpet-bag.

We were now allowed one tent between two subalterns, and my companion was W. B. The allowance of tents was at the rate of one for the commanding-officer, one for two majors, one for company officers, and fourteen men to each tent; the men's kit (in knapsack)

was ordered to consist of one shirt, one pair of boots and socks; the remaining articles being left behind in those most useless of inventions, the squad-bags, which were confided to the care of a rascal at Pera, and were, I believe, never seen again; at least I never got back the articles which I left in his charge.

One of our captains (S.) left us for England on the 25th, on account of his health.

The 79th (Highlanders) landed on the 27th, and encamped near the Rifle Brigade.

Chapter 2

May 29th to August 31st

At three a.m. on the 29th of May we struck tents and packed baggage. I went on board the *Cambria* steamer at eight a.m. in charge of the baggage-guard, and the regiment embarked at noon.

We left Scutari at three p.m., taking in tow an artillery transport at Kulali. The remainder of the Light Division preceded us in steamers, but we passed several of them. This move made all in the best of spirits; on the previous evening the men of the Light Division made bonfires, and shouted and yelled like savages. It was a beautiful evening as we passed up the Bosphorus, and the scenery was very fine. We entered the Black Sea about seven p.m. Here we passed two Greek vessels, which were fired upon by the Turkish batteries, as it is against rules to enter the Bosphorus after sunset.

About three p.m. on the 30th, after a foggy morning, we reached Varna, where we landed, and encamped outside the town, near the 19th Regiment and 2nd Battalion Rifle Brigade. We had a fine evening for pitching tents, which was not accomplished until nearly dark. The whole Light Division, with some Horse Artillery and the 8th Hussars, were encamped about a mile from Varna, near a large lake, where some of us bathed every morning after early parade and drill, which generally took place at six a.m.

We found it very difficult to obtain eatables in the neighbourhood. When first we arrived, eggs and poultry were plentiful and cheap. You could buy a goose for 6*d*.; eggs, twenty-four for 1*s*.; chickens, 3*d*. a pair. The natives soon, however, began to raise their prices, and we were very glad of the arrival of stores from England, which enabled us to obtain various articles of food from the commissariat at a cheaper rate than in the neighbourhood.

The French always treated the inhabitants in a very summary way, putting down whatever money they considered sufficient, and walking off with the goods.

The British fleet lay in the Bay of Kavarna, but the *Bellerophon* and a French man-of-war were off Varna.

Our *bât*-ponies came from Scutari in the *Trent* steamer, under charge of Lieutenant Ernst. The dirty town of Varna was enclosed by "lines," with various "outworks" dotted about the vicinity. The country around seemed very woody. Our camp was situated on a plain, bounded by a range of lofty hills, covered with vineyards, gardens, and occasional villages, all falling into decay, owing to the absence of so many men at the seat of war. The Bulgarians were a fine-looking race. We frequently rode or walked about the neighbourhood, passing through many villages. The men came out to stare at us, but the women hid themselves, although their natural curiosity prompted them to take a sly peep. The days were very hot and the nights damp. Every day passed very similarly; some of us bathed early in the morning; we had a parade at ten a.m., and afterward we rode or walked out into the country to forage. At this time porter was issued to the troops by the commissariat.

Shortly after our arrival in Bulgaria a provost-marshal was appointed to the army in the field. In order that this important personage might be easily distinguished from the remainder of the staff, his uniform was described in orders as consisting (besides cocked hat, &c.) of "*a blue infantry officer's frock coat.*" This announcement was somewhat embarrassing, as none of us had ever heard of a *blue infantry officer.*

The French camp, which was situated close to ours consisted of various arms of the service, and great cordiality existed between the two armies, although the intercourse between the privates was carried on by signs, and conversation seemed limited to the comprehensive word "*bono.*" One afternoon I paid a visit to the French camp, and talked with some of the officers and men, whom I found very polite, and ready to enter into conversation. We walked through the camps of the 7th Regiment of Foot and Chasseurs de Vincennes. The men were small, but seemed smart, active fellows.

I also saw a regiment of *Zouaves* (dressed in Algerian costume, but all Frenchmen) march in and pitch their *tentes d'abri*. They were fine, soldier-like looking men. I was much struck with the practical way in which they settled down after encamping. The vicinity of the camp was soon covered with men picking up sticks, grass, or anything that would make a fire; then the fires were soon seen burning, and coffee and food were cooked. Our men, when encamping, always seemed (from want of habit) less prompt in adapting themselves to circumstances.

I cannot say much for the behaviour of the men of the division, either here or at Scutari. Many were the acts of misconduct, and several men were flogged, flogging being the only punishment which could be awarded to soldiers on service in the field. The "Rangers," however, still maintained their high character for good conduct. A small force of Turkish cavalry and infantry was also encamped near us—fine-looking men, and apparently smart in their field movements.

The scene, in Varna, of English, French, and Turkish troops mingled together was very singular, and the consequent confusion of tongues was remarkable.

On the 4th of June Captain Wallace, 7th Fusiliers, died from the effects of injuries received by a fall from his horse. His funeral was very numerously attended.

Some of the 17th Lancers arrived the same day.

We used to frequently practise packing tents and baggage upon the ponies, some of which were very troublesome; mine, fortunately, was very quiet

About three a.m. on the 5th we struck tents, and commenced packing the *bât*-ponies, of which a captain was allowed two and a subaltern one; such a scene of confusion I never before witnessed; ponies kicking portmanteaus, &c. flying one way, tents another, ponies galloping through the different regiments dragging their loads under them. At five a.m. the columns moved off in succession preceded by the 8th Hussars, the Horse Artillery and field-guns, followed by the seven infantry regiments, with the pontoon-train and obstreperous baggagers to bring up the rear.

Our route lay along a beautiful country of undulating ground, bounded by lofty and steep hills, covered with low trees and brushwood. About seven a.m. the day began to get very warm, and the roads were exceedingly dusty, the soil in this part of the. country being entirely sand. We halted after the first half-hour, and then every hour; the halt generally took place near a watering-place, or fountain, in which Turkey abounds; sometimes the water was drawn from wells, but more frequently it flowed into a trough from a spout in the rock. Very few remarkable incidents occurred during the march, except occasional repetitions of the morning scene among the *bât*-ponies. Everybody looked very warm and thirsty, and while with the clouds of fine dust;

I trudged along with my cloak strapped on my back, and heavily armed with a pocket-pistol in my haversack, to quench my thirst. The progress of a large body of men is necessarily slow and tedious: the captains were allowed to ride; in fact this indulgence was extended to all officers, but as few subalterns had more than one pony each, not many could take advantage of the privilege.

About half-past eleven a.m. we reached our new camping-ground, beautifully situated between two lakes—*i.e.* at the end of one extending to Varna, and at the head of another. In the vicinity of the camp was a small Bulgarian village, called Aladyn, consisting of low, thatched, whitewashed hovels, surrounded by gardens, very prolific in the growth of weeds; these houses seemed clean, but all about them appeared neglected and in poverty. Through the misconduct of some soldiers these quiet, inoffensive people became panic-stricken, fancied we wanted to rob them, and refused to sell anything. The first time I visited the village, in quest of something to improve our dinners, the inhabitants ran into their houses, and, with difficulty, I at last bought a gosling; but they afterwards became reconciled to their new neighbours, and used to supply us with poultry and eggs; and hungry captains and subalterns might daily be seen returning to camp, with poultry in their hands and eggs in their haversacks.

Being surrounded by plenty of trees, the men amused themselves in constructing avenues of boughs in front of their tents, and various little arbours; in front of my tent was an arbour, in which three of us dined every evening, seated on saddle-bags, or cross-legged with our knees for a table, discussing brown bread and salt rations, varied by a chicken or goose, and finishing up with a *chibouque*. The regiments, while at Aladyn, attempted making and baking bread; field-ovens were constructed, but the difficulty of obtaining a supply of flour, I fancy, put a stop to these June, bread-supplies. The view from our camp of an evening was very beautiful; the calm-looking lake in the distance, with its woody banks rising up gradually into hills, and the golden tints of the setting sun lighting up the landscape, formed a suitable subject for a painter or a poet; but, being neither the one nor the other, I have confined myself to a matter-of-fact description in prose.

On the evening of our arrival some of us enjoyed a bathe in the lake: the same evening a Horse artilleryman, while bathing, got out of his depth, and, being unable to swim, was unfortunately drowned.

On the 5th I had a long ride with two others on a foraging expedition; our costume was cool though decidedly peculiar, consisting of a suit of flannel and a wide-awake encircled by a turban.

The day was calm and intensely hot: our road lay through a woody and sandy country along the borders of a large lake; the hills rose abruptly on either side covered with trees, and occasionally a bold rock peeping out. After riding about five miles we reached a large plain, on which some wheat was growing: near here was a Turkish cavalry camp, and a mile further on we reached the camp of the 8th Hussars. After remaining here a short time we went on to the village of Devna, where we failed in obtaining provisions; although there were plenty of fowls and cows about the place, still all our demands met with the perpetual reply, "*Yok, yok*" (Turkish for "No").

At the Hussar camp we picked up the Turkish names of articles which we required, and among them what we were told was the term for *flour*. At the first hut we reached the word was put in force, but those we asked tossed up their heads, saying "*Yok;*" they were Bulgarian women, and, being Christians, they had their faces unveiled, displaying prettier features than we generally saw in the country. After sundry fruitless attempts to make ourselves understood, one of the women presented me *with a rose*, and it then occurred to us that *flower* and not *flour* was what we had been demanding.

In my rambles about the country I was always struck with the scarcity of human beings; doves abounded, and numerous larks rose from the corn as we rode past, warbling forth their pretty notes, reminding us of country scenes at home; but inhabitants were few and far between. The small lakes and general scenery reminded me of some parts of Canada, and the park-like arrangement of trees, in clumps, made us sometimes almost fancy that a country-house must be near.

We used to march out very frequently, starting about six a.m. and returning at nine a.m. At this time there were great complaints about the want of regularity in the postal arrangements; the letters frequently lay at Varna for a day or so for want of conveyance up country. Occasional wet and blowing weather gave us cool days; on the 7th, which was hot and windy, the whole Light Division, with artillery, was drawn up about mid-day to receive Marshal St. Arnaud; after waiting under arms more than two hours, in perpetual gusts of wind and fine sand, very trying to the eyes, a message was received to say that he was not coming.

Every day showed more and more how faulty our arrangements were, not only in *one* particular but many particulars: for instance, the hospitals; when we left Varna there was no place in which to leave the sick, whereas the French, who had arrived only two days previously, had appropriated a large building as a hospital, thoroughly cleansed and whitewashed it, rendering it capable of containing many patients.

For practice, an "outlying picket" was established, the duties being carried out strictly, as if before an enemy. I was on picket one day with my captain; as a protection against an imaginary attack, we made the men construct an *abattis* of the trees, &c., by which we were surrounded; for it must be borne in mind that we were not provided with spades, &c., so as to practise throwing up some further kind of defence. We (officers) had a patrol tent, into which we crept for shelter. On the morning of the 10th we received sudden orders to march, destination unknown; about three a.m. my servant put his head into my tent, saying in true Hibernian accent, "Are you awake, sir?" I roused myself, and found it was pouring with rain in torrents as it had been all night; happily in the midst of my deliberations about the propriety of packing up, an order came postponing the parade until eight; a little more sleep, and all packed by seven a.m.

I then sat on my baggage, wrapped in a cloak, listening to pitter-patter of the rain against the canvas, until despatch from Sir G. Brown, at Varna, relieved suspense, by postponing the march until further orders, circumstances having arisen which rendered our move unnecessary; then arose the usual camp "shaves" as to the whys and the wherefores of this counter-order; it was currently reported that the Russians had advanced sufficiently near to cut off our division from that of the French; some wiseacre remarked that it was only a scheme of Sir G. Brown so as to keep us on the *qui vive*. Another report, that the defective arrangement of the commissariat was the cause, seemed to us far from improbable.

There was a great sameness in our everyday camp life, so very different to our first taste of "life under canvas" at Chobham in 1853; here we had not any British public in drags, busses, cabs, donkey-carts, &c.; no sounds of popping champagne, cries of "ginger-beer, lemonade, soda-water, oranges, apples, nuts;" that was *a pleasant picnic, but it taught us regimental officers nothing whatever in the way of practical soldiering.* We paraded every morning at half-past six, and the day afterwards passed in walking, talking, reading, writing, or bathing, and by a few in sleeping and grumbling, the latter pursuit said to be a privilege peculiar to Englishmen. The meat of the country was very bad, and rendered still more unpalatable by salt being very scarce. Divine Service took place every Sunday, to which, being a Roman Catholic regiment, we contributed few men, but principally officers; our chaplain was the Rev. Mr. Egan.

In my daily rides I was much struck with the beauty of the country, and I used to think how much could be made of it, if colonised; there was abundance of water, and the land, where cultivated, seemed capable being made very productive; as it was, it appeared denuded of inhabitants, and you might ride for miles without seeing a creature, only occasionally passing small villages, droves of cattle and *arabas*, or country carts. The birds reminded me of Old England—the cuckoo, lark, and some kind of thrush, besides numbers of doves. In some places violent convulsions of Nature seemed to have occurred—probably volcanic; and we frequently saw huge rocks so displaced that at first glance they presented the appearance of an ancient ruin. The climate was very variable: one day intensely hot, frequently followed by pouring rain and cold nights; and at other times there was a heavy dew at night.

It was surprising to observe what a complete change the French effected in Varna; from being a wretched town, badly supplied with anything eatable or drinkable, and inhabited by beings who seemed to say little else but "*Yok, yok,*" it soon became well filled with French shops, the streets named and repaired, and even *cafés* established. '

All this time we were constantly practised in packing up everything at a moment's notice, and marching out a few miles, under the superintendence of Sir George Brown, who used to come from Varna to see us.

By way of encouragement, we were told that during the Peninsular War the Light Division could then be roused from their sleep, strike tents, have everything packed, and get under arms *in fifteen minutes*. One morning in particular, the general complimented the officers of the 88th upon the excellent way in which their baggage-ponies were loaded.

It was notified to our division that no dependence could now be placed upon the commissariat arrangements, beyond the daily supply of the rations—bread and meat. At this time it very frequently happened that no supplies of tea, sugar, &c., could be obtained, and the men had to breakfast off dry bread only. The defective arrangements of the commissariat arose from the great difficulty of obtaining transport; in one night all the *araba-jees* (*araba*[1] drivers) deserted; those:

---

1. An *araba* was a rudely-constructed country waggon without springs.

to our regiment fortunately did not do so, thanks to our excellent quartermaster (Moore), who, by feeding the two old men with ration bread, managed to retain their services, and they remained with us until they both died of cholera at Devna, where the oxen also died of old age and starvation.

On the 13th the camp had a holiday, and the Light Division races came off. An open space near the camp was converted into a course, and the day's amusements consisted of hurdle races, mule races, &c., and foot races for the men; in the hurdle race a horse was killed; it belonged to Major Norcott, Rifle Brigade; several bands played some nice selections during the day. Altogether it was an agreeable change from the monotony of camp life.

The porter and ale, with which we were to have been supplied at a cheap rate, were issued at Varna, as already mentioned; but, after our departure from that place, the difficulty of transport caused the supply to cease, and with the talked-of cheap provisions, it relapsed into a fiction, so that only the troops at Varna continued to enjoy the privilege of such luxuries. Plenty of milk and eggs were, after a while, obtainable in the country; the country bread was brown and coarse, the meat was very bad, and the wine—a kind of claret—though rough, was wholesome, and could be purchased at fivepence per quart. Any article purchased at Varna was very dear; still it was Hobson's choice, "that or none."

One day I had a long ride to Varna, and returned about ten p.m., with my saddle-bags, like panniers, on each side of my pony, filled with candles, soap, tea, sugar, bacon, &c. It was very difficult to obtain change for large coin, and you might as well be penniless as have a sovereign; the commissariat issued pay in nothing but gold, which could be changed at Varna only, and that too with difficulty and at a loss: our canteen man, to insure customers, issued penny tokens made of tin, upon each of which were stamped the words, "*Bono per one pens*"—*Anglicè.* "Good for one penny."

On the 16th we received orders of readiness to proceed to Silistria, five days' march, and but little baggage was to accompany us; this was afterwards counter-ordered; the Russians, having been defeated in their assaults on Silistria, had retreated, and Omar Pasha (report said) did not require the assistance of the British Army; and it was as well, for it seemed doubtful whether the confusionary (not expeditionary) army in the East was ready to move in a country where all supplies must accompany the march. This counter-order disappointed us very much.

The days were occasionally intensely hot, and we endeavoured to keep our tents cool by putting our blankets outside them, and it certainly had the desired effect.

About this time nearly all the troops had left Scutari and were encamped near Varna, together with a large force of French.

On the 18th we were inspected by the Duke of Cambridge, General Canrobert, and Sir George Brown, attended by a large escort of French cavalry and 8th Hussars. As the French general passed, each regiment cheered him—a singular circumstance to have happened on the anniversary of Waterloo. It was a tedious and hot parade; we were under arms five hours. Although we knew that Canrobert had proved to be a fine and gallant soldier, yet, to our English ideas, his long hair did not give him a soldier-like appearance.

An order was now issued that all ponies were to be marked with the initials and regiment of the owner. Our adjutant desired his *bât*-man to get his pony marked; he afterwards found it marked with his initials, &c,. but underneath them the letters B. *R*. "What means this?" he inquired.

"Why, shure it British Army," replied the servant; the fact was, that the servant, who was *Irish*, had got some *English* gunner to mark the pony, giving him to put the letters B. *A*.; but having, as he was wont, pronounced *A* like the letter *R*, hence the blunder.

On the 20th the second Aladyn race meeting came off; pony races for the officers and foot races for the men. The day was very fine but hot, with an occasional breeze; among the spectators was one lady, whose husband was a captain in the Rifle Brigade. Captain Connolly, 23rd Fusiliers,[2] was thrown in a flat race, but not hurt, and a sergeant of the 33rd Regiment broke his leg in jumping.

The division went out to drill almost every morning at eight, and remained until one p.m.; the ground was about two miles from camp, very prettily situated, commanding a fine view of a woody valley, in which was a long, narrow lake resembling a river; in the far distance the Balkan range of mountains rose boldly up, and their blue form stood out majestically against the clear sky. The weather was intensely hot, but our heads were protected from the sun by white capcovers similar to those worn by the troops in India; these early and lengthened drills during the hot weather were very fatiguing; added to which, owing to the continued defective commissariat arrange-

---

2. Killed at Alma, September 20th, 1854.

ments, the rations did not arrive in sufficient time for the men's breakfasts to be prepared, and they frequently were obliged to go through these long and fatiguing parades without having previously broken their fast; it will however, be subsequently observed that, thanks to the careful foresight of our excellent colonel (Shirley), arrangements were made to remedy the defect, which, in this somewhat treacherous climate, undoubtedly sowed the seeds of much of the sickness which afterwards attacked the troops.

In one of my many exploring rides I came across what were apparently some ancient ruins, consisting of a row of several massive pillars and other *débris* of a building, which had the appearance of great age.

The vicinity of our camp was covered with wild flowers, and the trees were chiefly oaks of stunted growth; small snakes and lizards occasionally visited our tents. While sitting one evening in my tent, smoking my pipe, I felt something up the leg of my trousers; having been out for a long walk I thought it was a bramble, but, on putting up my hand. I pulled out a long centipede, which very fortunately did not sting me.

An officer from each regiment was selected to assist in purchasing horses for the commissariat; the pay was to be good and the duty pleasant, affording an opportunity of seeing the country &c.; Lieutenant Maynard, of my regiment, was one of those selected for this post The band of the 77th Regiment used to play every evening, and caused a pleasant change in our monotonous life by playing familiar *valses*, polkas, &c.: the so-called "army of *occupation*" might more truthfully have now been termed the "army of idleness."

Besides the ordinary routine of drills, &c., we continued constantly to practise packing tents and baggage upon the *bât*-ponies, and some, which had hitherto been very obstreperous, were becoming gradually reconciled to their loads.

On the 26th a Turkish infantry regiment passed our camp, escorting *arabas* filled with sick and wounded from Silistria: the Turkish loss during the siege of that place had been 2000 men.

On the 27th I went on picket with my captain, and we relieved a party of the 77th Regiment We sat nearly all day in a hut made of boughs of trees, with no enemy to annoy us except myriads of mosquitoes and flies. Our picket lay completely concealed among trees and bushes, commanding a distant view of lofty, woody hills. In the evening we sat and smoked round a good log fire until we nodded off to sleep or took refuge in our patrol-tent.

At four a.m. on the 30th the whole division marched to a place called Devna, about seven miles west of Aladyn: the morning was very warm; our march lay through an open and sandy country, and the clouds of dust tended considerably to induce thirst

Our brigade with the Rifle Brigade, went by one road, and the remainder, with the artillery, marched by a different way; there was a clear sky, scorching sun, and no breeze; and after a very hot and dusty march we reached our camping-ground about nine a.m.. situated on the side of a hill about a mile from the tumble-down straggling village of Devna, Immediately below us flowed a narrow river, traversed in many places by small bridges, and, above our camp, broken up into smaller streams, where several mills were placed. We now had no wood near us, and our lofty position rendered us exposed to every breeze; being encamped in a fallow field, the frequent clouds of dust were intolerable, every article in our tents being filled with fine sand, which rendered our stay here anything but agreeable.

In a large plain, about two miles below us, and bounded by lofty hills, were encamped the cavalry and artillery; it was, however, not so prettily situated a camp as that of Aladyn.

The Duke of Cambridge's brigade, Guards and Highlanders, moved to Aladyn on the 1st; the *Times* correspondent, when dining in our camp, was puffing up the marching of the Duke's brigade from Varna to Aladyn, as compared with that of the Light Division, which he termed disgraceful from the number of stragglers. At last he was obliged to acknowledge that numerous Guardsmen and Highlanders were left on the road, and *arabas sent to bring them in*; in our march between the same places there were numbers of stragglers from all regiments, but more especially from one, which was consequently nicknamed *the milestones*. With the Rangers there were none, a fact accounted for in this way; that through the foresight of our good colonel (Shirley) the cooks were preparing coffee on the previous night, and each man had some bread and coffee before starting in the morning; besides which there was no drunkenness in the regiment On the previous evening, owing to our colonel adopting the wise precaution of closing our canteen at an early hour; and it is also a fact worthy of record that in subsequent marches in Bulgaria and the Crimea, while other regiments had many stragglers, we had very few; the few that did fall out invariably joined after a halt.

About this time we heard of the death of Captain Butler, the hero of Silistria. It was said that at his funeral Omar Pasha stood at the head of the grave, and said, "There lies the defender of Silistria;" at the same time he drew his sword, and, kissing the blade, swore to maintain the friendship of Christians, and never to speak ill of them; an example which was followed by all his staff.

At this time we officers adopted the orthodox fashion of an army in the field, and had our hair cut as close as possible, presenting a somewhat peculiar appearance; but we found it a great comfort during the hot weather.

On the 3rd we received five minutes' notice to turn out and parade before Omar Pasha on his way from Silistria; he galloped down the line, colours flying, bands playing; we then drilled before him. He afterwards saw the Light Cavalry, consisting of the 8th and 11th Hussars, 13th Light Dragoons, and 17th Lancers, who manoeuvred before him, finishing with a charge, in the middle of which, amid clouds of dust Omar Pasha was to be seen trying the speed of his horse, but was soon left behind. He was a fine, soldierlike, and intelligent-looking man. Omar Pasha expressed his great admiration of the troops, and said that with such an army he could conquer the world After the review he rode through the camp, and was greatly cheered by the different regiments.

We used to bathe every morning in a large tank, which was kept full by a spring of icy-cold water, a great luxury in the hot weather. This tank was intended to supply water to turn the wheel of an adjoining flour-mill, the proprietor of which was, no doubt, considerably astonished at the unexpected use into which his reservoir was converted. Returning from a bathe one day, I fell in with a regiment of Bashi-Bazouks, under the command of a French officer, who inquired the way to the commissariat camp. I rode with him at the head of this motley column, as ruffianly a looking set as could be seen anywhere.

On the 5th we paraded for Sir George Brown, and drilled from five to eight a.m. The following day I went to see the Heavy Cavalry and Artillery inspected by Omar Pasha: after waiting three hours he came at last from Varna, accompanied by Lord Raglan, and rode down the line; the Horse Artillery galloped past, and afterwards performed several evolutions. The cavalry finished with a charge. Omar Pasha afterwards sent for a dragoon, examined his helmet and put it on; he left in the evening for Schumla and Silistria. At Omar Pasha's request a ration of rum was issued to all ranks on the occasion of his visit. One of the heroes of Silistria, when afterwards talking to a young cavalry officer, asked him if he did not find "camping-out" a very rough kind of life? "Oh, no!" replied the cornet, "we are accustomed to it; *we were at Chobham!*"

In my rambles about this part of the country I was often struck with the fine appearance of the inhabitants.

The Bulgarians are a handsome race, men as well as women, with swarthy complexions and intelligent countenances; very different to the Turks in the latter respect. The men wore large, well-folded turbans, of a shawl pattern, placed jauntily on one side, and arranged so as to project beyond the head, like the brim of a wide-awake; they wore the usual Turkish loose dress, of coarse cloth, with a broad sash, in which were carried a pistol, knife, and ink-bottle. The men used to pass daily through the camp, selling milk, eggs, &c., and by way of speaking English they cried out, "*Milko bono,*" "*Egg-es bono;*" sometimes a facetious Ranger would say to one of them, "*Bono bad egg-es,*" which the Bulgarian repeated through the camp, much to our amusement. Occasionally I saw women weaving at a primitive kind of loom.

During a ride one day I stopped at a roadside fountain, where was a group of women and children; they were quite unappalled at my approach, and one gave me a draught of delicious cold water from her pitcher, while I sat on my pony under the gaze of many black eyes: the picturesque group around me, and the beautiful light peculiar to an Eastern sunset, presented a fine subject for a painter.

I once lent a Bulgarian man my telescope; he could not shut one eye at a time, and therefore pulled his turban across one while he looked through with the other. He appeared astounded at the result, and returned the telescope, exclaiming, "*Bono johnny.*"

One day I amused myself in writing the following doggerel verses, descriptive of one of our many marches in Bulgaria, which I headed with this brief preface: *The exhilarating air of Bulgaria inspired a youthfull son of Mars to indite the following description of a march of the Light Division generally, and of the Connaught Rangers in particular.* —

Camp Devna, Bulgaria, July, 1854.

The clouds of night were scatt'ring,
The day began to dawn,
When from a doze Phoebus arose.
Sat up and said 'twas morn:
The mists on Euxine's shore
To his proud summons yield,

44

While England's sons still snore,
Stretched on the tented field

A deathlike stillness reigns,
When loud the bugle sounds,
Its stirring call
Wakes slumberers all.
And through the vale resounds:
Then sleeping faces quickly through
The tents appear, a motley crew,
And heads, of every shape and hue,
Of many a Connaught Ranger.

A servant then his head thrusts in,
"Get up—'tis time to rise;"
"Oh! what a bore,
'Tis scarcely four,"
Some sleepy sub. replies;
"I'll not get up"—and then turns round.
But bugles without number,
Close to his ear, with doleful sound,
Disturb his peaceful slumber.

But all in vain, ye sleeping few,
For to the stirring rattle
Of beaten drum,
Forth, forth, they come,
As though led on to battle:
'Tis duty calls, and in a crack
Each son of Mars puts on his pack,
And to the tune of "Paddy Whack,"
March on the Connaught Rangers.

What means this sudden cry of "Stop,"
This dust and perturbation!
A pony loose—
Ah! 'tis no use—
The saddle turns—what aggravation!
All ranks their loads are vainly sticking
On ponies rearing, neighing, kicking,
'Mid bâtmen pulling, shouting, licking,—
A perfect chaos scene.
'Tis then you see, in sad dilemma.

The restive nag of Ensign Stumps,
Which on the road
Kicks off its load.
While he looks on in doleful dumps.
That all was firm himself he flattered.
But soon his kit is widely scattered.
His goods and chattels sorely battered;
A sorry sight to view.
This dust and din well leave behind.
These ponies and their pranks.
And swallowing last
A light repast.
Well join the moving ranks;—
On, on they press, a warlike train.
O'er hill and dale, thro' wood and plain
Each band's enlivening martial strain
Re-echoes from afar.

The dust like powder flew that day.
Red hot the sun's bright beam;
Perchance you think
We stopped to drink
At every rippling stream?
Of course we did, like swarms of flies,
Each captain, sub, and private vies
(With whiskers white and blinded eyes)
Some fountain cool to gain.

At length our camping-ground we reach,
The tents soon deck the plain.
The fires are lit,
Unpacked each kit,
Which some ne'er thought to see again.
A few complain how they have toiled,
Others bewail a dinner spoiled.
While some discuss a chicken boiled,
And smoke a mild chibouque.

Full oft you heard the merry note
Of some enlivening song.
The hearty laugh,
The witty chaff,

Amid a jovial throng;
And thus the hours quickly flew,
While comrades, to a listening few,
Recounted tales (they said were true)
Around the warm camp-fire.

The shades of evening gather.
The stars begin to peep,
When Phoebus bright
Puts out his light,
And soon[3] drops off to sleep;
While on the calm lake's marshy shore
Loud croak the frogs (a dreadful bore!)
The moon her silvery beams sheds o'er
The slumbering tented field.

The sentries' solemn cry, "All's well!"
Disturbs the calm of night,
While all around
Are sleeping sound,
Snoring with all their might;
Dreaming, perhaps, of some kind mother,
A bosom friend, or absent brother.
And, if in love, someone or other
In England's peaceful land.

On the 13th we received intelligence of the repulse of the Turks at Giurgevo, and were very sorry to hear that Lieutenant James Burke, R.E., had been killed on that occasion; he was well known to us all, and had been staying in our camp a short time previously, when *en route* to the Danube; we all felt much sympathy for his brother in the 88th, to whom this sad occurrence was a heavy blow.

Lord Cardigan at this time returned with his reconnoitring party, having been as far as Trajan's Wall between Rassova and Kustendjie; nearly all the horses were knocked up.

On the 11th the Devna races came off, in which a pony belonging to one of our officers won two races; the course was next to our camp, and the attendance was very good.

The weather now became excessively hot, the thermometer being frequently 108° in our tents. On the 13th we had a long and hot drill from half-past four to eight a.m., which considerably sharpened our

3. The absence of twilight is thus poetically mentioned.

appetites for breakfast In the afternoon I rode over to see M., 47th Regiment, who was encamped with the 2nd Division, under General Sir De Lacy Evans, about four miles from us. After a delightful ride across the valley of Devna, up hills and through woody ravines, I reached their prettily situated camp, which they had improved by the erection of bowers to keep off the sun. I dined there, and after sunset I started home; and after losing my way in the fine but very dark night, I reached my tent shortly after tattoo, and was soon numbered among the many dreamers.

With the aid of our *bât*-ponies some of us brought boughs from a distant wood and made an arbour, in which we dined every day; it contained rushes for a carpet, pack-saddles for chairs, and two small tables; here we sat every evening smoking our *chibouques* under the feeble light of Turkish lanterns, and retired to roost at nine o'clock. About this time the news reached us of the Russians having evacuated the principalities; and we read in the papers that the people of England urged the necessity of attacking Sebastopol; the general opinion with us was, that it was getting too late in the season for commencing what would be likely to prove a work of time. The French said that an attack upon Sebastopol would be a great sacrifice of life attended with no profitable results. The only fighting we had at this time was about *the wearing of moustaches*; and, after sundry discussions among generals and brigadiers, all who had commenced cultivation were politely requested to remove the incipient growth.

Some of us were very proud one day in having achieved the manufacture of a plum-pudding, made of coarse country flour; and though, in England, it might have been despised, in Bulgaria it was pronounced excellent; our kitchen consisted of a hole dug about three feet long and deep and one fool wide, with a fire raised at one end; the cooking was carried on in every branch of simplicity, without the aid of a cookery-book; a canopy of trees protected the *chef-de-cuisine,* but a shower of rail frequently extinguished the fire. Sometimes we purchased fish from the natives. On the 16th it was cold, and poured incessantly with rain, deluging us all, and stopping our dinner-parties in the bower outside our tents.

The receipt of the mails now became more regular; horses were employed to convey the bags in charge of a Turkish *tâtar* (courier).

The forage for our ponies consisted of barley and cut straw, issued by the commissariat, and our *bât*-men cut grass in the neighbourhood; the ponies were marched down to water every morning and evening under the orderly officer; we nicknamed them the Bashi-Bazouks, or "Irregulars."

I heard a very interesting account of the siege of Silistria, from an officer who had just returned from that place; he censured the apathy of the Turks in not repairing the forts, &c., damped by the Russians; the siege had been raised twelve days, and nothing had been done, not even the Russian batteries destroyed. Had the Russians been aware of this they could easily have captured the place. Silistria itself was not the scene of action, but the nine forts by which it was protected, of which one—called Arab-Tabia—was the principal.

This officer described Arab-Tabia as bearing no resemblance to a fort now, but as having the appearance rather of a ploughed field, from the severe bombardment to which it had been exposed. It appeared that the Russians were anxious to gain Silistria for the sake of its strong position, as a base for future operations against our expected approach.

Numerous reports respecting our future movements continued to flow in daily; first, that we were to go to Sebastopol, then to Anapa, and so on—all equally true.

Some Turkish lancers were encamped near us; their tents being made of cotton were conspicuous by their whiteness; they were bell-tents, but lower and wider than ours; the soldiers were smarter looking men than the generality of the Ottoman cavalry which I had come across; they had the advantage, however, of being dressed in new clothing.

Lieutenant Maynard returned from his trip to purchase horses for Government; he went as far as Tirnova, and found the inhabitants most hospitable and kind.

At this time I had a slight attack of intermittent fever, which confined me to my tent for several days.

On Sunday, the 23rd, the cholera made its first appearance among us, breaking out in the grenadier company; Sergeant Dempsey, a very fine healthy young man, was carried off in a few hours; in fact, I saw him practising jumping in the morning, and he was buried in the afternoon. Sergeant Fortune also fell a victim, and before the next morning we had lost five men, and throughout the camp about twenty had died.[4]

As cases continued to increase daily throughout the division, we

4. Deaths by cholera in the 88th:—Sergeants John Dempsey and Fortune, 23rd July. Privates Charles McKee and Thomas Carty, and Corporal Bernard Cunniff, 24th.

received orders to shift our ground at nine o'clock on the morning of the 24th: weak from the effects of a recent attack of intermittent fever, I rode Maynard's pony. Our march lay through a woody and hilly country, with fields of golden corn; the sick were left at Devna. We encamped on the side of a hill, near a village called Monastir, picturesquely situated, with its flat-roofed houses surrounded by fruit gardens.

We changed our ground very often, but still we continued to lose two or three men every day. Immediately in front of our camp was a deep ravine, thickly wooded, through which ran a small stream; on the opposite side were encamped Sir G. Brown and staff; beyond this— among thickly-dotted walnut trees, in which this place abounded— were placed the 1st Brigade of our division; behind us the hill rose abruptly, and at the top was a large fruit garden, now forbidden ground; to our left the Rifle Brigade were encamped—this encampment, in a wood as it was, had a very beautiful appearance when lighted up with the rays of the setting sun.

We much felt the want of books to while away the many spare hours; and newspapers were most eagerly read and re-read.

On the 26th we received a draft consisting of 150 men, small and very young, with Ensign Webb.[5] Two men (James Walsh and Thomas Barnes) died of cholera today.

On the 27th I lunched with my old 20th friend, Captain Hallewell,[6] D.A.Q.M.G. Light Division, and in the afternoon I rode with my captain to the village of Pravadi. Our road lay across the extensive down or plain which stretched along the top of the hill, above our camp, where the Rifle Brigade were placed. This plain was the site of the Russian camp in 1828, and numerous tumuli marked the graves of hundreds who fell victims to the plague at that time. All was stillness; vultures soaring above our heads and perching upon these mounds; otherwise no sign of life. The view around was magnificent As far as the eye could reach rose hill above hill, bounded by the Balkan range of lofty mountains in the far distance; many of these hills, being covered with cornfields, afforded a pleasing contrast to the generally woody scene

After jogging along the undulating plain, our road descended suddenly into a deep rocky and woody ravine, where we crossed a nar-

---

5. Killed at the attack on the Quarries, June 7th, 1855.
6. Died November, 1869, Colonel unattached, and Commandant Royal Military College, Sandhurst.

50

row stream—a mountain torrent in winter. Here were the ruins of a bridge, no doubt blown up in 1828. Our rugged path now lay along the side of this deep vale, which gradually widened as we ascended the hill.

In about half an hour we reached a Turkish fort, standing on the summit of a lofty position above the precipitous ravine, through which wound the stream we had previously crossed. We scrambled up to the fort, a tumble-down-looking place, garrisoned by a few Turkish soldiers. Here we resigned our ponies to a soldier, and walking across the fort a new scene broke upon our view. Immediately below us, at the depth of some hundreds of feet, lay the picturesque-looking town of Pravadi; so that, as we stood in the fort, we were between two deep vales—the one we had previously crossed, the other containing the town.

Leaving the fort we continued our walk along the rocky hill between the two valleys, until we reached the ruins of an old castle, where we stopped to take breath, and, leaning over a ledge of rock, we contemplated the singular view below us; while the setting sun diffused a ruddy hue over the peaceful scene. It was curious to *look down* upon flat-roofed houses, with the inhabitants looking as small as flies, and to hear the sounds of children crying, dogs barking, cocks crowing, &c., so far below us; but still there was not the busy hum of an English town.

On the opposite side rose another hill, crowned by a fort; the place, we heard, was considered very unhealthy. At one end of the town was a large marsh, beyond which extended a line of fortification across the valley from hill to hill, with a Turkish camp. At the other end of the town was a line of trench and parapet, connecting the hills, and behind it Turkish hut-barracks.

Continuing our walk along the precipice we sat down at the end of the hill where the two valleys joined; here the view was magnificent; on one hand a rocky and woody valley, on the other the vale of Pravadi, with mountains rising in the distance. A dark cloud in the distance—and frequent experience that thunderstorms rise suddenly on the finest days in this climate—acted as a warning, and we hurried back to camp in time to escape a heavy shower. The next day we had a severe thunderstorm, and heavy rain continued throughout the following night.

At this time the cholera also appeared among our troops at Aladyn and Varna, as well as among the French, who suffered severely; between July 23rd and August 4th we lost twenty-four men,[7] and in the whole Light Division two officers and 100 men.

On the 1st August we shifted our ground about a mile towards Pravadi, to a fine open situation among large walnut-trees. At this time the troops were employed in making; gabions and fascines, and also in throwing up trenches; a list of the officers who had been educated at Sandhurst was called for, to act as assistant-engineers in superintending the works. This change from the ordinary routine of camp life was, apart from the useful nature of the employment, considered most beneficial to the men, as it tended to divert their minds from the terrible sickness which was raging among them, and to keep them in health. During the remainder of our stay in Bulgaria the regiment (with the rest of the division) was daily employed at the works, nicknamed "the diggings," and there was but little drill.

Our working hours were from nine to twelve and from three to six. Some days we had no work, and I took advantage of a holiday to pay one or two visits to Pravadi. Like all Turkish towns, it seemed on its last legs—shops few, streets narrow and dirty, and abounding in dogs, frogs, and stagnant pools. In one of my visits to Pravadi I found it full of Arnauts—Albanian soldiers—who had fought so well at Silistria. Some of them were very fine men, dressed in a short white kilt, crimson stockings, an embroidered jacket, with a large sash round the waist, containing two pistols and a *yataghan* (sword).

On some spare days parties of us went out foraging and occasionally succeeded in getting eggs and rancid butter. As Lieutenant E. (a quondam Sandhurst cadet) had refused the appointment of an assistant-engineer, I volunteered my services, and, being struck off regimental duty, was employed daily in superintending the construction of field-works, without pay.

On Sunday, the 6th, I rode with Captain Hallewell to the Guards' camp, about fourteen miles off; the day being very warm we went leisurely, and when about halfway we stopped to lunch at one of the many fountains which we passed, and Hallewell produced a bottle of

7. Privates—Robert Dadley, Patrick Joyce, and Thomas Davis, 27th July, at Varna, and William Burley, in camp; 28th, Daniel O'Brien, in camp; 29th, Michael Sullivan, John McDermott and John Horrigan, in camp; 1st August, W. Lewis, John Lyons, Anthony Fahey and Patrick Buckley, in camp; 2nd, John McCarton in camp and Timothy Cooney, at Varna; 3rd, James Connell and John Gall in camp; 4th, John McHugh in camp.
Corporals—T. Hammond, 31st in camp and Lynch, 4th in camp.
Total between 23rd July and 4th August—2 Sergeants, 3 Corporals, 19 Privates=24.

champagne, which was cooled in the icy-cold water. After attending Divine Service in camp we dined with Major South,[8] and returned home about midnight We heard that the 20th Regiment, in which my brother George was then serving, had reached Varna on the 5th, but had been ordered back to Beikos Bay, opposite Therapia.

Rumour at this time said we were going to move somewhere— the general destination fixed upon by such an informant

On the 6th an order was issued permitting moustaches to be worn, and we were much amused at the wording of the order, which prescribed the exact number of inches to be shaved between the moustache and the whiskers, as if every man's face was the same size.

The weather was oppressively hot, and on the 11th we again shifted our ground towards Pravadi, on a high position near the camp of the 77th Regiment The regiments of the Light Division were now all encamped separately, and not by brigades, as previously; our ground was very stony, and consequently bad for pitching tents. Close to us was a desolate-looking village; it was much knocked about by the Russians in 1828, and the ruined mosque, &c, still remained as emblems of the destruction then made. Many of the Bulgarian farmers were said to be rich, but, as any semblance of wealth was set upon by the *pashas* for heavy taxation, all lived in the same style of apparent poverty.

On the 10th a large fire broke out in Varna, and destroyed a good deal of government stores, both French and English. The men now got a half-ration of rum daily; our colonel had urged the advisability of issuing this when the cholera first broke out, but it was not then done. An extra half-ration of meat was also issued daily; but as the commissariat persisted in killing meat *by day,* half of it became bad before it was required to be cooked: meat, at this time, would only keep for about twelve hours.

On the 16th we were inspected by our brigadier (Buller). The same day I was very glad to receive a letter from my brother with the 20th Regiment at Beikos Bay.

On the 17th Sir George Brown came from Varna to inspect the various regiments of the Light Division as to their fitness for active service. This fine old soldier returned to Varna after the inspection. A ride of fifty miles was no bad day's work for one who was no longer a young man. He pronounced the 88th to be the healthiest regiment

---

8. Major S. had been many years paymaster of the 20th Regiment, and was at this time paymaster of the Brigade of Guards. He was the son of Colonel S., who succeeded my father in the command of the 20th Regiment in 1818.

he had seen. The cholera was now rapidly disappearing. Sir George Brown, on this occasion, asked our colonel to tell him candidly if he considered the 88th fit for service. The colonel replied that most certainly they were quite fit for work; and also that he was sure that the excitement of a move, and the prospect of active service, would very much tend to improve the men's health, and to drive away the cholera.

The regiment continued to be engaged daily at the field-works by wings. I had charge of the left brigade—19th, 77th, and 88th Regiments—and employed them in constructing parallels and zigzags of approach, under Captain Gordon, R.E.,[9] who recommended me to be permanently attached to the Royal Engineers, with pay. My daily routine now was—breakfast at eight, proceed to my engineering work at nine a.m., return to camp from twelve to three, and then again to my earthy occupation until five p.m., when a ride until dinner-hour, at seven, finished up the day, and I was quite ready for bed at nine o'clock.

In consequence of the loss sustained by the commissariat at the fire in Varna, our ponies were put upon half-rations. We heard that at the fire the French soldiers behaved very badly, plundering whatever they came across.

On the afternoon of the 22nd we (88th) again changed our position about 200 yards, to less stony ground, better suited for pitching tents. We were close to a small village called Jasma.

The cholera still kept to us, though cases were comparatively few. On the 22nd we lost a sergeant.[10]

The weather now became much cooler, and we had heavy rain and thunderstorms, which rendered camp life anything but agreeable, putting out the fires and spoiling the dinners.

Besides field-works some of the division were now employed in excavating one of the numerous *tumuli* near the camp. A very perfect

---

9. Afterwards Lieutenant-General Sir William Gordon, K.C.B.; he died in 1873.

10. Colour-Sergeant Clarke, one of the best men in the regiment; up to this date we had lost by cholera since the 4th inst. 2 sergeants, 2 corporals, 8 privates, and 1 by fever = 13—*viz.*;

Privates—John Houlihan, 5th August, in camp; John Barlow, 7th in camp; William Fox, in camp, and John Home at Varna 8th; John Jellicoe and B. Doran, 13th in camp; William Allen, 19th in camp of fever; Michael Maloney in camp and Charles Houran, at Varna 31st.

Sergeant Boylan 9th in camp; Corporal Harkin. 10th in camp; Corporal Ward, 16th in camp; Colour-Sergeant Clarke, 22nd at Varna.

skeleton was discovered, and a soldier found a coin of Constantine.

Now that the regiments were scattered, Divine Service was read at regimental parades. Being a Roman Catholic regiment, our number of Protestants was very small—more officers than men—and our colonel (Shirley) generally read the service.

On the 25th the Light Division received orders of readiness to march to Varna for embarkation, *destination unknown*: the same day Captains Maynard, Mauleverer, and Ernst, just promoted, left us for the *depôt* in England. In consequence of the paucity of *arabas* to convey the sick, and blankets and knapsacks (!!!) the 1st Brigade only could march on the 26th for Varna; at one p.m. on the 27th our brigade (the 2nd) struck tents, and, after a hot and dusty march of seven miles, we encamped at Yuksukova, where we found our 1st Brigade and part of the 2nd (Sir De Lacy Evans') Division.

In our marches towards Varna the want of conveyance for the blankets and knapsacks invariably prevented our brigade marching until the afternoon: this was very inconvenient, and threw everything out of order: we never knew the hour of starting, and consequently the men's dinners were frequently spoiled, and thrown away.

I accepted an invitation to dine with M. (47th Regiment), who was encamped some way off, our own larder being very empty. On the 28th we continued our march towards Varna, and pitched our tents about seven p.m. at Karagole, two miles from Varna. Having had a sudden attack of intermittent fever I was quite unable to march, but rode upon an *araba* on the top of knapsacks, and as the road was very rough and the waggon had no springs, I was nearly jolted to pieces; it was an ordeal I can never forget.

Poor Shegog, one of our assistant-surgeons, here died of cholera after only five hours' illness, and was buried in the evening: the regiment experienced a heavy loss by his sad death, and none can ever forget his unremitting exertions and devoted attention to the sick during the outbreak of cholera.

On the 29th we marched at three p.m. and joined the 1st Brigade near Varna: in the morning our senior captain, Brevet-Major Mackie was seized with cholera and died while being conveyed to Varna: he was greatly liked and respected in the regiment, and his unexpected death was a great shock to us all.

At mid-day on the 30th we marched to the south side of the harbour, and at three p.m. embarked on board the sailing vessel *Orient*, transport No. 78; she was quite new, having been built to run to

Australia.

The harbour was now a great scene of bustle and excitement, and a perfect forest of masts with the numerous transports, &c.We left many men in hospital at Varna, who, together with *bât*-ponies, were under charge of Captain Corbett and Ensign Little.[11]

We embarked 774 rank and file, 27 officers, and 16 women: up to this date we had lost 43 by cholera.[12]

---

11. Ensign Little was one of five non-commissioned officers of the 88th promoted to commissions in the regiment during the campaign. (*Vide* Appendix D.)

12. Between the 22nd and 29th we lost the following officers and men, *viz*.;—Privates George Broom, 27th August, and James Cuddy, 29th; Assist.-Surgeon Shegog, 28th; Brevet-Major Mackie, 29th. Total loss between 23rd July and 29th August was—2 officers, 4 sergeants, 37 rank and file = 43.

CHAPTER 3

September 1st to November 5th

Various and absurd rumours were of course current at chap. this time respecting: our destination, but on the 2nd a very quiet; but explicit, order was issued by Lord Raglan, intimating that the invasion of the Crimea was to be made, and that the Light Division was to land first The weather at this time was very fine and admirably adapted for the embarkation of so large a force, and by the 3rd all the army had embarked.

On the 4th Captain Hallewell came on board, and told me that he had seen my brother on board the *Colombo*, some way astern of us.

On the 5th we were taken in tow by the *Himalaya* (steamer), and joined the fleet of vessels assembled off Baltschik. The cholera still kept to us; since embarking we had lost seven by that fatal scourge, and one of fever;[1] besides sending to hospital ashore several men very ill.

On the 6th we were at anchor off Baltschik; it was a wonderful sight to see such a vast assemblage of vessels of all kinds—a perfect forest of masts—and to reflect how many human beings they contained During the day the *Colombo* passed close to us; I recognised my brother, and we waved our handkerchiefs; much to my joy and surprise, he came on board in the evening, accompanied by some of my old friends—Butler. James, and Peard—of the 20th Regiment.

About daylight on the morning of the 7th the expedition started in six lines, headed by the *Agamemnon*; we go under weigh about nine a.m., and H.M.S. *Fury* towed our vessel as well as one contain-

---

1. Privates Lorrigan, 31st August, at Varna; John Hagerty, 2nd Sept., on board ship, Varna Harbour; Wm. Hogg, 3rd, on board ship, Varna Harbour, (of fever); John Jones, John Tully, Reuben Rowley and Jas. Hutchinson 4th on board ship, Varna Harbour; Wm. Ruttle, 5th on board ship, Varna Harbour. This made our total loss (of all ranks), before quitting Bulgaria, to be—49 by cholera and 2 by fevers=51.

ing the 19th Regiment; the departure was a splendid sight and one never to be forgotten; as far as the eye could reach the sea was covered with a vast assemblage of some of the largest steamers in the world, conveying and convoying one of the finest armies that England ever possessed. It was a most beautiful morning; the six lines in which we moved consisted of the Light Division leading, and then the 1st, 2nd, 3rd, 4th Divisions and Light Cavalry, followed by magazine and store-ships, the whole flanked by our men-of-war: the several divisions were distinguished, respectively, by a particular flag, carried at the foretop of each vessel. The distinguishing flag of the Light Division was square, chequered blue and white. A plan of the order in which the various divisions were to anchor off the Crimea, previous to landing, was is-sued to each commanding-officer; I copied the one received by our colonel, and sent it home.

We had most lovely weather for our progress across the Black Sea, with a cloudless sky and smooth sea, which continued until we land-ed. Various were our daily occupations on board ship; some practising with pistols, others trying to climb aloft and to reach the main-truck, while many scanned the horizon with their telescopes. Our "skipper" (a Scotchman) happening to let out that he had champagne on board, we had it produced, and daily drank success to the expedition, until the stock was exhausted

On the 9th we anchored in open sea, about fifty miles west of Odessa; here we remained at anchor all day on the 10th.

The cholera did not leave us, and from the 7th to the 10th we lost six men.[2]

We remained here until one p.m. on the 11th, when we weighed anchor and progressed slowly; meanwhile, the *Agamemnon*, with Sir George Brown on board, had reconnoitred the enemy's coast; the weather still continued calm and warm, and we had bright moonlight nights.

At daylight on the 12th, we made the coast of the Crimea; the weather now became colder, and we had a violent storm of rain and hail. On the 13th we were off Eupatoria at noon; the *Retribution* ran in and anchored, demanding the surrender of the town, under threat of bombardment, and of course it was given up.

We now moved along slowly, keeping close to the coast, and could clearly discern villages, cattle, &c., and but few inhabitants, the coun-

---

2. Privates John O'Neill, Thos. Shughrue and James Donohoe died 7th September; Joseph Steel, 9th; Denis Loughnan and John Quinn 10th.

try appeared very flat and barren. One man (Private John Egan) died of cholera today.

The *Colombo* passed us during the day; I recognised my brother on board and we waved our caps.

At eleven a.m. on the 14th the army landed, under the protection of the fleet, at a place called Old Fort, near Lake Tongla; no opposition was made to our landing; a few Cossacks hovered about, but they kept at a respectful distance; the day was very calm, and it was a beautiful sight to see the boats from the different transports landing the troops under the protection of our men-of-war, which were drawn up broadside-on to the shore.

The Light Division landed first on the flat, sandy shore, followed by the remaining divisions and part of the artillery; almost the first thing I saw after landing was an *araba*, laden with pears, full of soldiers pocketing the contents, while the *arabajee* (driver) was on his knees, apparently asking for his life to be spared, but we calmed his fears by making the men pay for the pears, wishing to keep the friendship of the Tartars. Several country waggons, with drivers, and a few dromedaries were also seized and pressed into the service of our commissariat department.

The officers had no baggage, but only such as each could carry; I carried my cloak strapped to my back, and a water-proof haversack,[3] containing extra shirt and socks, my writing materials, and three days' rations; I soon found that the easiest way of carrying my cloak was by rolling it, fastening the ends together, and making it in shape like a horse-collar; thus it was quickly changed from shoulder to shoulder, and readily taken off when I halted; the men's knapsacks being left on board ship, each man carried only a shirt and a pair of boots wrapped in one blanket, and also three days' rations, consisting of salt pork and biscuit. [4]

The first person I met ashore was Major Sharpe, 20th Regiment,[5] who landed close to us, and shortly afterwards I saw my brother for a few moments. We heard that Sir George Brown, shortly after landing, narrowly escaped being captured by some Cossacks.

---

3. This haversack I had made at Bury. It was in two divisions; and, as it was made of waterproof material, the contents were kept quite dry during the many wettings which I underwent, and I found it invaluable throughout the campaign.

4. This was one of many other mistakes. The few things brought ashore by the men got wet the first night; and as for the knapsacks, very few saw them again; and those that were lucky enough to get them found that *everything useful had been stolen.*

5. He was mortally wounded at the Battle of Inkermann.

Our division marched up country two or three miles, and, after advancing and retiring several times, we at length halted at dusk, tired and hungry, and bivouacked. This, our first experience of lying down to sleep in the open air, can never be forgotten. It rained in torrents all night, and was extremely cold. As nothing but grass and furze could be procured, a fire lasted only a few minutes, and cooking a dinner became a hopeless proceeding. Wrapped in my greatcoat, I lay down on the cold ground, excessively tired—for my recent attack of fever had left me very weak—and I slept soundly, in spite of the pouring rain. The regiment lay down in quarter-distance column, each man sleeping by his arms (piled).

The dreadful cholera still continued with us, and two of our poor fellows (Privates John Duncan and Thomas Burke) died of cholera during the night. We were under arms before daylight the next morning. I woke up very stiff and cold, and perfectly wet through, my cloak having been blown over my head. The colonel was more fortunate than most of us; his horse, called " Protection," had been landed with saddle-bags, one of which contained a patrol tent, in which he and Henning passed a *dry* night. The 15th turned out a fine and warm day which helped to dry our uniforms *on our backs*, as we had no change of clothes.

A few miles from us was a small village, where an advanced picket (of the Rifle Brigade) was posted. Close to this place we obtained water for cooking, &c. and fatigue-parties were marched there, under an officer, several times a day. The house occupied by the Rifle picket had belonged to a Russian colonel, who, of course, had taken to his heels. It contained large rooms, with polished floors, and in the draw-ing- room was a very good piano, and upon it a pile of music. I tried the piano, but found my fingers very stiff. A Russian housekeeper still remained there with her family; a fat old lady she was, too, and looked very calm and unconcerned, with a bunch of keys at her waist From her we purchased some country wine, with which the cellar was well stocked. We heard that when the French came up after we had vacated this picket-house, they pillaged the house, ill-treated the inmates, and burnt down the place. The nights now were very fine, but the dew was very heavy.

One day our colonel purchased a pony from a Tartar, for which he gave *six sovereigns*, having no small change. The Tartar wanted only *six dollars,* it was thought, and required much persuasion to accept gold money, which he had never seen before.

On the 16th we got a few tents. In our tent M. and I made a bed of furze, and slept that night rather comfortably, though not undisturbed, as, while wrapped in soft slumbers, we were suddenly aroused in the middle of the night by the "alarm" being sounded along the lines. Such a scene as ensued baffles description. The night was almost too dark to enable us to distinguish friend from foe, if necessary; everything was confusion; men, half-awake, fancying the Cossacks were among them, were ready to fire at anybody and anything, and it took some moments to establish order and to form the ranks. After scrambling about in the dark for my *chaco* and sword, and experiencing sundry collisions with M., I emerged from the tent, and the first thing I could just distinguish was the stalwart figure of our drum-major, who, in a paroxysm of excitement, had drawn his sword, fired with military ardour. It so happened that the first individual whom he encountered was a stray drummer-boy, whom he was apparently proceeding to slay, as he was brandishing the sword above his head, while the bewildered drummer, on his knees, was calling out, "Och! spare me. Dthrum-Major, sure I'm a friend."

After a little helter-skelter work, we formed up to receive the enemy, who, however, did not appear; it seemed that the alarm originated with some French picket. Cossacks were continually hovering about the pickets, and we frequently heard shots at night. Two men (Privates Patt. Monohan and Nicholas Gaffney died of cholera today. On the night of this alarm, Sir George Brown, it was said, was lying down under an *araba* full of engineers' tools; one of the pickaxes protruded from the bottom, and the gallant general, in jumping up suddenly, struck against the pickaxe and bruised his face.

On the 17th, fresh meat was issued to us. Church parade took place at eleven a.m., and in the afternoon I walked with E. H. M. to Lake Tongla. a brackish pool; here we attempted to bathe, and the water being only ankle-deep, we got our servants to pour water over us from a camp-kettle. About ten p.m. we were aroused by a false alarm. After the occurrence of the previous alarm and its scene of confusion, the brigadier complimented the regiments of the brigade upon the orderly way in which they had behaved.

The Tartar peasantry were quite willing to sell us supplies, although it was said that the Governor of Eupatoria endeavoured to prevent them doing so. One day I purchased two small sheep for six shillings, and very good mutton we found them.

As far as we could see of the country it seemed a vast plain of coarse grass and weeds, well calculated for military manoeuvres; but the scarcity of fuel and water was a great drawback: at this time we had to march two or three miles to get water. One of our drummers (Corkerry) died of cholera on the 17th. On the 18th our tents were suddenly taken away,[6] preparatory to marching, and about six a.m. on the 19th we left our first bivouac, as the landing of the cavalry, artillery, and commissariat had now been completed; we advanced towards the river Bulganak, and after marching three miles, we halted for some time, awaiting the arrival of the 4th Division. Just before marching, we gave the men of our company some mutton; but, what with the antipathy to increasing the weight they had to carry, as well as on account of the difficulty of cutting it up, it was left behind; these were early days in the campaign, and they learnt to be more provident afterwards.

The French marched parallel to us, on our right About five p.m. we crossed the Bulganak, a small stream, an object of great delight to us thirsty beings, as we had only the small quantity of water carried in the wooden buckets to last throughout the day; the weather being warm, we suffered much from thirst, and a stream of water (muddy though it might be) was a welcome sight to all, at the end of the day's march. We lost three of our poor fellows by cholera on the 18th,— *viz.*, Sergeant Murphy, Privates Peter McLoughlin and John Ford; and one on the 19th, Private Thomas Quinn.

At the Bulganak we got our first sight of the enemy, with the exception of a few Cossacks when landing; great was the excitement: our Cavalry and Horse Artillery, supported by our 1st Brigade and the Rifle Brigade, had a skirmish with a a small force of Cossacks and artillery, who fired a few rounds and retired: several on our side were wounded. Before going into action the Horse Artillery threw away some nose-bags of oats, which our men picked up, and the colonel's horse found the contents very palatable. With the aid of our glasses we could this evening observe the strong position taken up by the Russian army, about five miles in front of us, on the heights of the Alma.

THE BATTLE OF THE ALMA

At 3.30 on the 20th we were under arms until dawn; the division marched about 7.30, flanked by cavalry and artillery, with the Rifle Brigade covering the front. Our progress was necessarily slow, and whenever we halted it was a splendid sight—never to be forgotten—

6. It will be seen that we did not get any tents again until October 5th.

to see such a vast force of French, English, and Turks, as far as the eye could reach, all quietly lying down, eagerly awaiting the next order. The divisions advanced towards the Alma in double columns of brigades from the centre of divisions, the Cossacks on the adjacent hills retiring as we approached. On the hill before us we could distinctly discern the Russian army, strongly posted in dense masses, with batteries of artillery in position. Marshal St Arnaud passed along the line and was loudly cheered by all. We gradually advanced towards the river (the Alma) which flowed across our front, and the frequent halting and moving forward for short distances was most fatiguing. Between twelve and one o'clock we arrived in front of the position. Having hitherto moved in quarter distance column, the regiments here deployed into line, and, after lying down a short time, advanced, covered by a wing of the 2nd Battalion Rifle Brigade, under the command of Major Norcott.

The enemy at once opened upon us a smart fire of round shot and shell, but we advanced too rapidly for them to fire at us with any accuracy of aim, and, hurrying towards a burning village in our front, we took shelter under a wall, where we remained for some time. As we lay snugly under the wall the roar of round shot, shells bursting, and the whistling of bullets was almost deafening. I saw one round shot come plump into the middle of the battery of Horse Artillery, in action close to us; wonderful to relate, the shot passed *under* the horses of one gun and *over* those of the next gun, *without touching a man or a horse*. Captain Norton (88th), who had been left behind ill at Old Fort, overtook us as we advanced into action.[7]

Meanwhile, Major Norcott, with his skirmishers, dashed through the burning houses and a vineyard, whence he dislodged the Russian riflemen and crossed the narrow stream of the Alma.[8] Our colonel

7. When we left our bivouac at Old Fort, Captain Norton was too ill to march. One of his numerous friends allowed him to ride on the limber of a gun, and, when the battery went into action at the Bulganak, he was put down at a neighbouring post-house, where Lord Raglan and his Staff were going to pass the night Captain N , feeling very unwell, had, it seemed, gone into the post-house, whence he was sent out by an A.D.C., who said that he must make room for Lord Raglan. His lordship met him at the door, and sent him back again, saying to one of his Staff, "You must not turn him out, but find a corner for him somewhere." Lord Raglan came up to see him, brought him a cup of tea, and asked if he could do anything for hint, subsequently sending him an armchair, and, the next morning, same tea and toast.
8. Just at this moment a battery of artillery was ordered up to fire upon some men, on the other side of the Alma, who were believed to be Russians. Fortunately, our colonel, seeing that these men were Rifle Brigade (continued next page),

asked Sir George Brown, who was then close in rear of our line, if we had not better support our skirmishers, when the words "*over the wall*" were given, and over we went, rushing hurriedly through the vineyard, under a perfect hail of grape-shot and bullets; and thus lessening our chance of casualties, we jumped into the stream, which was more than knee-deep in some places, being the first of our brigade to cross the river; here we halted and re-formed the line under the shelter of the opposite bank. It was now about one p.m.

Our colonel was riding a horse called "Protection," which in the hunting-field would not cross water, at least without some trouble; today the horse jumped into the river, as if she liked it We observed that where we crossed the Alma the trees had all been cut down to enable the Russians to fire their guns with more effect; higher up, where the 77th Regiment crossed, it appeared that the trees were left standing. After remaining for a short time under the bank, we received the order to advance, and at once we moved forward in line, under a well-sustained fire of round- and grape-shot, to say nothing of bullets whizzing about our ears, for the roar and din of a great battle had now fairly begun; and I can never forget the peculiar noise, made by round shot passing over and around us, which I heard for the first time today. Upon this advance part of our right wing became temporarily separated from the remainder of the regiment, and, as they diverged to the right and came more under the severe fire of the enemy than the remaining companies, they therefore had many casualties.[9]

---

skirmishers, and not Russians, drew attention to the mistake, and the battery was ordered to limber-up. Thus was averted what might otherwise have resulted in a deplorable blunder.

9. When we received the order to advance, these men, with their natural Irish impulse, rushed forward at the "double;" in fact, there was no holding them; and thus they became, for a short time, separated from the remainder of the regiment. During their advance they came upon a step in the ground, under cover of which they lay down in company with some skirmishers of another regiment. Not very far from this spot was a Russian field-work (with guns), in which, at this time, the colours of the 19th Regiment were distinctly visible; and a column of Russians, in a wavering condition, was also observed (within easy shot), with their officers in front waving their swords, and gallantly urging on their men.

The major in command of this portion of our right wing ordered his men to open fire upon these Russians; but the officer in charge of the skirmishers called out, "No, don't fire; they are the French;" and thus a golden opportunity was lost, as, had they fired, no doubt the advance of this column would have been checked, and the severe losses in the subsequent struggle for the enemy's intrenchment might have been prevented.

The regiment continued to advance under a heavy fire, especially from two guns placed in a field-work not far from us; as, however, we moved rapidly we suffered but little loss. Two columns of Russian infantry could be observed about 800 or 900 yards in front of us, which retired when we had advanced about 400 yards. We had reached a hollow in the ground, nearly parallel with the right flank of the Russian field-work, when, while still advancing, our brigadier ordered us to form square in this exposed position, having, it was said, mistaken the helmets of the Russian infantry columns for those of cavalry. We had hardly completed the movement when a round-shot came into the middle of the square.

The regiment was in the act of re-forming when the 1st Division (the Guards and Highlanders which supported the Light Division) passed us, and, in fact, subsequently took that part in the action which we should have taken, had it not been for the delay, in our advance, caused by the unnecessary formation of the square; this was a very galling and annoying occurrence to us all, especially as the regiment was working so steadily, and might have rendered valuable assistance to the 19th Regiment (on our right), who, as it afterwards appeared, was hard pressed at that particular time, and was being terribly cut up. When we re-formed line our colonel waited until the 1st Division had passed, and then moved the regiment a little to the left, so as to place it in the interval between the Guards and Highlanders, who, as stated, were marching up the hill where we ought to have gone; as the 42nd passed us the enemy in our front could be seen retiring up the hill.

The regiment suffered but little loss in this action; we had four privates killed (all of the Grenadier Company), and Quartermaster Moore,[10] two sergeants, and sixteen privates wounded.[11] Colour-Sergeant McNally,[12] No. 2 Company, lost a leg, one man was missing, and Lieutenant Baynes was struck by a spent ball, though not returned wounded.

Nearly the first bullet from the enemy, as we lay under the wall

10. Quartermaster Moore, having no issues to make, had—like a brave old soldier, as he was—volunteered to join one of the centre companies as a subaltern. He was hit by a spent grape-shot in the knee, causing great pain, but no fracture.

11. *Vide* Appendix A.

12. Sergeant McNally, being one of the first wounded men to arrive in England, was treated very liberally by the Government, being awarded an *annuity of 20l., in addition* to whatever pension he was entitled to receive. He was afterwards barrack-sergeant for many years, and died in 1877.

previous to crossing the river, pierced our colonel's holster, and, after the action, was found *lodged in his prayer-book*. [13]

Cheer succeeded cheer as we ascended the hill; the enemy retreated rapidly, and our artillery made great havoc among their columns; it was a heartrending scene as we passed along, the ground being thickly covered with dead and wounded, among them a Russian general and his A.D.C. lying wounded upon a pile of hay.[14] As we were moving along we met the *Times* correspondent, by whom one of our officers sent a letter to his friends at Cheltenham; and as my parents resided in the same place, I took the opportunity of sending a message to them, saying I was "all right." The action was all over by three p.m., in spite of the: very strong position held by the Russian army; their columns lined the lofty heights, which rose up from the plain, across which our advance was made, and their artillery, intrenched in various advantageous positions, fired their guns *too well*; meanwhile the French troops, crossing the Alma between us and the sea, scaled the heights there, which were more precipitous than the ground attacked by the English, and turned the left flank of the Russians, assisted by the Allied Fleet which shelled the position; but the brunt of the action fell upon the British army, whose bull-dog courage inflicted a severe defeat upon the right and centre of the Russian line.

After the action Lord Raglan rode down the line amid the cheers of the troops, and conversed with those commanding officers whom he knew, in his usually kind and affable manner; amongst the number he spoke to our colonel. Through some oversight our colours remained *cased* during the engagement, and were not *uncased* until Lord Raglan passed along the line.

A strong feeling of resentment was roused among the army towards the wounded Russians, who had been detected pretending to be dead, and, after our troops had passed, rising up and firing at them; I heard of one case in which a Russian killed a sergeant (British) who had given him some water; I saw a Russian in this way fire at one of our artillerymen as he passed by; under these circumstances it was

---

13. This prayer-book, *with the bullet in it*, is, (at time of first publication), I understand, carefully preserved by Sir Horatio Shirley's nephew, E. P. Shirley, Esq., Ettington Park, Warwickshire.

14. Surgeon Dunlop—then in the 4th Foot, and afterwards in the 88th—told me that, being called upon to attend this wounded man he proceeded to examine the wound, but was delayed in doing so as a consequence of being unable to unfasten what seemed to be *a very complicated pair of braces*. This appeared to amuse the general very much, and he smilingly solved the difficulty.

impossible to prevent the men expressing (although in terms unintelligible to a Russian) their anger at such conduct as they passed by any wounded, whose firelocks were soon carried off.

Although the action was over early in the afternoon, we did not finally reach the ground on which we bivouacked until long after sunset; much to our annoyance, we had been moved backwards and forwards until at last we rested our weary limbs near the Highland brigade; after a welcome supper of coarse beef and hot tea I rolled my cloak around me, and, with my feet to a large fire, I slept very soundly on a heap of hay; we had been fifteen hours under arms, with no opportunity of eating anything: the night was very dark.

The next morning we moved and rejoined the Light Division; the day was passed in burying the dead collecting the wounded.[15] After sitting, under an *araba* (cart) with my friend J. W., and *writing a letter home upon Ike top of my chaco*, we walked over the field of action, which was thickly covered with dead and dying Russians, and many of our brave fellows; a truly sad scene. The 23rd Fusiliers lost many, officers, and I was very sorry to find that Captain Connolly, whom I had known for some time, had been killed; I had been chatting with him at his bivouac only a few evenings before the action.

I also heard, with much regret, that two officers (Wardlaw and Stockwell) of the 19th had fallen; I had known them both very well, and the latter had been employed with me as assistant engineer in Bulgaria. Having had a bathe in the river (Alma) I paid my brother a visit to report myself safe and sound, and found him and all my old 20th friends well, full of inquiries about the action. Today our colonel

---

15.

Total numbers on the Field of Alma (engaged)

British ...... 27,000 ⎫ 50,000[1] | Guns ⎰ British ...... 54 ⎱ 126
French...... 23,000 ⎭ | ⎱ French...... 72 ⎰
Russians—Men...... 37,000 | Guns...................... 96

Casualties of the British Army at the Battle of Alma.

	Killed.	Wounded.	~~Taken~~.
Officers........................	26	73	99
Other ranks	327	1557	1884
Total.............	353	1630	1983

French Casualties.

Officers...........................	3	54	57
Other ranks	253	1033	1286
Total..................	256	1087	1343

[1] Exclusive of 6500 Turks not engaged.

rode over the position attacked by the French, going to the telegraph-house, down the hill, and across the river; he saw very few dead, only two or three near the telegraph-house; he then passed by the burnt village, intending to return by the course which we had followed on the previous day, but *several musket-shots were fired at him* from one of the houses, by whom fired he could not say; so he came back by the Russian redoubts, where fatigue parties were engaged in burying the dead, hundreds of whom still remained above ground.

I went on picket in the evening with my captain; the night was intensely dark, and, after wandering about for some time, we at last found our ground; a patrol of the 17th Lancers passed us, which had also lost their way. During the night General Pennefather visited us, and when, in reply to his inquiry why we had no fire, he was informed that we had received orders not to light one, he told us to do so, saying, "If anyone asks who gave the order, say it was General Pennefather."

The night was cold, with a heavy dew, but all passed off quietly, no signs of any enemy; in fact, as it afterwards appeared, the enemy, panic-stricken, had fled precipitately, *leaving (unknown to us) guns, &c.,* close to us. Some of the men brought the colonel a quantity of the black bread found in the Russian knapsacks, thinking his horse would eat it, but old "Protection" would not touch it.

One man of ours (Private John Frazer) died of cholera today.

On the 22nd September I came off picket, and in the course of the day walked with W., B., and H. to see the position attacked by the French. At the telegraph-tower, captured by them, were the *débris* of a severe struggle, but all the killed had been removed: on the tower the French had inscribed "*Bataille de l'Alma, 20me 7bre 1854,*" In the evening I walked to the river with my brother and B. (20th Regiment), I was in charge of a watering party.

On the 23rd we paraded before daylight, and at seven a.m. the army commenced its march towards Sebastopol. About one p.m. we reached the river Katscha, a narrow stream, which we forded, and, after a dusty and tiring march of six hours (the fatigue of which was much enhanced by the scarcity of water) through flat, open, and un-interesting country, we bivouacked about dusk on the hills beyond. On the river was a pretty little village, surrounded by vineyards of delicious grapes, which the troops punished, in spite of the vigilance of the provost-marshal.

About eight a.m. on the 24th we resumed our march, and about one p..m. reached the river Belbek, which we crossed by bridges. Here the country changed from perpetual plain to a deep valley and hills covered with wood, presenting a view worthy of an artist's pencil: a village and nice houses—all deserted—were prettily situated in the valley, through which the river flowed, and were surrounded by vineyards and orchards. As we marched along we could hear heavy firing from the fleet, which was bombarding some fort. We bivouacked on the heights beyond the river without being molested by the enemy. The days continued fine, though very hot, and there was a heavy dew at night. This day's march was very fatiguing; the water-buckets, filled before starting, were soon emptied; and today, as well as on previous days, water could not be obtained until the day's march was over. The scarcity of water was a circumstance of constant occurrence throughout our marches; we were frequently many hours under arms without being able to obtain any, and, on reaching our bivouac we often were obliged to go a long distance in order to get water for cooking, &c.

As I was trudging along today I fell in with Mr. McGee, quartermaster in the "Royals," whom I had known in the reserve battalion of the 20th Regiment, in which he was sergeant-major when I joined that regiment at Bermuda in 1846, and taught me my drill. We walked together for some distance, and chatted about old times and friends.

The following day (25th) is notable for a clever manoeuvre on the part of Lord Raglan to delude the enemy, who, it seemed, fully expected an attack upon the north side of Sebastopol. About eleven a.m. we commenced our march, moving in a south-easterly direction—having relinquished the idea of attacking the north side of the town—and thus making a circuitous route so as to clear the harbour, and, by a flank march, to reach Sebastopol on the south side, which was said to be quite unprotected. Our march lay through a thickly wooded country; and so dense was the under-wood that regiments became broken up and companies mixed, and buglers were constantly sounding to keep regiments together, until at length we emerged from the wood and reached open country at a place called Khutor Mackenzie (*Anglicè*, Mackenzie's Farm); here word was passed that the enemy was in front; formations were quickly resumed, the Horse Artillery dashed to the front, and we could hear the sound of firing, but could not see any enemy.

Great was the excitement: although much fatigued and suffering from thirst—as no water could be procured, and the sun was intensely hot—we soon forgot our discomforts, and it was most satisfactory to find, on halting here, *that every man in the regiment was present.* We now learnt that Lord Raglan and Staff, on nearing Mackenzie's Farm, had unexpectedly fallen in with the rear-guard of a force of Russians *en route* to Simpheropol, and that our cavalry and artillery had captured a considerable quantity of baggage and ammunition, which latter was destroyed. Several Russian officers and soldiers were here taken prisoners; among them I saw one officer, sitting in a waggon, who was in a very *excited state*, which was explained by the fact that some champagne had been found among the captures. The road, as we hurried along, was strewed with various articles of wearing apparel, uniforms, furniture, &c. After halting some time our division pushed on towards the river Tchernaya: we now descended by a road (deep in white dust) which wound down a steep hill, called the Mackenzie Heights, into the valley of the Tchernaya. The country here was chalky and barren, and the dense clouds of dust, which we raised, nearly blinded and choked us.

About sunset we crossed the river at Traktir bridge, and, after being unnecessarily marched about, up one hill and down another, through some blunder on the part of the Staff, we at length bivouacked on the hills beyond (called the Fedukhine Heights); right gladly did I attack my salt rations, and, after a cup of hot tea, slept soundly before a good fire. *Every man of the regiment was present when we bivouacked*, although the day's march had been a most severe one, seventeen miles in all, nearly five of which was through wood sometimes so thick, that it was very difficult to force our way through it Not far from us was said to be a camp of 16,000 Russians, and at night we could distinctly discern their fires. By this flank march we intercepted all reinforcements from reaching Sebastopol.

On the 26th we were under arms, as usual, before daylight, and about eight a.m. we marched towards Balaklava, five miles distant.[16] As we neared the village, our skirmishers opened fire; leaving our packs in the plain our division advanced, the 1st Brigade ascending the heights on the right, overlooking the harbour and town; the 2nd (our) Brigade marched up the heights to our left, on which was a ruined Genoese fort, held by a small detachment of the enemy; our fleet, as well as some of our artillery, opened fire upon them, but they soon surrendered. The 77th Regiment, being on our left, was nearest to the fort, and their Colonel (Egerton)[17] was deputed to receive the

---

16. Having written my impression at the time of the various occurrences, I will not vouch for the accuracy of distances, &c.
17. Killed in the capture of the rifle pits, April 19th, 1855.

commandant's sword; a finer specimen of a British officer could not have been found for this purpose, for Colonel E. was a remarkably tall, soldierlike man.

We did not fire a shot but lay snugly under the brow of the hill above the fort; a few shells burst over us, and one of our men (Private William Fannon) was slightly wounded by a splinter, and that too, it was said, from a shell fired from our flagship, the *Agamemnon*. Just behind us was a fine vineyard, where we feasted upon delicious grapes, now quite ripe. I recollect picking one bunch of Muscatel grapes so large, that it completely filled my *chaco*. It was thought that these *very ripe* grapes were most beneficial to all, and, in a great measure, tended to drive away cholera. At one of the houses near us some of the men found a cart, and horse in it, which they presented to our colonel,[18] and it proved very useful afterwards; the wounded man was now placed in it; in one house was found a bag of copper coins, secreted in a bed. The inhabitants did not, apparently, begin to decamp until we had nearly reached Balaklava; and we could see some of them making off across the hills, with their worldly goods and chattels.

Rumour said that Sebastopol had been summoned to surrender, and that the Russians were panic-stricken.

We bivouacked on the plain near a village called Kadikoi, where we remained until the 29th. Behind our bivouac was an extensive vineyard, the paths of which were lined with almond-trees. Grapes and almonds! what an agreeable prospect to salt-pork-and-hard-biscuit-fed campaigners! The grapes were delicious, but *the almonds were bitter!*

On the 28th, while making purchases at Balaklava, there was an alarm, and the division was under arms, but it proved to be nothing. Sergeant Creaven and Private John Boughan died of cholera today.

About midday on the 29th, the Light Division advanced to the heights above Sebastopol; one of our captains remained behind at Balaklava in change of weak and sickly men of the regiment. About four p.m. we took up our position three miles south-east of the town, not far from a house belonging to a Mr. Upton, an Englishman, who was taken prisoner.

---

18. Strictly speaking, I believe that the colonel saw the cart, and sent some men for it, as at that moment he wanted to put our wounded man into it The colonel had some difficulty in obtaining permission to keep the carriage, as it is the rule on service that all captures of horses, waggons, &c., are to be handed over to the commissariat department.

The fleet was shelling the town as we arrived, but only for a short time; we bivouacked on very stony ground, where wood and water were scarce; there was a false alarm during the night; the nights were now very cold, with a heavy dew.

On the 30th, I was sent with forty men of various regiments to loophole, and render defensible, a house, belonging to an old Englishman, named Willis, and held by one of our pickets; the old man was very deaf, or, as I believed, pretended to be so; he seemed strongly to object to his house being knocked about his ears, and made frequent fruitless appeals to me; when I inquired whether there was a well where we could obtain water, he assured me there was none; this I did not, of course, believe: and, after searching his garden, I discovered a well, apparently recently filled up with stones. I reported the circumstance, and the well was cleared out; this Englishman had lived in Sebastopol many years in government employ. We were turned out again in the middle of the night by a false alarm; it was a very cold night.

At seven a.m. on the 1st of October we changed our position a few miles to the right of the line, and bivouacked under a hill, which commanded a fine view of the town; the left of our brigade rested on the Woronzoff Road; on this position we remained throughout the remainder of the campaign.

Above us at the top of the hill was a house, occupied by a picket of our brigade, whence we had a fine view of the town; it was a very handsome-looking place, built of white stone, containing some fine buildings, &c.; we could see the Russians strengthening their fortifications, and throwing up earthworks round a Martello tower, called the Malakhoff Tower. A desultory fire was kept up by the Russians upon our pickets, with little loss to us.[19]

We used to feel very much disgusted at seeing how comfortable the French officers were in comparison with ourselves; while we were loaded like donkeys with provisions, besides a change of clothes, and a heavy cloak, so that at the end of a day's march we used to feel more inclined to sleep than to attend to the many duties which devolved upon us, the French officers had mules provided for them; they always seemed to us to have been so instructed as to be more practical soldiers than we were.

On the 3rd I went on picket in front of our position; our right rested on a ravine (called the Middle Ravine) which led towards Se-

19. Our casualties at this time were—Corporal James O'Rourke, killed Oct. 1st and Privates John German and Thomas Kirk, killed Oct 2nd

bastopol, and our left on the picket-house; the picket consisted of a company of the 19th, 77th, and 88th Regiments; the 19th was on our right. It rained all night, so there was no lying down, and I passed the night in walking about, and visiting my line of sentries: the enemy was very quiet. During the day several Cossacks hovered in the distance, and a few shells were fired at us from the Round Tower (Malakhoff); a splinter struck close to my feet as I lay down. A Russian officer with an escort of Cossacks came and reconnoitred on the opposite side of the ravine; our brigadier happened to be visiting the pickets at the time, and as none of the pickets fired, he reproved us for not doing so, saying it was a most daring reconnoissance; but we had at that time received such strict orders not to betray our position by showing ourselves or firing, that it was very puzzling for us, new hands at campaigning, to know how to act.

At this time the 2nd Division occupied a position some distance to our right, called the Heights of Inkermann; in rear of them were the Guards and Highlanders (1st Division), and our 1st Brigade was on our right front, across the Middle Ravine.

On the 5th we received a few tents; the men were very closely packed, and there were three officers in a tent: I was in one with our quartermaster and Lieutenant, G. Vigorous preparations for the siege continued to be pushed on at this time; the heavy guns from the fleet had all been landed, as well as 1000 marines, besides sailors; some of the latter were encamped near us, and it was very amusing to watch them dragging the heavy guns, &c., singing merrily and evidently enjoying their land occupations.

On the morning of the 6th we were turned out, before daylight, by a picket of the 23rd Fusiliers firing upon some Cossacks, who retired. Today I drove to Balaklava with J. W. in the colonel's *drosky*[20] (waggon) to make sundry purchases and to fetch the mail. The place was a scene of bustle and confusion; parties of soldiers and sailors landing ammunition and dragging away guns to the front. A few speculators (robbers would be a more appropriate term) from Constantinople had opened stores, which were beset with customers; and one shopkeeper told me that he had sold 400*l.* worth in one day; no wonder, considering the exorbitant prices charged for everything. Here we might be seen, in full uniform, staggering along through streets deep in very adhesive mud, with a sack of potatoes between us, our coatee-pockets (then shaped like jelly-bags) crammed full, and bars of yellow soap in our

---

20. The one captured at Balaklava.

hands, besides a bag of letters, fit subjects for a caricaturist; while our carriage (?) followed us, driven by our coachman (a bearded grenadier), belabouring a *very* lean pony with what Paddy calls "a bit of a stick."

At length we started homewards; our road from camp had been almost impassable from the depth of the very tenacious mud, which had severely tested the strength of our somewhat rickety conveyance. We had hardly left Balaklava when our trap fairly broke down, and we felt in a terrible fix, not knowing how to reach camp; but, as good luck would have it, a midshipman with a party of blue-jackets happened to come up, and, seeing our difficulty, at once set to work to repair damages; lots of rope-yarn was soon produced, and, after hammering and splicing, they rapidly braced up the waggon, and made it stronger than ever.[21]

At length we reached camp very tired and stiff; no wonder, as our cushions varied between potatoes, onions, and cheeses, and the cart had no springs; all which, combined with the roughness of the road, was enough to loosen our teeth and dislocate our bones. Privates Edward Green, Gorman, and Diggan died of cholera in camp today. On the 8th, while our brigade was drawn up at Church parade, and Mr. Egan, the chaplain was officiating, a shell pitched among us, but injured no one; a second shell, however, coming up, Sir George Brown removed us further off.

When the shells pitched, we all endeavoured to lie down, and it was remarked that the only one who did *not* try to do so was the chap shells were fired from a Russian man-of-war, called *The Twelve Apostles,* which had been moored at the end of one of the creeks in the town, called the Southern, or Military Harbour; as the guns could not be elevated, in the ordinary way, sufficiently to send a shell into our lines, two miles distant, the enemy adopted the novel expedient of slinging a gun, and in this way they managed to throw several shells up to our camp, but I never heard that they caused any casualties.

This evening the first ground was broken by a detachment of the 2nd Brigade, Light Division, under the command of our Colonel (Shirley); they were employed throwing up a small battery near the picket- house; it was afterwards known as Hoare's Battery, being under the charge of Lieutenant Hoare, R.N., brother-in-law of my old 20th

---

21. This waggon continued to be very useful for some time, but the frequent journeys and bad roads broke it to pieces, and it was eventually burnt as firewood, nothing remaining but the axle.

friend, Hallewell, the Deputy-Assistant-Quartermaster-General of the Light Division; the battery contained one Lancaster gun, intended, among other things, to fire upon *The Twelve Apostles* man-of-war. The ground where the battery was constructed was very hard, and as the men worked from eight p.m. until six the next morning, they were thoroughly tired out.

Up to this time I had felt in the best of health, and ready for any work; very different were my feelings in Bulgaria, where I found the climate rather enervating, (though of course we had not the excitement of active service then,) and had one or two attacks of intermittent fever, which were very weakening. I now began to feel the effects of constant exposure to wet and cold, sleeping night after night in the open air and on damp ground, and I was not at all well. Not the least uncomfortable thing which I experienced at this I time was sleeping in a coatee and epaulettes; in fact, it was impossible to lie down with epaulettes on; a very suitable dress for a ball, but not by any means adapted for rough work on service.

I used to pay my brother almost daily visits; his regiment (the 20th) was in the 4th Division, and encamped about a mile to our left. We heard that some of the fleet, with commissariat officers, had just made an excursion to the south-east of the Crimea, to procure cattle; the scenery was described as magnificent; they visited several palaces of the nobility (owners and plate gone, but the servants remaining), and said they were very handsome. Our days passed very much alike; after being under arms before daylight (exceedingly cold work !), the remainder of the day, when off duty, was passed as best we could in camp visits or trips to Balaklava. Dinner came off at three p.m., regimental parade at four p.m., the evening being finished up with a cup of tea (no milk, of course), a pipe, a glass of grog, and then to bed (?), effected by lying on the ground in ones clothes, wrapped in a blanket and cloak—the hardest of beds!—this was accomplished at eight p.m.

On the 9th I was on outlying picket at the Middle Ravine; there was a little shelling from the town; the nights now were very fine, with bright moonlight, but very cold and windy, and as I was far from well, I felt the nights rather trying. The next day I was relieved by a party of my regiment under Lieutenant G. The duties on picket were very fatiguing to all, but especially so to the officers. The line of sentries was extensive, and as, from the nature of the ground, the position was easily assailable by the enemy, extreme vigilance was very necessary, and this could not be insured unless the officers were continually visiting the sentries by night; during the day the necessity was less, as the number of sentries was reduced, and they could be seen from a secure place[22] above the caves in which the picket was placed. I once had occasion to go round the sentries in the daytime; the men in files lay down under shelter of low piles of stones at intervals of about twenty yards.

As I walked along the line I presented a tempting mark for some Russian riflemen, who, concealed in caves about 500 yards off, opened fire; their bullets whistled about me, and struck the ground at my feet, but I nevertheless got back to my sheltered lookout untouched. The enemy's riflemen used constantly to fire at the sentries of this picket, and occasionally men were wounded at their posts; so that the relief of sentries (by day) had to be gradually carried out, but it was always attended with the risk of men being shot.

On the 11th I was obliged to go on the sick-list for a few days; the whole regiment was out this evening and the following day as a covering party; there was a good deal of firing during the night which was very fine; during the day the Russians occasionally sent a round-shot bounding through the camp.

On the night of the 13th the regiment covered a working party, which was employed in breaking ground for the 21-gun battery, called Gordon's Battery, after Captain Gordon, R.E., who commanded the Royal Engineers, Right Attack. On this occasion Captain Gordon, who superintended the work, pointing to a hill afterwards well known as the Mamelon, said to our colonel, "That's where we ought to be." Captain G. was undoubtedly quite right, and if we had established our first battery there, it was thought by many that the place might have been taken the same year. The working party continued to work away all night unmolested, and made good progress in throwing up cover. During the night there was an alarm that a large body of Russians were coming out; but it appeared that the men had mistaken *a patch of burnt furze* for a column of Russians.[23] Towards daylight the Russians discovered what we had been doing, and opened a very severe fire; more than 100 rounds were expended in about two hours, causing, however, but little loss on our side, as the enemy fired very wildly.

---

22. The remains of a butt used for target practice by Russian gunners in the Mala-khoff Tower.

23. This said patch did duty for an enemy during the winter; and It was always a sign of a newcomer if he reported this burnt furze as a column of "Rooshians," adding, confidently, "Shure, I saw 'em move."

We had two men slightly contused by splinters of shells; the regiment returned to camp about four a.m. on the 14th. On the 15th the regiment was again out as a covering party, but nothing particular occurred; on this occasion two of our men were wounded.[24] On the previous day there was a skirmish on the right of our position, which a few Russians were killed and wounded.

The pickets and covering parties were now very frequent, and the duties severe, with scarcely even a night in bed. The English batteries were said to be finished, and the first bombardment was to have opened on the 16th, but the French were delayed in their preparations by the damage which their batteries had sustained from the heavy fire of the Russian guns. We had now been seventeen days before the town, during which time the enemy fired at us perpetually, but we had not yet fired a shot. The nights were very foggy and damp, and sleeping, as we did, in our clothes, wet or dry, we found a tent very comfortable. Our coatees and epaulettes began to look the worse for wear, and our once white belts dirty and stained—in fact, we looked a shabby set; but though rough, we were always ready. The ground about the camp was very stony, but the barren appearance of the plateau was much enlivened now by the ground being covered with crocuses.

At this time our rations consisted of fresh and salt meat alternately, ship-biscuit (of the toughest description), tea, rice, and rum; occasionally we (officers) had a few additional *luxuries* in the way of vegetables from Balaklava, but for which we paid exorbitant prices.

The position around Balaklava had been much strengthened by the erection of redoubts, &c., both by the English and French engineers, and a strong force of marines was encamped there, besides the Turks and British cavalry; the place had been made an invalid depot for the army.

Between six and seven a.m. on the 17th the first bombardment opened upon Sebastopol, and was kept up continuously all day; the Malakhoff Tower was knocked to pieces, and the batteries in front of it were shut up in a few hours. In the afternoon two French magazines exploded, which made their fire very slack; in our Right Attack an ammunition waggon was blown up, killing and wounding many men; part of the 88th was out as a covering party and had a great many killed and wounded; among the former were a sergeant and two privates, who were, poor fellows, blown to atoms at the explosion of the ammunition wagon, under which they had taken refuge as a safe

24. Sergeant Michael McDonough, slightly, and Private James Kenny severely.

77

place.[25] The fleet opened fire, engaging the enemy's batteries on the sea front. I was not out, but saw the bombardment from the picket house.

Soon after daylight on the 18th the firing was renewed briskly on both sides. Several guns were opened by the Russians in new places; there was no firing during the night, but an attempted sortie by the enemy was repulsed.

On the morning of the 19th firing was renewed on both sides, but our guns made little impression, apparently, upon the Russian batteries. There was some skirmishing between our Light Division sharpshooters, under one of our officers (Lieutenant Webb[26]), and the Russians, in which several of the latter were taken prisoners; this corps of sharpshooters was formed of volunteers from each regiment of the division; the whole were under the command of Captain Bright, 19th Regiment, with Webb as his subaltern. Webb happened to be very short-sighted, but an excellent officer; he, however, used the eyes of a smart and plucky fellow of the light company, 88th, who always kept close at his elbow.[27] These men were intended to keep down the fire of the Russian batteries by firing into the embrasures, as well as that of the enemy's riflemen, who annoyed us in the trenches; after the Battle of Inkermann this corps was broken up, as the men could not be spared.

Today (19th) a draft from England arrived with two officers, Pearson and Day;[28] the latter took up his quarters in our tent.

The fourth day of the bombardment opened briskly on the 20th; I went out with a working party to Green Hill Battery (the Left Attack) at half-past eleven p.m., and remained there until daylight the next

---

25. The names of our men killed and wounded were—
Killed—Sergeant John Matthewman, Privates Michael Hynes, Robert McDonald, Michael Ferryman, Peter Leonard, John Griffin. Total—1 sergeant, 5 privates.
Wounded—Corporal David Anderson, severely, Privates Timothy Doherty, Thomas Foley slightly, Maurice Savage slightly, Patrick Leonard slightly, Patrick Burns slightly, Maurice Ferris severely, Patt. Morris slightly, James Nowlan slightly, Thos. O'Brien slightly, Edward English slightly; died 9th Dec, 1854, Patrick Cullen, Daniel Moriarty severely, Patrick Morrissey, John Daly, Michl. Connolly severely, Thos. Bastable slightly, Acting-Corporal James Rush slightly. Total—18 Rank and File.
26. Killed 7th June, 1855.
27. Michael Wrenn (afterwards sergeant), killed 8th September, 1855.
28. This officer was most fortunate in his promotion, getting his company, without purchase, after only twelve months' service. His military career was, however, destined to be a short one, as he was killed, poor fellow, at Cawnpore, in 1857, during the Indian Mutiny.

morning; at that time we used to furnish working parties for both the Right and Left Attacks, but after the Battle of Inkermann our duties were confined to our own (the Right) Attack. The cholera still continued to make its appearance in camp, and one of our men (Private John Considine) died today of that fatal disease.

Firing was renewed on the 21st, and some of the Russian batteries seemed much knocked about: the day was very warm; the enemy were very busy throwing up fresh batteries inside the town.

Today about 100 Russians—shouting as they always did—came out against our sharpshooters, only fifteen in number but when they saw the Rangers with fixed bayonets coolly awaiting them, they turned tail and ran like stags; many were then picked off, and a Russian officer wounded and taken prisoner; I saw him brought into camp, he had been shot in the mouth. During the night of the 22nd the French fired rockets and shells into the town, which set it on fire in one place.

Every day we could see crowds of people leaving Sebastopol, and the road on the other side of the harbour was covered with conveyances.

Deserters frequently came over to us; they were Poles, and among them was an officer; they represented that the place was in a very sorry state, the garrison half-starved and disaffected; but all such statements were usually received with caution. Skirmishes between our pickets and the enemy were of daily occurrence, in which the latter were always repulsed. I was on a working-party from half-past ten p.m. on the 23rd until the morning of the 24th; this day there was a good deal of firing on both sides; the town was on fire in several places, which lasted all night

At half-past two a.m. on the 25th I went out with part of the regiment as a covering party at Gordon's Hill, the Right Attack; I was sent with a company to the most advanced trench, afterwards called the Third Parallel, where we remained all day; the work was only partially finished, and the cover was so scanty that we could not stand upright without being exposed to the enemy's fire; the Russians favoured us with a hot fire of grape, round-shot, and rifle-bullets, but we kept very snug, and fortunately had no casualties. The captain in command of the company had a narrow escape; while sitting under the shelter of the partially finished parapet, with his back against a gabion, a round-shot made a breach in the parapet, and sent him sprawling on his face with the contents of the gabion on the top of him. At sunset we were relieved, and remained all night in rear of the 21-gun battery; the following morning we were not relieved as usual, and thought that it arose from some blunder, but the sequel will explain the cause.

During the day the grenadiers, No. 2 and 4 companies of the 88th, and a company of the Rifle Brigade occupied some caves above the Woronzoff Road, in rear of the battery; we then heard of the cavalry action at Balaklava on the; previous day, in which, it was said, that some of our cavalry regiments had been almost annihilated; a few of the 88th, belonging to the invalid depot, with the detachments of weak and sickly men from all the regiments of the Light Division, under Captain M., joined the Highland Brigade, and assisted in repelling (in line) a charge of Russian cavalry during this action.

Today (26th) the enemy came out in force towards the position occupied by our 2nd Division, under Sir De Lacy Evans, but were repulsed with great loss; this brilliant little action was called "Little Inkermann." At the same time they advanced upon our Right Attack, under cover of a very severe fire from their batteries. We were ordered up suddenly from the caves, and, scrambling across the open ground behind the battery under a heavy fire, found shelter wherever we could in the crowded trenches, I hurried up with my company (No. 4) and we occupied a trench (leading out of the battery) called the Right Boyau, which from its dangerous position was not used except to pass through; the fire was terrific, round-shot and grape pouring around us; the *boyau* was so crammed that I was obliged to sit down, opposite the men, in a hole, into which I fitted comfortably.

One of my men (named Richard Walsh) said to me, "Don't sit there, sir, the round-shot are coming over every second; we'll make room for you here." I was in the act of moving, when a round-shot came over the parapet (passing so close to my back that I felt the wind of it), *and dashed into the hole in which I had just been sitting.* Richard Walsh remarked, "Well, sir, I wasn't far wrong when I asked you to move"—a providential escape indeed! I saw one poor sailor killed in the battery; he was sitting on a gun-carriage: a Russian shell ("Whistling Dick," as we called them, from the noise they made in the air) fell under him and exploded, blowing him up into a hundred fragments.

Our adjutant (Maule), while standing close to me, had his left arm carried off by a round-shot.[29] We also had one man killed and five wounded before we had been there many minutes; the remainder

---

29. Lieutenant Maule suffered amputation, but did not do as well as was expected, and was sent to the hospital at Scutari. I went to see him before he left camp, and was shocked to see the poor fellow lying on a heap of straw (continued next page)

of the regiment was under arms in the Middle Ravine. We returned to camp on the evening of the 26th, very glad of a little rest after a fatiguing spell of more than thirty-six hours in the trenches.[30] The following day numbers of Russian horses were to be seen wandering about between the Redan and our works; the Russians coolly came out and drove them into the town. Our colonel drew General C.'s attention to the fact that where *horses* could get over the enemy's works, *our men* could likewise do so. Very little went on from day to day, and the bombardment seemed to be gradually passing off. The firing of our batteries was daily diminishing, and the Russian guns, so far from being silenced, still kept up a well-sustained fire. We enjoyed warm, cloudless days, but the nights were cold, with heavy dew.

The cholera had now almost disappeared, and the regiment was pretty healthy. One of our men (Private Denis Mannix) died of cholera today. Up to this date our total loss by cholera, since it broke out on 23rd July, had been two officers, six sergeants, one drummer, and sixty-eight rank and file; total, seventy-seven.

Writing materials were very scarce at this time. I seemed to have been almost the only one who had brought ashore pens, ink, and paper. I was obliged to be very stingy, and stoutly to refuse all applications for loans from my scanty store. My envelopes had entirely vanished, and I was obliged to resort to the expedient of using *envelopes received, by turning them inside out.* Until the arrival of the *Orient* the colonel had not any writing materials, writing his letters on the backs of envelopes received: nor had the companies, nor orderly-tent any pens, paper, &c., and consequently some courts-martial were obliged to be held without the proceedings being written down.

Our various duties now came round very frequently. On the evening of the 27th I was in charge of a working party at Gordon's Hill, and on the 29th I was in the trenches all day, and came off at daylight on the 30th; the same day I attended the sale of effects of some officers killed at Balaklava, and was glad of the opportunity of adding to my scanty kit At half-past four a.m. on the of November I went on picket at the Middle Ravine, in company with Captain Bayley.[31]

in a wretched hovel—a Tartar cowshed, I believe—while dead and dying Russians were in the next part of the hut. Our colonel—the most tender-hearted of men—burst into tears when he saw his poor adjutant in such a place, looking very ill. Lieut. M. died at Scutari Hospital, Nov. 14th, 1854.

30 *Killed*—Private James Kildea. *Wounded*—Lieutenant and Adjutant Maule, severely; lost left arm, Privates Thomas O'Brien, slightly, Bartholomew Purcell, severely, Michael Connolly, severely, John McMahon, slightl,. Patt. Leonard, severely.

The picket was formed of two companies, sometimes by regiments, sometimes by different regiments of either 1st or 2nd Brigade: the detail for this duty was by companies, regardless of strength, and when during the winter the companies were reduced to a mere skeleton (eighteen or twenty men perhaps, the full strength being nearly one hundred), and the number of sentries required was not reduced, the duty became very severe.

The officers on picket had a cave to sit in, which afforded good shelter from the rain and cold winds; the day was passed in writing letters, with one's knees as a table, besides sundry naps, as at night we were obliged to be vigilant, frequently visiting our sentries to keep them on the alert, so that sleep was not thought of: the cave being very low we could only sit upright, and that too with the chance of occasionally knocking our heads. Here we always remained twenty-four hours; in the trenches we were at this time kept about twelve hours, either day or night.

Just before being relieved on the morning of the 2nd the Russians opened a very smart fire upon us, but we had no casualties. On the previous day part of the regiment were in the trenches, and had several killed and wounded.[32]

The weather now began to get very cold, especially at night, but fortunately we had as yet had but little rain; those who luckily had any warm clothing gladly put it on; I had none, so could only shiver and bear it. Our cookery was gradually improved by the addition of supplies purchased from the ships at Balaklava: I might occasionally be seen busy in *curing a tongue*, or in superintending the manufacture of a *boiled suet pudding*, being the *chef* of our small cuisine. I had a capital and attentive servant in John Higgins, a genuine native of the Emerald Isle; he was ready and willing to do anything or go anywhere for his master. When on picket or in the trenches our meals were brought to us by our servants, and the arrival of J. H. with something good to eat was anxiously awaited by me.

When I returned to camp on the morning of the 2nd, I found I had been appointed an assistant-engineer in the Right Attack, with

---

31. Killed 7th June, 1855.

32 Our casualties at this time were—28th Oct.—Sergeant James Goggins, slightly wounded; 1st Nov.—killed—Private John McHugh. Wounded—Sergeant Edward Simmons, and Corporal William Knowles, both slightly, Acting-Corporal Thomas Kelly, dangerously; died 3rd Nov, Privates James Adamson, Michael Geraghty, John Downie, all severely.

the pay of 7s. 6d. per day—a nice addition to the pay of a needy subaltern. I shifted my quarters (a very simple matter, having little to move besides myself) to the Engineer Park, which was situated to the right of our 1st Brigade, not far from our camp: here I lived in a tent with Captain V., 33rd Regiment, and in the next tent was a Captain G., of the Indian Army. The same evening I went out to the trenches as a supernumerary, in order to learn my particular duties, and returned early.

On the 4th, at five p.m., I went on duty in the trenches, and superintended a party of Turks strengthening the parapet of the advanced work, afterwards the Third Parallel: it was a miserably wet night and very foggy: during the night we heard a great deal of stir going on in the town, and a continuous rumbling of wheels; thinking that perhaps a sortie might be in preparation, I went out in advance of our line of sentries, and lay down with my ear to the ground,[33] when I could distinctly hear the sound of heavy vehicles moving along; but the Russians had been working hard every night at their works, so that the sound of moving waggons was of frequent occurrence and attracted little attention. [34] My party of Turks worked very well for a short time, but had scarcely begun to do much good towards rendering the parapet stronger, when they quietly walked off, in spite of my gesticulations, which, in the absence of an interpreter, did the duty of remonstrances.

About four a.m. on the 5th I walked back to camp with Lieutenant Baynes, R.E.[35] The morning was wet and foggy; the church-bells in Sebastopol were all ringing, and we stopped to listen to them, for they sounded so very musical. I gladly reached my tent, and, being very tired, I soon fell asleep, though my bed was hard enough, only a blanket between me and the ground. About seven a.m. I was roused by my servant saying there was a terrible battle going on, and I then heard heavy firing on the hill above the camp of the 2nd Division: at first we thought that it was an affair between the pickets, but the hurried advance of troops past our camp soon showed that the attack

33. I had frequently heard my father say that this was the method adopted during the Peninsular War for detecting the sound of footsteps, and I often tried it successfully during the Crimean War.

34. Little did we then imagine that this sound was that of the march of Russian batteries of artillery (belonging to General Soimonoff's Division), preparatory to the struggle the following day on the field of Inkermann.

35. Lieut. B. was, poor fellow, severely wounded in the attack on the Rifle Pits, April 19th, 1855, and died of his wounds.

made by the Russians was a serious matter: this firing proved to be the commencement of the Battle of Inkermann, and I will narrate in the next chapter the part taken by my regiment on that memorable occasion.

CHAPTER 4

November 5th to December 31st

THE BATTLE OF INKERMANN

Sunday, the 5th of November, 1854, was ushered in with a continuance of the incessant rain, which had prevailed throughout the previous night, and the heights above Sebastopol were enveloped in a fog, so thick that it was scarcely possible to discern objects more than a few yards in front.

The usual early brigade parade had taken place before daylight; four companies of the 88th (Connaught Rangers), *viz.*: Nos. 4, 6, 8, and 9, had gone to the trenches, Right Attack, where Lieutenant-Colonel Shirley—commanding the regiment—was the field-officer in charge of the Divisional trench guard; No. 3 company, with Captain Bayley and Ensign Pearson, had proceeded to relieve No. 2 company at the Middle Ravine picket; and the remainder of the regiment—some of whom had only just returned to camp, after passing the night in the 21-gun battery—were engaged in preparing their breakfasts, when the sound of musketry was heard from the direction of the hill above the camp of the 2nd Division, and the "alarm," followed immediately by the "assembly," was sounded throughout the various camps.

The whole of the Connaught Rangers in camp at once fell in, consisting of the following companies, *viz*:

Grenadier Company, Captain E. J.V. Browne.
No. 5 Company Lieut Grogan and Ensign Day.
No. 7 Company Lieut. Baynes.
Light Company Captain Crosse;

. . . . . mustering (approx) not more than 290 men. These companies were ordered by the brigadier (Buller) to march off immediately, without waiting for the remainder of the brigade, consisting of the

19th, 77th, and 88th Regiments, and they accordingly proceeded in the direction from which the firing was heard, under the command of Brevet-Lieutenant-Colonel Jeffreys (the senior major), with Major G. V. Maxwell and Lieutenant Riley, who was acting as adjutant for Lieutenant Maule, who. as before narrated, had been dangerously wounded—lost an arm—on the 26th of October. Near the windmill, at the head of the Careenage Ravine, these four companies overtook the Guards; and, on reaching the camp of the 2nd Division. General Pennefather, commanding the division, riding hurriedly past, ordered the Rangers to press forward—-keeping to the left of the road—and to reinforce the pickets of the 2nd Division: at this time they came under the fire of artillery, and shortly afterwards under that of musketry, though it was not severe; the Guards had, meanwhile, taken ground to the right.

The companies continued to advance, in fours, until they reached the summit of the sloping ground, to the left of the hill,[1] above the 2nd Division camp, where they formed line, and moved steadily forward; but, owing to the brushwood, with which the plateau was covered, as well as from the broken nature of the ground, the close formation of line could not long be maintained, and the ranks were obliged to open out, and thus became virtually in skirmishing order.

At this time such a dense fog prevailed, that no enemy could be seen; still the Rangers pressed on, struggling among the thick brushwood and over the broken ground, until they arrived near the head of a precipitous ravine,[2] leading into the Careenage Ravine. Here they fell in with some of the pickets of the 2nd Division; one of them passed close to the grenadier company, and, as the enemy had not yet been seen. Captain Browne asked the officer in command of the picket what was going on; he replied, "Oh! you will soon find out, for there are about 6000 Russians on the brow of the hill."

In consequence of the direction in which this ravine[3] ran, the two companies on the left (No. 7 and light) were the first to reach it; and, as they were descending the steep ground, they suddenly encountered the advancing forces of the Russians, who rushed down the opposite side of the ravine in such overwhelming numbers, that they forced their way through the centre of the Rangers' slender line, completely separating No. 7 and light companies, from those on their right, and

---

1. Called "Home Ridge," by Mr. Kinglake (*vide* Map).
2. Called "Mikriakoff Glen" (*vide* Map).
3. Mikriakoff Glen.

at the same time compelling the latter (grenadier and No. 5 companies) to give way, and they consequently fell back for a short distance (less than 150 yards) where they were halted and re-formed, ready to resume their advance, as will presently be seen.

In this attack the 88th lost several men, amongst whom was the sergeant-major (O'Donnell), who was one of the first to fall, and whose body was found, on the following day with eight bayonet wounds.

Notwithstanding, the partial success attending the vigorous attack which the Russians made upon the centre of the Rangers' line, they could not arrest the steady and determined advance of No. 7 and the light companies. These companies (as previously narrated) were descending the rugged slope of the Mikriakoff Glen, when they suddenly met the advancing forces of the enemy, upon whom they at once opened fire; the Russians returned the fire, but soon broke and retired, closely pursued by the two companies, which charged down the hill, driving the Russians before them, along the bottom of the ravine, across a road,[4] and up the side of a hlll,[5] near the top of which their further advance was arrested by a wall about five feet high, where the retreating enemy evaded pursuit, and on the other side of which could be distinctly discerned several columns of Russian infantry,[6] with a large force of artillery.

Many of the Rangers got over this wall; of these men—some sixteen in number—none survived; the bodies of these brave fellows were found on the following day thus far in advance, all bayoneted.

On the left the light company became closely engaged with the enemy; Captain Crosse was bayoneted in the leg, and, as he lay on the ground surrounded by Russians, he was fortunately enabled to defend himself with a revolver, and eventually succeeded in getting away in safety,[7]

4. Shown in the map as branching off from the Careenage Ravine and up a hill called "The West Jut."

5. West Jut (*vide* map).

6. Mr. Kinglake states that there were at this time eight columns of Russian infantry, besides artillery, on this hill; this statement is corroborated by Captain (then Lieutenant) Baynes, who, whilst standing on the top of the wall, distinctly saw *the same number* of infantry columns, besides several batteries of artillery. Through a clerical error when preparing this narrative, I misled Mr. K. as to the number of columns counted by Lieutenant Baynes on this occasion. *Vide* Cabinet Edition, vol. vi, p. 120 footnote.

7. Captain Crosse had a truly wonderful escape; when the light company and No. 7 retired, he found himself surrounded by a knot of Russians, who advanced to attack him; having just taken out his revolver, to (continued on page after following map)

SEBASTOPOL ROADSTEAD

Lower Light

Cape Trolisky

Wladimir
Chersonese

Little Redan

Line of approach for
the Sebastopol Army

Malakoff T.

Cascadi
Stulh Hill

Saddl
Rea.

Right Lancaster
Battery

To the 21-gun
or Gordon's Battery
Right Attack

R.N.
Camp

Scale of 1 mile   Furlongs

Camp of 1st Brigade
Light Division

Camp of 2nd Brigade
Light Division

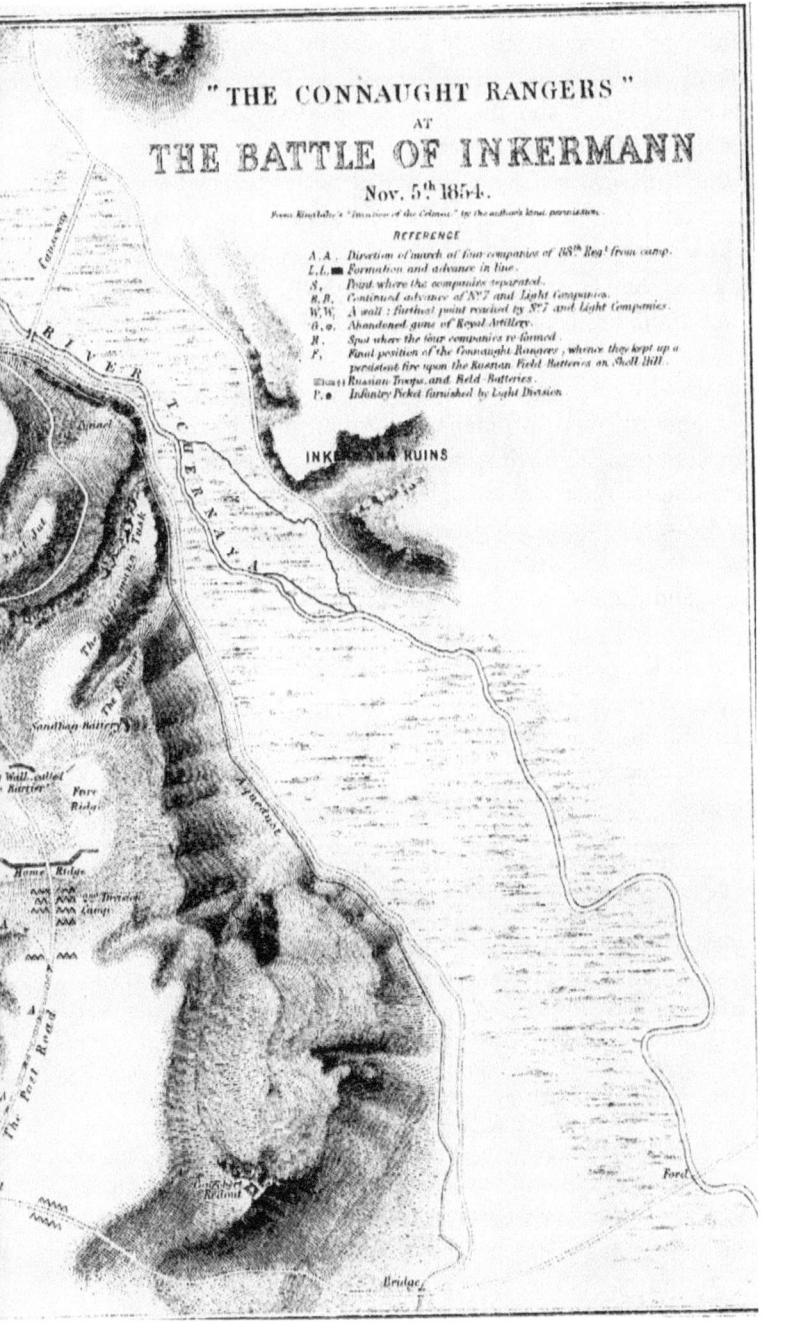

Before any more men could cross the wall, a bugler in the rear sounded the "retire," and the two companies at once fell back across the bottom of the ravine, closely followed by the enemy, some men occasionally turning round to fire, almost without halting. Although hotly pursued, No. 7 and the light companies retired, steadily and without any confusion, up the hill down which they had previously driven the Russians, and when they had nearly reached the plateau they came unexpectedly upon part of a battery of the Royal Artillery, with which were an artillery officer and some gunners, but no horses nor tumbrils. Here an attempt was made to rally, which was successful only for a moment. Major Maxwell, Lieutenants Baynes and Riley, with Private Dunmody,[8] of the light company, and another private, gallantly stood by the guns, and used their utmost endeavours to assemble a body of men to defend them; but, in consequence of the thick brushwood, and the broken nature of the ground, having caused the companies to open out considerably, as well as on account of the rapid and overwhelming advance of the enemy, it was found utterly impracticable to collect suddenly a sufficient number of men to protect them, and therefore they were reluctantly—though inevitably—abandoned.

Borne back by the enemy, these two companies continued their retreat for a short distance[9] beyond the guns, where they rejoined the grenadier and No. 5 companies, the regimental "call" and "assembly" having been repeatedly sounded. No. 7 and the light companies, now became aware (for the first time) of the separation which had taken

---

save one of the men (Lance-Corporal M'Donough, No. 7 company), he was luckily ready for this sudden onslaught, and shot four of the enemy; a fifth bayoneted Captain C. in the leg, and fell over him, bending the bayonet in the wound, and at the same time pulling Captain C. on the top of him; a sixth man then charged him, but, with his sword, he was enabled to cut along the Russian's firelock on to his hands, compelling him to turn back. Captain C. at once got up and made off, but was again attacked by the Russian whom he had just encountered, and again drove him back; he then fell in with his colour-sergeant (Cooney), Privates Samuel Price and John Gascoigne, light company, and Pat Daly of the grenadier company, and another man, who had come to look for Captain C.; as there was no officer with the company. Sergeant Cooney was sent to rejoin it, but Privates Price, Gascoigne, and Daly, retired with Captain C., and defended him against the continued attacks of Russians; they then met some bandsmen of the 49th Regiment with a stretcher, who carried Captain C. to the camp, the three privates of the 88th, rejoining their companies.

8. *Vide* Appendix B, Sardinian War Medal.
9. Less than 150 yards.

place between themselves and the other two companies; up to this time they had been under the impression, that the *four* companies had driven back the Russians to the West Jut; the dense fog, however, had prevented them seeing that the grenadier and No. 5 companies had been forced back, on the first encounter with the Russians at the Mikriakoff Glen.

It was now found that the Rangers, in their recent encounter with the Russians, had nearly exhausted their ammunition; for it must be borne in mind that, upon the first alarm in the morning, the brigadier (Buller) had been so urgent in hurrying off the four companies to the scene of action, that no time had been afforded for completing the men's pouches with ammunition before leaving camp; Major Maxwell therefore rode off to ask General Pennefather where reinforcements or ammunition could be obtained, but was told by him that he did not know where to put his hand on a man or a round, and that the four companies of the 88th "must stand their ground, give the Russians the bayonet, or be driven into the sea." Lieutenant Riley was also despatched to camp on a similar errand.

As Major Maxwell was returning from his interview with General Pennefather, he fell in with General Canrobert, commander-in-chief of the French Army, attended by Colonel Rose,[10] our chief commissioner at the headquarters of the French Army, and a numerous staff; the French general desired Colonel Rose to inquire from Major Maxwell what was going on in the front; Major Maxwell (addressing General Canrobert) said that the Russians were in large force in the front, and that 'he was returning from an unsuccessful endeavour to obtain ammunition, of which the Rangers stood so much in need, that they could scarcely keep up any fire upon the enemy; General Canrobert replied, "*N'importe—rétournez—déployez en ligne—fixez les baïonettes—faites une apparence.*" The French general and staff then advanced to the spot where the four companies of the 88th were lying down, and, on being told that they had nearly expended all their caps, he observed, "*C'est une position très importante—il faut faire une apparence.*" (See note following)

Note:—This incident is thus narrated by Baron de Bazancourt, in his account of the Crimean expedition:—

The commander-in-chief (Canrobert), washing to ascertain how far the right of the English was united with

---

10. Later Lord Strathnairn.

the left of General Bosquet's troops, accompanied by no other persons than the English General Rose, the chief of the staff. General de Martimprez, and a single *aide-de-camp*, Lieutenant-Colonel Cornely, advanced among the brushwood which covered the slopes at the head of Careening Ravine. In one of those intervals when the mist cleared up for a moment, he perceives a Russian line drawn up in order, and is struck with the danger which might result from allowing such an opening to remain undefended.

As he returns to send a body of troops to that point, he meets an Irish regiment, which, after an heroic encounter, has burnt its last cartridge, and is retiring, at ordinary marching step, to get fresh ammunition. 'General Rose,' said General Canrobert, 'tell the colonel of that regiment to post his men here, and, if they have no ammunition, let them raise their bayonets above the brushwood, to show the enemy that the passage is guarded. We will send him cartridges.' The English colonel bowed, and, with that calm intrepidity which distinguished our brave allies, placed his soldiers in the position which had been indicated.

One of the officers of the regiment present when this incident occurred, maintains that the above account is quite correct, and that when Canrobert met the 88th they had not a round of ammunition, and were in the act of moving back a few paces to a spot more sheltered from the Russian fire. As, however, those present on this occasion are divided in their opinion respecting the order in which events took place, I adopted the version introduced in my narrative of the action.

The line having now been re-formed, though not in the same order of companies, the four companies of the 88th at once moved forward, and found the guns (which had been left a short time before) abandoned by the enemy, who, by that time, had commenced to retreat from that portion of the field of action. The ground over which this advance was now made was covered with killed and wounded Russians; one of the latter attempted to shoot Colonel Jeffreys, but was quickly bayoneted.

After advancing for a short distance, the companies halted, and, lying down in the brushwood, fired occasional shots at the Russian infantry and artillery in their front, until they had expended all their caps, and therefore could no longer maintain this desultory firing; the four companies now continued to retain their position, without being able to fire a shot, and anxiously awaited the arrival of ammunition.

While all these occurrences were taking place, Quartermaster Moore—a brave old soldier, who had experienced many a hard fight when serving in the 31st Regiment during the Afghan and Sutlej campaigns—as he listened in camp to the distant and protracted sounds of a severe action, was not unmindful of his comrades on the field of battle; but thought, from the duration of the engagement, and from the continuous firing which had been maintained,—that the four companies must have nearly exhausted the contents of their pouches; he therefore, with his characteristic promptitude, loaded the *bât*-ponies, and gallantly appeared upon the scene with the much-wished-for ammunition, at a time when (as has been narrated) the companies stood greatly in need of it

The pouches being now replenished, Colonel Jeffreys at once ordered the men to extend in skirmishing order, to lie down among the brushwood, and, sighting their rifles for 800 yards, to keep up an incessant fire upon the Russian field-batteries posted on an opposite hill,[11] aiming wherever they saw puffs of smoke, for by this time the fog had cleared away.

This brought down upon the Rangers a heavy fire of grape (thereby decreasing the fire directed against the centre of the British position), which became so severe in its effects, that Major Maxwell suggested to Colonel Jeffreys that the companies should retire for a short distance, so as to throw out the enemy's fire; but, as General Canrobert had ordered Colonel Jeffreys to keep his ground, he therefore would not move the companies without special authority to do so. Permission to retire was shortly afterwards obtained, and the four companies moved back about twenty paces; whilst in the act of retiring with his company Lieutenant Baynes was severely wounded in the leg by a grape-shot, and thus placed *hors de combat*.

Notwithstanding the perpetual discharges of grape shot to which the four companies were here exposed, the fighting reputation of the old regiment was nobly maintained by this mere handful of brave fellows, who kept up such a steady withering fire, upon the enemy's

---

11. Called by Todleben "Cossacks' Hill," and by Mr. Kinglake "Shell Hill." (*Vide* Map.)

artillery, that Todleben states, in his account of events at this period of the action,[12] that in consequence of the persistent and accurate firing of the English riflemen, concealed in the thick brushwood at about 800 paces distance, almost every artilleryman in the batteries on Cossacks' Hill was either killed or wounded; and as it is fully believed that these four companies of the 88th Regiment were, at this time, the only portion of the British forces within musketry range of this hill, they may claim the credit of having nearly silenced these batteries.

During the time that these events were occurring on the field of Inkermann, No. 2 company, under the command of Capt. the Hon. J. J. Bourke, having been relieved off the Middle Ravine picket by No. 3 company, was detained there for some time after daylight by the field-officer on duty (Colonel Unett, 19th Regiment), and the ammunition having been all expended from encounters with the Russian pickets during the previous day, the company was ordered to go to camp for a fresh supply. This having been accomplished, Captain Bourke proceeded with his company to join the Rangers on the field of action. On the way he met a staff officer, who instructed him to press on with his men to the extreme right of the position.

When No. 2 company arrived at the right the French troops were advancing in force, and the Guards, having retired for a short distance, were getting a fresh supply of ammunition. The company remained for some time a little in rear of the Sandbag Battery, and, though not engaged with the enemy, here lost several men. Captain Bourke was then ordered to march his company to the left, and to join his regiment. While passing through the 2nd Division, then in action, Captain

---

12. *Défense de Sevastopol:*—*"Trente-huit de nos bouches-à-feu, placées sur le mont des Cossaques, leur repondirent. Le combat corps-à-corps avail cessé pour faire place à une vive canonnade. Notre artillerie, separée de celle des Anglais par deux ravins, ne pouvait, en égard aux conditions mêmes du terrain, agir contre les batteries Anglaises autrement que par un tir de plein-fouet à boulets et à obus, à une distance considérable surtout pour les bouches-à-feu légères. Notre artillerie causait, néanmoins, d'assez graves dommages à celles des Anglais. Mais ces avaries ne pouvaient compenser, que très-imparfaitement, les pertes énormes que le feu des carabiniers ennemis faisait subir à l'artillerie Russe. Une véritable nuée de tirailleurs, cachée dans les buissons épais, ouvrit contre nos artilleurs, à la distance d'envlron 800 pas, un feu violent d'une grande précision. Quelques unes de nos pieces seulement faisaient de temps en temps pleuvoir de mitraille sur les tirailleurs Anglais; mais ce tir n'arrêtait que pour un moment le feu des carabiniers ennemis; car après s'être remis de leur effroi momentanée, ils n'en recommençaient que plus énergiquementà décimer nos rangs.*
"En même temps les batteries Anglaises lançaient sur notre artillerie et notre infanterie des obus-à-balles; mais c'était plutôt par les armes rayées de l'ennemi, que par le feu de son artillerie, qu'avaient été atteints nos artilleurs, dont la plupart furent tués ou blessés."

Bourke offered his services to General Pennefather, who, however, instructed him to proceed further to the left, and to find the four companies of the 88th, which he succeeded in doing about noon, having suffered a loss of seven killed. By this time the action was nearly over.

Late in the day Lord West came up with part of the 21st Fusiliers, saying he had been ordered to support the 88th, but all firing had then ceased. On the final retreat of the Russians the five companies of the Connaught Rangers received an order to remain where they were until the following morning; but this order being subsequently withdrawn, they returned to camp about sunset.

It is a remarkable fact that, after General Pennefather passed the four companies of the 88th going into action, no general officer (except General Canrobert), nor any staff officer came near them until late in the day, long after the engagement was over; and it is also worthy of record, that the four companies of the 88th Regiment were the first of the reinforcements from camp to reach the field of action, where, for several hours, they sustained unsupported a trying conflict with the Russians; and also, that two of the companies penetrated further into the Russian position than any of the troops which subsequently came up.

In this action the Connaught Rangers suffered severely, having had 119 killed and wounded, *viz.*;—

Four sergeant and twenty-five rank and file killed, of which sixteen were reported missing, and, as previously stated, their bodies were found on the following day beyond the wall on the West Jut (*vide* map), all bayoneted; also three officers, ten sergeants, one drummer, and seventy-six rank and file wounded, amongst whom were—

Brevet Lieut.-Colonel Jeffreys	slightly
Captain Crosse	severely
Lieutenant Baynes	severely.

Lieut.-Colonel Jeffreys and Major Maxwell had their horses shot under them; there were also five men taken prisoners.

The greater part of these casualties fell upon the grenadiers, Nos. 5, 7, and light companies; No. 2 company, as has been stated, not having come up until the action had nearly ceased.[13]

During the time that the action was going on, all in the lines of the Royal Engineers were confined to camp, and ready to fall in if required, I felt very down-hearted at thinking that I was not with the

---

13. *Vide* Appendix A.

regiment at this time, and thought myself very unlucky in being with the Royal Engineers; but when Lieutenant Riley passed through our camp, on his return from going for ammunition, I ascertained that my company (No. 4) was in the trenches and not in the engagement, and therefore that even if I had been with the regiment I should not have been present in the action. The din of the battle was a sound never to be forgotten; besides the continuous roar of musketry-firing and shells bursting, the Russians kept up an incessant screeching yell, quite distinguishable from the ringing cheers of the British troops, which were frequently heard during the engagement About ten a.m. the French troops passed our camp at the *pas de charge*, drums beating and bugles blowing; an exciting scene.

After the action was over and the troops were beginning to return to camp we were allowed to leave our lines, and I hurried off, being most anxious to hear how my comrades in the 88th had fared. Near the windmill (behind our camp) I met General Sir Richard England, who, seeing "88" on my cap, inquired if his friend, young Browne, of my regiment had been in the action, and I told him he had not;[14] shortly afterwards I met the Rangers returning, and was rejoiced to find that among others my friend Grogan was safe and sound. I eagerly questioned him; he told me they had had a terrible time of it, but that he would not have missed the action for anything; he spoke as if all hands had done their work well, though not without leaving many a brave fellow behind them. I walked to camp with him, and visited Crosse and Baynes, both lying wounded in the same tent I was still kept in anxious suspense respecting my brother, and did not ascertain until the following day that he was in the trenches during the battle.

While Colonel Shirley was in the trenches during the action he could distinctly see the Russian reserves on a hill about two miles off; he was highly amused by some forty sailors, who manned the 21-gun battery, coming up (armed only with ship's cutlasses) and requesting that he would lead them to attack these columns of the enemy, which looked about 10,000 strong; the colonel, putting on as grave a face as he could, asked what they would say if the Russians came out and took the battery and guns, while they, who were sent to defend them, were away; they saw the force of this remark and retired. When the troops in the trenches saw these Russian reserves beginning to retire,

---

14. In consequence of the 23rd Fusiliers having lost so many officers at Alma, officers from other regiments were attached to them; we supplied two, Lieutenants Browne and Beresford, who were with them at the time of the action.

and the fire of the allied troops to advance, they jumped up on the parapet and gave three cheers: this brought down upon them a few shots from the Malakoff, which caused, however, no casualties; an attempt was also made to hasten the enemy's movements with a few rockets, but the distance was too great.

After the engagement on the 5th it was considered advisable to throw up entrenchments, &c., upon the field of action; very like shutting the stable-door after the horse has escaped. On the morning of the 6th I was sent with a party of Turks to throw up a line of entrenchment on the battlefield; the ground was so thickly covered with dead and dying Russians that it was difficult to find room to carry on our work; it was a truly horrible sight; parties were busily engaged around us in carting away the hundreds of dead, and burying them in large pits in one of the neighbouring ravines.[15]

In one of the Russian infantry-pouches I found a small spike (with serrated edges) about an inch and a half long, which I understood that the men carried for the purpose of spiking guns. Colonel Cunynghame,[16] whom I had known in the 20th Regiment, happening to come up, I gave it to him, at his request, and unfortunately I did not succeed in finding another.

On the evening of the 8th I went up to Inkermann with Captain G., an assistant-engineer Right Attack, to trace a square redoubt and another work; it was a densely dark night, and, besides being ignorant of the ground, the place was covered with many dead Russians, wheels, broken timber, and other *débris* of the battle. Captain Gordon accompanied us to give the necessary instructions. Captain G. was sent off to another part of the field, and I was left to throw up a redoubt round a knoll (called Cossacks' or Shell Hill), where the Russians concentrated their batteries during the battle.

After Captain Gordon had given me instructions he disappeared in the darkness, and I was left to carry out the work with the assistance

---

15. Strength of the Allied Forces engaged at the Battle of Inkermann.—British, about 8000, French about 7000, Russians 47,000.
Casualties.—Killed—Officers 43 Other ranks 416 (Total 459). *Wounded*—Officers 101, Other ranks 1832 (Total 1933). *Missing*—Officers 1, Other ranks 197 (Total 198). 145 total officer and 2445 other rank casualties = 2590.
French casualties were 900 making the grand total of casualties 3490.
Russian casualties amounted to 15,000 (Copied from Colonel Adye's *Review of the Crimean War.*)
16. Now (1878) Lieutenant-General Sir Arthur Cunynghame, recently commanding at the Cape of Good Hope.

of a sergeant of sappers and 400 Turks.

It was no easy task to commence operations, as, besides the darkness, which rendered it almost impossible to see the tracing-tape, we had first to clear the ground of the brushwood and *débris*, as well as of numerous dead Russians; we were more puzzled than anything else as to how to dispose of the latter; the ground was too hard and stony for any pit to be dug in which to bury them, and, besides this, we had not many hours before us for getting on with the redoubt, so I adopted the expedient of placing these bodies in the spot where the parapet of one of the sides of the work was in course of construction, and before we left off work they were completely covered in—buried, in fact.

The Turks were a lazy set, working very fairly for two hours, and then betaking themselves to pipes and sedentary positions, so that my task altogether was no light one, especially as they frequently took to walking off. The Turkish officers used to enforce their orders by pulling and boxing their men's ears, and I saw one officer commence to beat a man on the head with a ramrod; this I could not stand, and interposed. I returned to camp about half-past four a.m. on the 9th, and I cannot say that our night's work made much show. In the afternoon I strolled with Captain G. to hear the band of the *Zouaves*, who were encamped close behind us. Today the 46th Regiment and some Guards landed, besides a few thousand *Zouaves*; men were much needed now. I was, as an assistant-engineer, entitled to forage for a horse. An officer of the Royal Engineers lent me a pony during his absence on duty, and I found it very useful, my own pony being still at Varna,

On the evening of the 10th I was out at Inkermann with a party of Turks, continuing the construction of the redoubt It was a bitterly cold and wet night; with no little difficulty I managed to keep the Turks at work until four the next morning; I pitied these unfortunate Turks, who, besides being badly clothed, seemed in many cases ill and unfit for hard work. The officers appeared to be a useless set, for whom the men apparently had great dread but no respect; it was said that the Turkish soldiers were half-starved (and they certainly looked so), their officers keeping for themselves a greater part of the good rations issued to their men by our commissariat.[17] I picked up a few Turkish words to assist me in giving directions, as, although an inter-

---

17. The privations endured at this time by the Turks in the Crimea were somewhat aggravated by our commissariat being unable to issue anything but salt pork to them, which, of course, as Mussulmen, they could not eat.

preter was supposed to be with me, he generally disappeared during the night, and was consequently absent when most required.

This morning I rode back to camp very wet and cold, and longed for a waterproof, for at that time I had none, neither had I any other clothes, except those on my back. I much wished for my baggage, left in the *Orient*, and would have given anything for a bedstead or something to raise me from the ground, upon which I had been sleeping for the past two months, my bed being only a blanket above and another below me, and very hard and cold it was too.

I was on duty with some sappers in the 21-gun battery all day on the 13th, and on my return to camp after dark I had an adventure, which might have proved a very disagreeable one. Sending the sappers home by the road which led from the battery, I thought I would try a short cut, and make straight for the camp, skirting the Middle Ravine. I had not started very long before it became very dark, and a thick fog set in; I still stepped out, but soon found that I had lost the slope of the ravine, and I had not the remotest idea where I was; I had no stars to guide me, all around was pitchy dark; I stopped occasionally and listened—not a sound; at last I saw some lights in the distance, and saying to myself "There's the camp at last," hurried on.

I had not proceeded very far when I tumbled down over a heap of stones, and to my astonishment a voice *behind* me called out, "Who goes there?" I was puzzled indeed! where could I be to be "challenged" from the rear! I soon picked myself up, and, *returning*, made for the voice, calling out who I was, and saying, "Don't fire." I then found that my challenger was one of the sentries *in front of the advanced work, right attack*.

After leaving the 21-gun battery I must have wandered in a circle, passed to the right of the battery, and thence gone (*unperceived*) *between* the sentries in front of the advanced work, when I *luckily fell over the heap of stones*: had this not occurred *I was walking straight into the Russian lines, and should soon have been a prisoner*, for the lights I *rejoiced* to see were those of Sebastopol, instead of those in our camp. I soon found my way back to the 21-gun battery, *returning to the very spot* whence I had started about an hour previously. I then went to camp *by the road*, and did not again venture upon any *short cuts*. We heard today that Sir George Brown, having gone on board ship wounded, the command of the division had devolved upon General Codrington, commanding 1st Brigade, and also that our colonel was to take command of the 2nd Brigade *vice* Buller, who had assumed command of the 2nd Division.[18]

On the morning of the 14th a terrific storm of wind, with torrents of rain and sleet, broke over the camp, levelling the tents and carrying everything before it; it was an event never to be forgotten by those who experienced it. I was fast asleep in my bed on the ground when my tent was blown down, and I was carried away in it for a few yards; with difficulty I managed to prevent my few things being blown away, while my servant, *most reluctantly*, abandoned a fruitless chase after my *chaco*, which he *would* run after, instead of assisting me to hold together what was of much more value—blankets and a shirt, &c.

With considerable difficulty some of us (Captains G., V., and myself) contrived to erect a shed of planks—intended for battery platforms—into which we moved our goods and chattels, and where we dined and slept; thanks to being in the Engineer camp, we were able to get shelter; never was there a more miserable day passed by any mortal being than the day of this storm, more especially by those on duty, on picket or in the trenches; it commenced about seven a.m., and raged for nearly twenty-four hours with the violence of a hurricane, accompanied with a deluge of rain and sleet; it was bitterly cold, and the force of the wind was so great that it was almost impossible to stand against it, and the ground soon became a vast expanse of deep and adhesive mud: lighting fires or cooking were out of the question.

The day after the storm was very calm, and I took advantage of the fine weather to pay a visit to our camp and also to see my brother, comparing notes with all my friends respecting the miseries of the previous day; the atmosphere being very clear, we could observe the distant mountains covered with snow, which, when tinged with the rays of the setting sun, presented a beautiful appearance. Much discomfort was, of course, caused throughout the camp, by the terrific gale of the previous day, but the worst result seemed to be the loss of several transports, fifteen of which were said to have foundered with stores and baggage belonging to the army; among the number was one called the *Prince*, which was lost off Balaklava with a quantity of warm clothing; a good deal of Minié ammunition also went down; we were very glad to find that the *Orient*, with our baggage, was safe.

18. Colonel Shirley had command of the brigade throughout the winter, retaining, however, the command of his regiment Colonel Lawrence, of the Rifle Brigade, also took command of our 1st Brigade. Lord Raglan successfully resisted an attempt on the part of the home authorities to send officers from England to take these several commands, and thus to supersede those who had borne the brunt of the campaign up to this time.

All hands looked anxiously for the arrival of warm clothing; the fine weather was breaking up, rainy and cold days began to tell upon *all* ranks, exposed as they constantly were to bad weather on trench and picket duties; having no change of clothes, both officers and men could not take off their wet things, which of course resulted in much suffering and sickness.

The firing from our batteries had gradually ceased, and, with the exception of occasional unsuccessful sorties upon the French trenches, the Russians were also very quiet, but at the same time very busy in strengthening their defensive works.

This evening (16th) I went to the square redoubt at Inkermann with two hundred Turks; we had a fine night; my covering party consisted of some companies of my old regiment (the 20th) under my friend and old captain, Lieutenant Colonel E. I returned to camp very tired about 4 a.m. on the 17th, having been on my feet all night, as unless constantly on the move among my working party, I could get nothing done; directly I turned my back they invariably sat down, and darkness favoured skulking. I went to the regiment in the afternoon of the 17th to pick up news, and was rejoiced to find that I had been gazetted to my company.

How we were to hut ourselves for the winter was now the topic of discussion, and various were the schemes and plans for doing so, but the prospect of any huts being erected seemed very remote; I understood that the authorities had only just applied for the necessary hutting materials, so that it would be some time before they could arrive; meanwhile the weather was becoming very wintry and damp tents were very undesirable residences, especially without any fires to warm and dry the wet occupants. Reinforcements continued to arrive daily, both drafts and some regiments from the Mediterranean. Being off duty on the 21st I rode to Balaklava with my brother. I now was employed almost every day in engineering duties either in the batteries, repairing the works, or at the square redoubt at Inkermann; when at work here a Russian battery (just erected at the lighthouse on the opposite side of the harbour) used frequently to fire shot and shell at us, but without injuring anybody.

At this time the miseries of the winter had begun, and the severe work and privations were now telling upon both officers and men; on the 21st the regiment had 270 men in hospital; to which 100 more might easily have been added if all not fit for duty had been taken off the roster; consequently the 88th could muster only 450 bayonets for duty.

On the 23rd, the 97th Regiment joined the Light Division.

The colonel had made frequent applications to the Quartermaster-Generals Department for the Orient to be sent round[19] to Balaklava, so that we might get the men's knapsacks, tents, and officers' baggage, but always met with a refusal; after the dreadful storm of the 14th, Major Jeffreys was very ill from the effects of forty-eight hours' exposure in the trenches during the gale, and was sent down to Balaklava to recruit his health under the shelter of a house; he there met Captain Boxer, who had been appointed to take charge of the transport arrangements at Balaklava; and, on Major J. representing to him how badly off the 88th were for clothing and tents, he ordered the *Orient* to come up immediately, and on the 24th she arrived at Balaklava; 100 men of the regiment were sent down to bring up as much as they could carry, and it was then found that the knapsacks had been pillaged of everything that was at all useful. I sent my servant down for my baggage, which he brought up on a *bât*-pony, and much delighted was I to receive a change of clothes, as well as my camp-bedstead, having slept upon the hard ground for the previous ten weeks.

The arrival of a few tents was a great boon to the regiment, and helped to lessen the discomforts experienced by all ranks; for at this time supplies were running short, owing to the road between Balaklava and the camp having been rendered almost impassable from incessant wet weather; added to which the transport service was in a state of collapse; consequently there was the greatest difficulty in getting anything up to the front; and the only way in which this could be effected was by sending parties occasionally to; Balaklava, to bring up as much as each man could carry on his back. The place was about seven or eight miles from camp, and the track (for road it could not be called) was in many places almost knee-deep in very tenacious mud; having to march this distance, with a return load, partly up a steep hill, was terribly hard work, in addition to the constant exposure and arduous duties on picket and in the trenches.

The arrival of the *Orient* would have been a much greater boon to the regiment had it occurred a month earlier, before the inclement weather had set in; the receipt of the tents and additional clothing then would have undoubtedly saved many poor fellows, who, from the want of these things, fell victims to the incessant exposure to rain and cold when on duty, as well as when being conveyed to Balaklava, sick

19. The fleet of transports was lying off the Alma.

or wounded, without any warm clothing to protect them from the severity of the weather, which, towards the latter part of the month, became very wet and cold. There was now but little firing from our batteries, and they were frequently silent for a whole day.

I lived pretty comfortably in my tent with V. We made sundry attempts to improve our cookery, and I might occasionally be seen, with upturned sleeves, making a roly-poly pudding, rolling the paste with a bottle on the top of an old ammunition-box; such *luxuries* were, however, rare.

Owing to the want of protection against the increasing inclemency of the weather, as well as from the scarcity of food, many of the horses died in camp, and, among the number, the colonel lost his old charger "Protection" towards the latter end of this month.

Up to the 26th the supplies to the regiment had been ample; but as there were no camp-kettles, except those brought out by the drafts—the others being lost or worn-out—there was now great difficulty in cooking the men's dinners; and the small mess-tins were useless for that purpose. The men were also in a sorry plight, poor fellows; they were very scantily clothed, and some of them actually in rags, not having had any change of clothes since they landed in the Crimea, except some of the trousers and boots stripped off dead Russians after the Battle of Inkermann.

My engineering duties kept me frequently employed, and I was out with working-parties, at the Inkermann redoubt, on the nights of the 27th and 30th. Whenever I had a spare moment I used to pay the regiment a visit, to hear what was going on, afterwards prolonging my walk to my brother; sometimes the bad weather and frequent duty prevented my seeing him for some days, but an occasional "*billet-doux*" between us made up for it

I understood that at this time some hutting materials had arrived at Balaklava, but the bad state of the track render it impossible to convey them to camp; some of the 20th Regiment had adopted the Turkish system of "burrowing," *i.e.* making huts by digging out the earth to the depth of three or four feet and then roofing it: the sappers also began building huts: none of my regiment attempted anything of the kind as yet; they were too hard-worked to find time to do so, and materials were not forthcoming. Having no fire to in my tent I began to find letter-writing very difficult work with half-frozen fingers.

The perpetual wet weather had now rendered the camp a sea of mud, and the track to Balaklava was next to impassable for *arabas* or waggons; and as neither guns nor ammunition could be brought up to the front, the siege seemed virtually at a standstill, and the batteries were almost silent. During this month five of the 88th died in the camp hospital.[20]

On the 2nd of December. V. and I shifted our quarters and were encamped near the square redoubt on the field of Inkermann; our party consisted of Captain Gordon, with another captain and two lieutenants of the Royal Engineers; with us were a company of Sappers, and a strong picket was furnished daily, from one of the divisions, for our protection.

Some very sharp musketry-firing was heard early this morning in the direction of the Middle Ravine picket and the shouts of the Russians could be distinctly heard; since the Battle of the Alma the enemy had tried to imitate the British cheers by keeping up incessant yells whenever they were in action. I was engaged every day from eight to four in the redoubt, and as I was not employed at night my work was very easy; we had three works in course of erection, a square redoubt, a battery, and a breastwork in advance; the French also had several works completed, and we flattered ourselves that if the Russians did come again, we could give them a warm reception. The redoubt, at which I was engaged, was intended to be armed with six 18-pounders and two 13-inch mortars, and was constructed as a work of defence, not offence; a good rallying place for pickets in case of attack.

The enemy, however, did not allow us to work in peace, but generally kept up a sharp fire of shot and shell all day from the battery recently erected, in front of the Inkermann lighthouse, on the opposite side of the harbour; this firing caused a few casualties among the pickets and working-parties. On the morning of the 6th a round-shot went through one of our tents, and a shell-splinter struck the ground at my feet as I stood at my tent door eating my lunch.

In the Light Division (for the other divisions were not nearly so hard-worked) matters seemed to be getting daily worse; the ration of salt meat was now reduced to a quarter of a pound, such was the difficulty of getting up supplies; and the artillery horses were employed in bringing up rations from Balaklava instead of guns and ammunition. The incessant hard work was beginning to tell upon all ranks, and the strongest men began to look most miserable, pale and worn-out; those

---

20. Privates No. 3006, James Egan, November 15th, No. 2278, Patrick Rooney, 19th, No. 3409, George Nicholls, 22nd, No. 3008, Michael Driscoll, 28th, No. 3074, John Wild, 29th.

who came off duty in the morning had frequently to go on again, sometimes, the same night, but invariably the next morning. About this time a supply of warm clothing arrived and was issued, for which our poor ragged fellows were most grateful; besides this our colonel procured some thick warm coats for the men.

A few huts also arrived at Balaklava, but could not be brought to the front for want of transport. The sickness among the troops was also appalling. On the 6th the 88th had 400 sick, and only 300 fit for duty, including a draft just arrived. The men suffered very much from swollen feet, brought on from not being able to take off their wet boots, and some could, consequently, hardly walk. The Light Division was now reinforced by the arrival of two regiments, the 34th joining the 1st Brigade and the 90th going to the 2nd Brigade.

The regiment was still obliged to send fifty or one hundred men occasionally to Balaklava for rations, to be stored in the Divisional commissariat tents, the transport being completely done up; besides this, parties were despatched there daily with the regimental *bât*-ponies, and the men were almost up to their knees in mud and water between Balaklava and the front; this work was too hard for them, in addition to the incessant and arduous duties on picket and in the trenches, and the number for duty began daily to decrease; this arrangement was therefore abandoned.

From our camp at Inkermann we had a commanding view of the town and harbour of Sebastopol. One afternoon (6th) we saw two Russian steamers venture boldly out of the harbour and shell the French trenches; one of the French steamers engaged them, and for some time they peppered at each other, until one of our large steamers bore down upon them, and the Russian steamers retreated into the harbour, under cover of their guns, which opened fire from Fort Constantine and other sea batteries; it was very exciting to watch this short engagement.

The Russians seemed very busy strengthening their town-works, and also had a force hutted on the north side of the harbour, above the Inkermann valley, strongly entrenched with redoubts and batteries; we feared that one of the batteries would cause us some trouble at Inkermann, as it took us rather in flank, but I do not suppose that they had found out our position exactly.

The 6th being the festival of the Russian patron saint, St. Nicholas, the troops were all under arms before daylight, in anticipation of any attack which the enemy might be tempted to make; the day passed off quietly, however.

On the 12th there was an alarm about midnight; all the camps were under arms; it appeared that the enemy made a sortie against the French batteries, but were repulsed after some severe firing.

We had some very heavy rain one day; and one night it blew so hard that I was afraid my tent would be blown down; still, in spite of occasional rainy days and cold nights, the temperature was comparatively mild for the time of year; but the weather began to break on the 16th, which was a very cold and wet day, the distant mountains being covered with snow.

I used generally to sit with the other officers every evening, and, while some read, I used to indulge in a pipe and in the manufacture of gaiters out of sacking, or in darning socks and mending my clothes. Necessity caused much liberty to be taken, both by officers and men, in the matter of dress; some officers were dressed in pea-jackets, with boots to the knees, besides being adorned with beards and moustaches, and armed with swords and pistols; the unwieldy *chaco* had long been discarded, being replaced by the forage-cap, which continued to be always worn throughout the siege.

My daily dinner was boiled salt pork and rice, and sometimes a pudding of pounded biscuit and currants, with a pipe for dessert. Being too much engaged to visit the 88th often, and to see my brother, I heard but little of what was going on.

We had frequent night-alarms while at Inkermann, and, as we always slept in our clothes, with loaded pistols by our sides, we were continually kept on the *qui vive*; these alarms generally arose from the fact that, on the arrival of any fresh regiment or drafts, there was a consequent influx of young soldiers; some mere boys, whose fears, when on sentry on a dark night, construed every bush into a Cossack, or enemy in some shape or no shape. One night we had no less than three alarms, and it turned out afterwards that the Russians had surprised and taken prisoners, five men and a corporal, who were in an advanced post in front of our camp.

Captain Gordon, R.E., a very tall, thin man, was always on the alert and reconnoitring in the vicinity of our works; one dark night he had gone to the front beyond the line of sentries, who had been warned accordingly; as he was returning, one of the sentries, a new arrival in the Crimea, became flurried at seeing a tall, dark figure stalking towards him, and fired at him when not more than five yards off; he fortunately missed Captain G., who, being the most cool and collected of men, quietly walked up to the sentry and said, "My good man, what were you firing at?"

Our hours were necessarily early, and I was always ready to roost at eight p.m. By one mail I received some rather good riddles; it was quite a relief to get something to laugh at, my daily occupation not being suggestive of any jokes.

Our field-works did not progress as satisfactorily as we could wish, but no wonder; we seldom had any men except half-starved Turks to work, with occasional assistance from the 2nd Division. Before going up to the redoubt of a morning I used to do a little reconnoitring, watching the Russians with my telescope; and often on a calm and quiet day I could distinctly hear the deep and musical tone of a bell in one of the Russian churches in the town.

I remained with the Engineers at Inkermann until the 18th, when, in consequence of the increased sickness in the regiment having reduced the number of captains to one (Captain Bayley) fit for duty, I was recalled and returned to my regiment.[21] My own company was at the *depôt*, but fortunately I was not sent home, but took command of one of the companies (No. 2) whose captain was on the staff at Scutari this company, which had left England 105 strong, could with difficulty muster *forty men* fit for duty at this time.

On the 20th I was in the trenches all day, returning to camp about nine p.m., very tired and wet; the same evening we were all turned out by an alarm. It appeared that the Russians had made a sortie upon the advanced work in the Right Attack, surprising one of the regiments on duty there, bayoneting many men and capturing their blankets; the regiment had only recently arrived in the Crimea, and the men were young to the work. At the same time the enemy attacked the trenches of the Left Attack, where they took prisoners two officers[22] and several men.

A few days after a flag of truce was sent into the town to inquire about the officers who had been taken prisoners. As soon as a white flag was hoisted at the 21-gun battery, and answered on the Russian works, all firing ceased; it seemed so strange being able to look over the parapet with impunity; the Russian riflemen came out of their

---

21. District Order, December 18th, 1854, paragraph 6:—"Captain Steevens, having been promoted to the rank of captain, will rejoin his regiment from his employment as Assistant-Engineer, in which he has conducted himself entirely to the satisfaction of Lieutenant- General Sir John Burgoyne."
22. Captain Frampton and Lieutenant Clarke, 50th Regiment.

hiding-places and walked about, our men waving their caps to them; but directly the flags were lowered the usual *ping-ping* of bullets was heard; it was a singular sight.

At the beginning of this month great exertions were made to bring up guns and ammunition from Balaklava, but the impassable state of the roads and badness of the weather rendered it almost impossible to do so now. Our batteries were being much strengthened, and the Russians also were very busy adding to their works, but there was very little firing on either side.

Our casualties at this time, and in fact during the winter, were comparatively few,[23] and at the early part of the siege the Russians did not fire many shells at us; some very large shells, however, used occasionally to be fired at us; they were larger than our 13-inch shells, and the sailors nicknamed the shell "Whistling Dick," from the peculiar whistling noise it made in passing through the air.

Our duties in the trenches and on picket came round much more frequently than in the other divisions. On the 21st I paid my brother a visit, returning to go to the trenches at five p.m.; here I passed a miserably wet night, getting back to camp about seven a.m. on the 22nd, very wet and cold (for I had no waterproof coat at this time); and finding there was no fuel to be got for a fire, the only alternative was to go to bed. Sometimes I was obliged to wear my damp clothes for several days, having no means of drying the little change I had.

Reinforcements still continued to arrive—*viz.*, the 17th, 39th, 71st, and 89th Regiments, besides the *Royal Albert* with some Guards and other troops.

A camp shave was current that the government contemplated adding second battalions to the regiments in the Crimea; we also heard that our good queen had presented each officer with the following most acceptable articles of warm clothing—*viz.*, a sheepskin coat, fur cap, some warm underclothing, and two pairs of gloves.

The night of the 24th—Christmas Eve—I passed in the trenches; it was a bright moonlight night, but frosty and very cold. One of our Majors (Lieutenant-Colonel J.) was the field-officer on duty; I walked up and down with him, and chatted about the different way in which our friends in England were passing their Christmas Eve. I returned to camp next morning (Christmas Day) at seven o'clock, and found a cold and fireless tent to welcome me; at this time I was sharing a tent

---

23. We had one man (No. 2752, Private John Lilley) wounded in the trenches on the 19th.

with Captain N. Although very tired, after a long and cold night's duty, I could not manage to get a nap; and I had barely time to swallow my breakfast, when I was ordered to take my company to Balaklava to bring up their knapsacks, and, after a fatiguing march in snow and mud, we returned to camp about six p.m. I was dead-beat, but quite ready to eat my Christmas dinner, solitary though it was, consisting of pork and biscuit. I had hardly sat down for nearly twenty-four hours, being obliged to be perpetually on the alert all night, besides a long march to and from Balaklava; I need scarcely say that I was very glad to turn in after my dinner. When in Balaklava I found that the prices asked for various articles were most exorbitant: 4s. per lb. for *salt* butter; 2l. for a ham; 4l. for a pot of indifferent marmalade, and so on; but we were completely at the mercy of a parcel of Greek, Maltese, and Hebrew robbers, for they were no better.

The following morning (26th) I was again in the trenches, returning to camp about seven p.m. Our morning parade for duty was generally about four a.m., but we seldom reached the trenches much before seven o'clock; for besides progressing very slowly in the deep snow, we used invariably to lose our way in consequence of the dense darkness, and the snow did not offer any landmarks to give us our "bearings." One of our sergeants had a wonderful faculty for easily finding the way to the Right Attack in the snow, and when it was densely dark. Officers of other regiments used always to call for him; he was placed in the front to lead, and never failed in guiding the covering parties correctly to their destination.[24]

One day a relief wandered about in the snow and could not find the way to the 21-gun battery; fortunately they fell in with a Jack Tar returning to his camp; on being asked the way to the battery, he replied, "Keep straight on till yer comes to a dead 'orse on one side and a 'orrid smell on the hother, and then turn to ya right." This was literally correct; at a spot on the Woronzoff road (to which the relief had wandered), where a track turned off towards the battery, were lying the remains of several dead horses, killed on the 17th October, and left unburied; these did duty as a *sign-post* throughout the winter, I returned to camp about seven p.m. on the 26th, right glad to get a little rest after some hot tea and a pipe.

On the 27th I was out in the advanced trench all night; here there

---

24. This sergeant was, I believe. Sergeant John Haverty (killed in the attack on the Quarries, June 7th, 1855); several other non-commissioned officers used frequently to act as guides to the trenches—*viz*. Savage, Cregg, Fitzgerald, Knox, and Taylor.

was no resting, as we were close to the enemy, having no other works beyond us. We had a chain of sentries between us and the Russians, and all had to be on the alert, but more especially the officers, who could not sit down all night, being obliged to be constantly with the sentries, who from overwork, poor fellows, could with difficulty be kept awake.

We came off duty at seven a.m. on the 28th, and on the evening of the 29th I went on picket with my company at the Middle Ravine; here I remained for twenty-four hours, returning to camp on the evening of the 30th, and on the 31st I was all day in the 21-gun battery with my company, being relieved at six p.m., and very glad to get back to our tents. The detail, in orders, for the trench and picket duties was always *by companies, not numerically*: this was done, I understood, with the view to mislead the Russians about the actual strength of the trench guards, &c., in case they might, through spies, procure any intelligence about the daily detail; a company was *supposed* to represent nearly *one hundred* men: a sad delusion at this time.

Dismal indeed was the state of affairs as the old year closed upon us; the increasing sickness amongst us was terrible to contemplate; what once was a strong and healthy regiment seemed to be gradually dwindling down to a mere handful of worn-out men; one day nine men were sent to camp from the trenches — belonging to a company of only thirty-eight men—attacked with choleric symptoms. The French, having their transport in good order, now gave our army a helping hand and took 1200 of our sick and wounded to Balaklava. Our transport service had completely collapsed, and field-officers were obliged to send their chargers to Balaklava for their own forage.

Besides the misery produced by the want of clothing and boots, the deplorable condition of the troops was much enhanced, by the continued deficiency of cooking utensils during the greater part of this month; requisition after requisition was made to the quartermaster-general's department for camp-kettles, none having been issued for many months; but the same reply was always given, " None in store;" and we were also told that we had brought this want upon ourselves, by throwing away our camp-kettles, when going into action at the Alma. This was partly true; but it must be borne in mind that these kettles (cumbersome things to carry, even when properly adjusted to the pack) had been issued without any straps, or other means of attaching them; and, moreover, a folded coat on the back (knapsacks having been left on board ship) increased the difficulty, even if straps or string had been available. No wonder then that many men threw them away, for the British soldier could hardly be expected to fight with a tin kettle tied to his tail and wobbling about at every movement. The day after the action at Alma all kettles, worth having, were picked up, and also some Russian ones of a better kind than ours.

As each draft brought only their own complement of kettles, company messes could not be formed, and consequently each man was obliged to cook his food, as best he could, in his mess-tin: and, to crown all the mismanagement by which the troops were being victimised, the commissariat issued to us *green coffee*. The men tried to roast it in their mess-tins, which of course fell to pieces, depriving the owner of the only means he had for cooking his food; grinding the coffee was attempted by smashing up the berries with a heavy shot on a stone; half-roasted coffee brought on illness, and increased the sufferings of all. Picture, then, the miserable conditions under which the men were compelled to try and cook their daily rations.

After returning from a long spell of duty in the trenches or on picket, thoroughly wet through and completely fagged out, a man must first collect fuel where he could, as none was issued by the commissariat at that time; to effect this he was obliged to go a long distance to Inkermann to dig up roots or to cut brushwood, which daily became more scarce, and where many a poor fellow was killed or wounded by the Russians, through being compelled to go too far to the front Many, however, were unfortunately too weak or over-fatigued to do this, and ate the salt pork *raw*, or lived upon biscuit; consequently numbers of men died from illness produced by this unwholesome and insufficient food, if not actually from starvation.

A man of ours hid himself in one of the caves on the Woronzoff road, where he would have died of starvation had he not fortunately been discovered. It was thought that he intended to desert, and consequently he was tried by a court-martial, but he was too weak to undergo the corporal punishment awarded, and subsequently died in hospital. He was a young soldier who had only recently joined the service companies.

Such was the deplorable condition of the 88th until towards Christmas, when our ever-vigilant quartermaster (Moore) heard from his colleague in the 19th Regiment that some large tin cans could be purchased at Balaklava. No time was to be lost, so our colonel sent him off at once, and he succeeded in purchasing sixteen; these tins were fixed up so as to form boilers, in which the men's breakfasts and dinners were cooked. Company messes were now re-established, and a few men struck off duty daily as cooks; although this arrangement entailed additional duty upon the remainder they did not grumble at it, as they saw how great was the advantage gained. The coffee being boiled early in the morning, each man now had half a pint of coffee and some biscuit before starting for the trenches or picket.

On the morning that the new boilers were first used, a deputation from the different companies, headed by the sergeant-major, thanked the colonel, saying that they had not felt so comfortable for many a week. Starting, as we did frequently, about four a.m. on bitterly cold and snowy mornings, I was very glad to join my company in a cup of hot coffee. Although at this time the officers constantly had to wear their wet or damp clothes for days, still they had an opportunity of drying them, when fuel could be obtained, having a change of things; but it was very different with other ranks: after, perhaps, being twenty-four hours on duty, they had to return *wet through to damp tents, without any fire to warm or dry them, and no change of clothes; besides having to pass the night on the cold, damp floor of the tents.*

During this month eighteen of our men died in the regimental hospital.[25]

---

25. December 2nd, Privates No. 2257, Thomas M'Donald and No. 3301, John Collins. 3rd, No. 2712, Daniel Hayes, 4th, No. 1250, M. Donohoe and No. 1173 William Barry. 6th, No. 2330, John Callaghan. 9th, No. 2842, John Harvey, No. 2924, Jeremiah Moriarty and No. 3033, James O'Brien. 10th, No. 2561, John Ryan. 12th, No. 3277, Daniel Dowey. 20th, No. 1477, Patrick Kelly. 21st, No. 3369, William Hogg. 23rd, No. 1404, John Kerrin. 25th, No. 2792, William Driscoll. 27th, No. 3254, Michael Lynch. 30th, No. 3228, Patrick Harrington. 31st, No. 2768, Michael Herlihy.

CHAPTER 5

January 1st to March 31st, 1855

Although the establishment of company messes tended to lessen considerably the miserable discomforts which the regiment had experienced during the previous month, the terrible sickness amongst us nevertheless daily increased; on the 6th we had *only* 250 *men fit for duty,* and there were *only* 14,000 *effective men in the British army then in the Crimea,* The transport service still remained in a hopeless state of collapse, and our cavalry were now employed in conveying sick to Balaklava. We seemed destined to continue victims to the apparently culpable mismanagement on the part of the quartermaster-general's and commissariat departments; medicines had become very scarce, and it was found that although there was an abundant supply of them on board the *Medway* at Balaklava, they could not be got at, *because they had been stowed away underneath a cargo of shot and shell;* stretchers also were much needed for the hospitals, but these also were not available, *because the canvas had been sent in one ship, and the wooden frames, legs, &c., in another.*

Our companies were now sadly reduced in numbers, and sometimes *could muster only six or eight file each fit for duty.* After a long and wet night in the trenches or on picket, it was pitiable to see my company, a mere handful of worn-out men, crawling back to camp through snow or mud; many poor fellows found it very difficult even to reach their tents, so weak and tired were they; and even in the comparatively short distance to be traversed, there were many stragglers, men who could not keep up with the remainder; but I never pressed them, letting them take their own time; having been on my legs all night, I was by no means the least fagged out of the party.

It is impossible to speak too highly of the noble conduct of the men throughout the winter, notwithstanding the hardships which they underwent. It was wonderful to observe how cheerful and merry the men were, even when matters were at their worst One of my company, named Dowd, used frequently to keep the men awake and amused, during some miserably cold night, with telling an absurd story, generally a fairy tale.

One day our colonel (Shirley) heard a man say, as he returned from the trenches, "The work is too hard; I can't stand it." His comrade, an old soldier, replied, "We can't complain when we see our officers as badly off as ourselves, and they are not accustomed to hardships." Such was the noble spirit which pervaded the regiment that you scarcely heard any poor fellows complain, but they perseveringly worked away until many of them succumbed to illness, produced by the hardships which they had patiently endured.

At this time the troops suffered much from cholera and diarrhoea, and many of our gallant fellows were thus carried off. Numbers, too, were invalided from frostbitten feet, caused by constant exposure to wet as well as to cold.

Besides these complaints, scurvy became very prevalent among the men, from the continuous diet of salt meat without any vegetables. Our ambassador at Constantinople very thoughtfully sent up a vessel full of cabbages and other vegetables for the use of the troops; *but because such articles were not included in the daily rations of the troops, neither the quartermaster-general's nor the commissariat departments would undertake to issue them, and consequently the vessel discharged these vegetables into the harbour.* Our ever-vigilant quartermaster, seeing numbers of cabbages, &c., floating about, brought up several loads of them, and they proved most acceptable.

One day our colonel saw a strong party of *Zouaves*, with carts, working in the ground adjoining the picket house above our camp. He found that they had discovered a quantity of parsnips in the garden, and were carrying them off. These parsnips had not been found out by our pickets, although they had occupied the house for many weeks. We thus lost the greater part of them, at a time when scurvy was prevalent for the want of vegetables.

A report was current at this time that an officer of the Indian army—a friend of Lord Raglan—was staying at headquarters, and seeking for some employment with the army. Lord R. was puzzled what to do with him; at last he was sent off, with a large sum of money, to purchase mules. When passing through the Dardanelles he fell in with a vessel laden with oranges. Thinking they would be good things for troops troubled with scurvy, he spent some of the money *on oranges instead of mules*, much to the astonishment and disappointment of the authorities.

At this time there was no superintending officer at Balaklava whose duty it was to report the description of supplies, besides shot and shell, brought by each ship which arrived there; and consequently many vessels *discharged their upper cargo of shot, &c., while the under cargo of warm clothing, &c., was taken back to Constantinople.*

As I have before remarked, we fortunately had a most active quartermaster with an equally active pony, and the amount of work that they both got through was marvellous. He went daily to Balaklava *throughout the winter, and in all weather*, with our ten bât-ponies, and always contrived to bring back something useful—frequently boots, rugs, blankets, warm clothing of some sort—in fact, anything he could lay his hands on, and, failing these, fodder for the ponies. He used to induce the Commissariat Department there to issue these articles, on condition that he sent them next day a requisition duly signed by the proper authorities. When the requisition was presented at headquarters for signature on the following day, the answer given by the quartermaster-general was invariably, "*None in store.*"

Sometimes our colonel took the requisition, so as to prevent the issuers getting into a scrape, and with difficulty got it signed, with the assertion, however, that "*it was of no use, as there was nothing of the kind in store.*" Before the report of the arrival of any stores reached headquarters, they had frequently been issued to the Cavalry, Guards, and Highlanders, who, being on the spot, of course kept a good lookout for all they could get It was, therefore, doubly necessary for those in the front to be equally vigilant, and, thanks to our excellent and indefatigable quartermaster, we always got our share.

Major (afterwards Colonel) Kenneth Mackenzie[1] was subsequently sent to superintend matters at Balaklava, and his excellent arrangements rapidly rectified the hitherto chaotic state of affairs in that place.

At the commencement of the winter we had our complement of ten bât-ponies, and, although our quartermaster managed to feed and shelter them during the very inclement weather, still the number

---

1. Colonel Mackenzie was unfortunately drowned during the autumn manoeuvres, at Dartmoor, in 1873. His untimely death was most deeply and universally regretted, more especially by those who, like myself, enjoyed the friendship of so estimable a man.

gradually decreased; many of the other regiments of the division not having adopted our quartermaster's plan of *storing* forage for the ponies, they could not feed theirs, and consequently they were turned out to pick up what they could find, and the neighbouring plateau therefore abounded in numbers of miserable, half-starved ponies, many with sore backs.

We had a man of the grenadier company, named Thomas Handley, who, when the number of the ponies had considerably decreased, used to go out before daylight and drive into our camp all the ponies he could find on the hills without sore backs; the best were retained to complete our numbers and, when fed, were despatched to Balaklava for loads; one chestnut pony, belonging to the 77th Regiment. was frequently claimed as he was being driven past their lines, and I do not believe that we got a *load out of him*, though he got *many feeds out of us*. Handley used frequently to come to our tents after dark, with a captured pony, to ask if any of us wanted "*a nice baste to ride to Ballicklarvy in the mornin'*," and he generally found an employer.

Our divisional commissariat had hitherto adopted the plan of keeping their *bât*-ponies up in the front, sending them daily down to Balaklava for supplies, to return to the exposure of wet and cold nights on the plateau; they were thus in a great measure employed in bringing their own food to the front, of which, however, judging by their lean condition, they did not appear to get much. At last our colonel persuaded the assistant-commissary-general to keep the animals at Balaklava, and consequently they came up fresh with their loads in the morning, and thereby the rations arrived by daylight, instead of in the middle of the night, and were therefore issued more regularly, which had not been the case for some time.

Although our *bat*-ponies seldom got back to camp until nearly midnight, we were lucky in not losing any loads except on one occasion, at the beginning of this month, when they were sent to Balaklava for boots; chap. they left Balaklava with their loads in good time, but were overtaken by a violent storm of wind and snow; as the ponies would not face it, the corporal in charge very properly made for the nearest camp, which happened to be a Turkish one, and deposited the boots at the guard-tent. We sent for the boots on the following day, but no boots were forthcoming; either the Turks thought that they were intended for them, or they could not resist the temptation of appropriating them; in any case we never saw the boots again, in spite of our colonel making a strong representation about it.

On the morning of the 1st January I went on picket at the Middle Ravine with Captain Bayley. This important position, which, from the nature of the ground, as I have already remarked, I always considered difficult to defend, even when held by *two strong* companies, was very inadequately protected now that our companies were so much reduced in strength; besides which the ground favoured surprises from the enemy, hence it was most necessary to be always on the alert On this evening I wiled away the long and weary hours, seated on the damp ground, a stone wall at my back for an easy-chair, my cloak around me, and a pipe to warm me. I visited sentries every half-hour; in fact, whenever I felt sleepy I immediately started on my rounds. Captain Bayley, one of the most vigilant and active officers I ever met, adopted a somewhat cunning plan for keeping himself awake in the trenches. He sat on a gabion laid on its side, so that, when he dozed and nodded, the gabion (being round) turned over and deposited him *wide awake* upon the muddy ground; a necessary precaution, as from our constant, hard work we felt over-fatigued.

On the 3rd I passed a miserable twelve hours in the 21-gun battery, up to my ankles in mud and water, with rain and sleet overhead. Whenever we were on duty in the "advanced work" (afterwards called 2nd Parallel) the Russian riflemen always fired if a forage-cap appeared above the parapet. One day I put my cap on the top of a stick and held it above the parapet, when "*ping*" went numerous rifle-bullets at it. Occasionally I used to return the compliment and fire at them with my servant's rifle, while he loaded; it was a long range, and I sometimes fired away for a couple of hours—rather a dangerous occupation, I must admit, as the Russians fired at me in return.

The 5th was about the coldest day I almost ever felt. Before going to the trenches I sat in J. W.'s tent writing home: we had no fire, and the snow and cutting wind blew into the tent-door; my fingers were so benumbed with the intense cold, that I could with difficulty hold my pen, and my letter was, consequently, a terrible scrawl under my congealed condition. Snow with severe frost had now set in, and we felt the inclemency of the weather the more severely, being exposed to every gust of wind in the trenches; and in camp a tent was a poor protection especially without a fire, as was frequently the case at this time, fuel being now very scarce. Warm clothing also was much needed; a little had arrived at Balaklava, but there was not any transport to bring it up.

The frost at night was now so intense, that the men's coats used to freeze to the ground as they lay asleep in their tents. The water in my jug was sometimes a solid mass of ice, and the snow was about a foot deep. At this time we read, with much interest, that all England had gone military mad, and while John Bull was thrusting his arms up to the elbows in his generous pockets, the fair ladies at home (old and young) were wearing their fingers to the bone in knitting all kinds of indescribables for the heroes of the Crimea.

On the night of the 6th I was again in the trenches; it was a bright moonlight night and a very hard frost. We could discern the Russian sentries as distinctly as if it were daylight. In the middle of the night some of them advanced towards our line of sentries, calling out, "*Bono Ingliz, bono Franciz, no bono Turco,*" but when we sent a party towards them, fancying they intended to desert, they retired into their rifle-pits. In previously speaking of the Middle Ravine picket I mentioned that the Russian riflemen used constantly to fire at our sentries; this was also the case in the trenches, and one of my men was wounded on his post today; I had always understood that firing at sentries was not customary in civilised warfare—at least, my father used to say that it was never done during the Peninsular War.

We returned to camp before daylight on the 7th; it was bright moonlight and intensely cold, the frozen snow sounding very crisp under our feet I was very sorry to hear today of the death of Major Sharpe, 20th Regiment, which had taken place at Scutari from wounds received at Inkermann. I had known him very well when I was in that regiment. One of our subaltern officers having gone away on sick leave, I took possession of his tent, the floor of which (being dug out) was sunk three feet below the surface: this was a very comfortable change from my previous cold tent.

Some of the huts, as well as warm clothing, were said to have arrived at Balaklava at this time, *but as there were no means of bringing them to the front they were placed in store!!*

On the 8th I was in the trenches all day; it was frosty and very cold, the ground being covered with snow, with a cloudless sky and bright sun. Seated on a gun-carriage, I enjoyed my breakfast of hot tea, bread and butter. I thought if my friends in Old England could but see me breakfasting *al fresco* in such cold weather, they would exclaim "poor fellow:" but I felt very comfortable. Hardly any firing took place in the batteries today, which seemed to make the Russian riflemen more saucy than usual, and they annoyed us much by firing into the embrasures of the 21-gun battery; consequently several of my men were wounded, one of them, named John Walsh, slightly.

The French and Russians kept up a desultory fire of shells and musketry regularly every night; in allusion to which a *Zouave* officer once remarked to me. "*La musique commence à sept heures précises;*" as for our batteries, they seldom fired a shot.

Such were the daily occurrences to which we became so accustomed as to think nothing of them—so much does custom become second nature. As for getting into Sebastopol, we seemed to have abandoned all idea of such a thing, and considered that it could not be effected without the assistance of a strong force, acting on the north side, and where were they to come from? England appeared to be draining herself of troops in sending out reinforcements; nevertheless, such was the continued increase of sickness amongst us, that our numbers seemed to *de*crease instead of to *in*crease.

The arrival of mails from England is always an object of constant interest to those who are away in foreign lands; but the circumstances in which we were now placed seemed to increase the anxiety and eagerness with which we looked forward to the receipt of "news from home." In spite, however, of the public journals holding out promises of great improvement in our postal communication with England, there was, nevertheless, great irregularity in the delivery of our letters and newspapers at this time; unlike our allies, the French (and later on the Sardinians), we had not, apparently, any organised postal arrangements.

On the 9th I passed a quiet night on picket; a thaw having set in, the ground was very wet; three of us wiled away the weary hours of the long night in the cave (under the light of a candle stuck in a bottle), and in frequently visiting our sentries, the French and Russians, as usual, firing all night. We returned to camp before daylight on the 10th. During this month I managed to get a second tent, which I put over the other, rendering my canvas residence warmer and more water-tight I also constructed a fireplace with a piece of Russian water-pipe for a chimney; but, what with wet fuel and a chimney that would not draw, I used constantly to sit in an atmosphere of wood-smoke, very painful to the eyes; added to which a spring appeared at the bottom of my tent, which was frequently covered with water.

Under these disadvantageous circumstances I often wrote my letters home by the light of a candle, while my servant (John Higgins) sat on a block of wood and prepared soup for my return from the trenches, or warmed himself before the small fire, indulging in some quaint observation, for he was a thorough Paddy. I used to feel a pleasure in talking with him about his friends in "Ould Ireland," and in making him write to them. I heard today that, among other things which had been sent out to the army, were *wooden legs at the rate of four per man*, which only showed *what donkeys our government took us to be*.

The duty, in the trenches and on picket, still came round very frequently; I was in the 21-gun battery all day on the nth, when one of my men (Corporal John Houlihan) was killed, and on the following evening I went out to the advanced work; there was very hard frost and it was bitterly cold, but a red nose was preferable to wet toes. During the night I heard a single shot, as if fired by one of my sentries; Captain Bayley, who was out with me, and I hurried out and found that one of my men, named Thomas Carroll, had deserted off his post, and the shot I heard was one fired at him by his fellow-sentry; we made a search to the front as far as we prudently could, for we could discern the Russian picket watching us, to see if he had been hit, but found only his belts, &c., which he had thrown off.

It was a very calm and dark night, and with the exception of this incident we had not heard a sound, when about midnight the well-known yell of the Russians broke out suddenly, in the direction of the French attack, followed by the enemy's batteries opening fire upon us, as well as upon the French. We all stood to our arms expecting an attack; for more than half an hour the shower of shells bursting over our heads was most brilliant, but, although they burst all round us, we had no casualties. The firing upon our Left Attack (Green Hill) was even heavier than upon us; at length all firing ceased, and the night resumed its previous stillness.

On the morning of the 14th, about five o'clock, I again started for the trenches; as I struggled out through the hard frozen flaps of my tent-door, a dreary scene presented itself to my view; it was intensely dark, and rendered more so by the thick fog and heavily falling snow, all around was one vast white expanse, not a sound, save the crackling of the crisp snow, as my company wended their snowy way to the place of rendezvous; the tents themselves, banked up by the drifting snow, seemed as if they must be shivering to the very poles; like a will-o'-the-wisp you saw the faint light of a candle glimmering through the fog, a beacon to show where, like myself, some sleepy "son of Mars" was getting himself up for the trenches.

As soon as all had assembled, we started for the 21-gun battery: a long line of men, in sheepskin coats and fur caps (which happily had been issued a few days previously), besides every kind of grotesque costume imaginable, might be seen wading through the rapidly deepening snow, and white from head to foot; leading the column was the field-officer[2] a very long man upon a very short pony; he was enveloped in furs, with little visible but his nose, while his legs dangled in the snow; we lost our way completely, and did not reach the battery until eight a.m.

Underclothing issued to us about this time, proving most acceptable to all ranks, but boots were much wanted; I succeeded in purchasing a very indifferent pair, *off the legs of a sea-captain* at Balaklava, for the exorbitant sum of 3*l*.

On the 16th my old Captain, M. joined us from the invalid *depôt* at Balaklava, and, as the ground was far too wet for pitching a fresh tent, I made him take up his abode in my smoky and damp residence; here we used constantly to sit blinking at each other, with our feet in water, until the increasing smoke from the damp fuel caused us almost to disappear from each other's view. When on trench duty on the evening of the 15th, I passed the coldest night I ever experienced, the snow was very deep and, early in the morning, a cutting east wind set in, which blew about the snow like sand. During the intervals between visiting sentries, I crept into an empty magazine and endeavoured to get warm, but the snow drifting in, covered me so that I was scarcely discernible. J. D., who was with me, lay upon the ground under a rug, which soon became thickly covered with snow, and he found it very warm; visiting sentries was no easy matter, so deeply had the snow drifted, and the night was very dark. The 18th being the Russian Twelfth Day, an attack was expected, but all passed off quietly.

Notwithstanding frequent drafts from England the regiment still continued to decrease. On the 19th we showed *only 291 fit for duty*. 1000 men were *detailed every night* for the trenches, but *our brigade could only* furnish 400; 800 men were *detailed* for the trenches *by day, but only* 300 *were sent*. Of course this strong detail was put in Orders, so as to deceive the enemy regarding our actual strength, under arms, in the trenches, &c, in case spies might give in- formation respecting our duties. For every fifty men received in the drafts, one hundred went away sick; the eight regiments of the Light Division, originally 850 men each, and therefore representing a total strength of 6800, could not at this time muster 2000, including numerous drafts which had arrived; but we looked hopefully for better times, remembering the old adage,

2. Lieutenant-Colonel Egerton, 77th Regiment, afterwards killed, 19th April, 1855.

Better to live in hope than die in despair.

The French having increased their force towards Inkermann took the pickets furnished by the 1st and 2nd Divisions, as well as the charge of all field-works on our right; this change enabled the 2nd Division to assist us in our trench and picket duties.

This week we received a draft from England, with some officers; all ranks had now a much easier time of it than hitherto. The weather having changed to a thaw, the snow rapidly disappeared; this made the ground around us very muddy.

Tattoo now was at seven a. m., after which not a voice was heard in the camp, all hands being too tired to be wakeful. I was on duty in the advanced trench on the 24th; one of our majors (Norton) was the field-officer in command; it was a very cold but fine night, and we made ourselves snug in an empty magazine, where we lighted a fire, and left some coffee to keep warm for our early breakfast. As I lay with my feet to the fire I unfortunately kicked over the pot, and we lost our coffee, much to the disgust of us both. Captain Corbett and Ensign Little[3] rejoined us from Varna this month, and our ponies also arrived from that place on the 24th.

The same day I rode to Balaklava with my brother; we went on board the *Imperatrix* and saw Major C, of the 20th, who had just arrived from England and brought me a parcel from home, the contents of which proved very acceptable, as everything was so exorbitant at Balaklava. The men were now sadly in want of more protection than that of a tent, which did not save them from frost-bites during the severe weather; huts began to spring up in many regiments, but we were unable to get any as yet; each hut consisted of *thirty-six pieces*, some of which were too heavy for men to carry, and all this time we had no other means of transport. Hitherto we had had no regular hospital-tent, and could obtain nothing except some bell-tents—most inadequate accommodation for our numerous sick and wounded.

The regimental hospital marquee was on board the *Albion*, and when that vessel first arrived at Balaklava we had no means, for some weeks, for bringing it up to the front, none of our ponies or mules being strong enough to convey it through the deep mud; but when our *bât* animals arrived from Varna, the colonel received amongst them a strong English horse, which easily brought up the marquee; and a great comfort it proved to our poor sick and wounded fellows. Subse-

---

3. Ensign Little had been made adjutant of the regiment (15th Nov., 1854), *vice* Maule, who died of his wounds.

quently our P.M.O. sent us another marquee.

During the greater part of the winter our days were principally passed on duty in the trenches, &c., or in sleeping off our fatigues, leaving little time or inclination for reading even a newspaper; it had been very difficult to obtain books of any description, but during this month I fortunately picked up some numbers of *Household Words*; and as, at this time, I used to be off duty for three or four days, I found this periodical very acceptable for reading in leisure moments. Matters generally were beginning to look a shade brighter; a parcel office had at last been established at Balaklava, and ships, laden with all kinds of useful things—the gifts of a generous British public—began frequently to arrive.

The days and nights were now very fine, the former with bright sun and hard frost; still the previous sudden and frequent changes in the weather caused a good deal of sickness, and coughs and colds were also pretty prevalent I luckily escaped and kept my health throughout the winter, in spite of the constant exposure to which I had been subjected, and I was fortunately enabled to keep steadily to my work. The force of French troops had considerably increased towards the Inkermann heights, and, on our right, there was a continuous expanse of tents as far as the eye could reach. Some deserters reported that the Russians intended to attack us shortly, but now that the right of our porsiton was strengthened we felt pretty secure.

The papers made out that the *Czar* seemed inclined for peace: so little did we credit such "shaves," that whenever we heard the Russians open a smart fire upon the French we always exclaimed, "There's the proclamation of peace."

The weather continued very fine, the frost had disappeared, and the ground was dreadfully muddy; the way to Balaklava still remained a muddy track; at last however, the authorities began to *talk* about repairing it. On the 28th we had church parade, which had not taken place for many Sundays.

Having at last received a wooden hut, we were busy in erecting it for a hospital, and we hoped, by taking advantage of the few fine days, to get up some more huts before the wintry weather again set in. The works in our Left Attack were now being increased and armed, and preparations were also being made for extending the trenches of our Right Attack, so as to join those of the French on our left; by this drawing closer to the town, and driving out of their pits and hiding-places the Russian sharpshooters, who still continued to cause us much annoyance in the batteries.

On the 30th I rode to Balaklava with my brother, and R. and M. of the 20th; the road was dreadfully muddy, and still remained unrepaired; we made a few purchases on board the *Firefly* and *Foyle*, How changed now was the once beautiful vale of Balaklava!—the vineyards all rooted up and the trees cut down!—all around one vast sea of mud, embellished with the numerous carcases of dead horses! The miserable villages of Balaklava and Kadikoi were increasing in size, as well as improving in appearance, by the erection of many wooden houses for shops, besides others for hospitals, barracks, stores, &c.

The scene which presented itself on entering these places was very singular; strings of mules and half-starved ponies (laden with every kind of article, from a bag of forage to an officers long-expected parcel), splashing through the mud, besides numerous English, French, and Turkish soldiers staggering along under some heavy load; to say nothing of the ubiquitous British officer, his costume more civil than military, jogging along to camp on a lean pony, his saddle-bags, besides all his available pockets, being crammed with articles of food purchased on board ship; such a figure did I often present We found that the shops at Balaklava had all been closed, and were soon, it was said, to be reopened with supplies from England (sent by government) to be sold at cost price; a great boon to us who had hitherto been victimised by a set of Maltese and Greek robbers. I returned to camp from my foraging excursion about sunset, finding a warm tent, a good fire (in a stove recently obtained), and my companion M. to welcome me.

All our sick, &c., had now been moved into our hospital hut, which proved very warm and comfortable, more roomy than the marquee hitherto in use, and therefore an immense boon to the patients. With a continuance of the fine weather we much hoped that the health of all would improve; but we still continued to lose, every week, many of our poor fellows, fourteen of whom died in our camp hospital during this month.[4]

The whole army was under arms long before daylight on the 1st

4. Privates—January 5th No. 1690, John Connell. 7th, No. 3063, Patrick McHugh. 9th, No. 3208, Joseph Campbell. 10th, No. 3202, Patrick McGovern and No. 3141, Daniel Clancy. 13th, No. 3012, Patrick Cassidy. 15th, No. 2569, Private Patrick Fox. 18th, No. 2994, Stephen Bailey. 19th, No. 2550, John Mullen. 20th, No. 1948, George Allen. 24th, No. 2784, Thomas Bennett. 31st, No. 1830, Michael Gordon and No. 2614, George Handcock.
14th, No. 2041, Corporal Patrick Burns.

of February, and we were confined to camp during the day, expecting an attack. Lord Raglan was at our camp at an early hour; all, however, passed off quietly. Hearing a voice outside my tent, remarking my stove-chimney, I looked out and found, to my astonishment that it was Lord Raglan. His Lordship said that he hoped I did not burn charcoal in my stove, as it was a very dangerous thing to do, an officer[5] having been recently suffocated in his tent through using charcoal as fuel. I was much struck with his Lordship's pleasing, affable manner. It was constantly regretted by all that he was so seldom seen in camp during the winter—so very different to what I had often heard my father say about the Duke of Wellington, who, during the Peninsular War, was always everywhere, and was known by everybody; our commander-in-chief lived only three miles off, and yet we almost forgot his existence.

During the early part of the day columns of French artillery and infantry passed our camp towards the field of Inkermann.

Having now obtained a stove, I found my tent much more comfortable than when I had a smoky fireplace; the change rendering my residence dry and warm without any smoke.

About this time we were ordered to be on the alert day and night, as it was believed that the Russians intended to make a final attempt to drive us into the sea, the *Czar* having said that Balaklava *must* be taken at any cost: the attack, however, did not come off.

A spy made his appearance one day in our Right Attack: he was a gentlemanly-looking man, and represented himself to be an assistant-surgeon just arrived to join the 3rd Division, excusing his appearance in mufti from his baggage not having come up from Balaklava. He minutely inspected the battery, and asked permission to visit the advanced trench, where he chatted with the officers in charge: watching his opportunity he suddenly sprang over the parapet and made for the Russian lines; the men in our trenches fired but missed him, and at the same time the Russian sharpshooters opened a smart fire to cover his retreat. He reached the enemy's batteries in safety, and was received with loud cheers. He spoke English fluently.

But little firing now went on in the trenches; the Russians were very busy strengthening their works, and deserters reported that the imperial princes (Nicholas and Constantine) had returned to Sebastopol: this report, and the enemy's continued silence, made us suspicious that some mischief was brewing.

---

5. This was Captain Swinton, R.A.

The French continued to push on their works rapidly, and eclipsed our apparently slow progress; the French always seemed to us much more practical soldiers than ourselves; and the more we saw of them the more we observed, how much we had yet to learn in the way of soldiering in the field.

The frosts continued to be very severe, but as our sick were now comfortably protected in huts, we could afford to think lightly of the weather; a hut was also erected for the light company; we were told that huts for officers would not be erected, and we were recommended to board our floors, the necessary materials being supplied; this I had already done, and found the comfort of it. Matters were beginning to look brighter; the "navvies" having arrived at Balaklava now *commenced* making a road between that place and the camp. With the exception of fresh meat occasionally, our rations still continued to be salt meat; and some facetious son of Mars observed, that if we continued to live upon pork we should grow bristles and grunt.

Our duties were now much lighter than they had been, coming round about once or twice a week; I was in the trenches on the 1st and 5th. The Russians very seldom fired at us, but they and the French kept up the usual fusillade every night. Frequently, when off duty, I used to make foraging excursions into Balaklava, returning well laden with "varieties" from the recently arrived ships; one evening when coming back alone I nearly lost my way in a fog, and as I happened to have a cargo of poultry, I should have proved a very acceptable prize to a hungry Cossack.

The French 25th Regiment of Infantry was encamped in rear of our lines for several months, and its excellent band used to play almost every day, affording a delightful relief for many of us. We heard today that the Russian princes had been accompanied on their way to Sebastopol by an army of 25,000 men, of whom one-half had perished in the snow as they came down. On the 8th I marched my company to Balaklava to bring up planks for flooring my men's tents, as a protection from the damp ground; it was a foggy, wet day, and the track was still in a terrible state of mud; on our return it poured with rain, but under cover of good waterproofs, recently issued by government to the whole army, we were kept dry, reaching camp about; sunset.

On the 9th I received a hut for my company, which was sufficient for part of the men, while the remainder lived in boarded tents. We began to be well supplied with warm clothing from private sources as well as from government, who besides the waterproof cloaks, issued warm underclothing. I now, at last, possessed a good mackintosh and stout boots, my forage-cap being covered with an oilskin cover which I picked up on the field of Inkermann; a brother officer also gave me some warm things, a relation having very generously sent him a large package, containing socks, comforters, &c, for distribution among the officers of the regiment.

What would we have given for all these during the worst part of the winter; they would have saved us from many a wetting, as well as from constantly sleeping in wet clothes for the want of a change! One of our men (Private Daniel McMahon) was wounded severely on the 9th.

An anecdote was told me concerning the *Zouaves*, who were always represented to be a very independent set, acting pretty much as they pleased. One very dark night a *Zouave* said to his comrade: "*Alphonse, allons faire la guerre.*"

"*Bien, mon ami,*" replied Alphonse. Upon this they armed themselves with as many loaded firelocks as they could carry, and crept towards the Russian batteries; placing the firelocks in a row upon the ground, they fired them in succession as rapidly as they could. The Russians, fancying it was an attack, opened a brisk fire, which, as Alphonse and his friend lay flat on their faces, left them untouched. When the enemy found that it was a false alarm and ceased firing, the two *Zouaves* shouldered their firelocks and returned to camp, highly delighted with their nocturnal exploit.

On the 11th we had Divine Service in a hut for the first time. In the evening I was in the advanced trench, and passed a miserably wet night; it was very dark, and the trenches were in a terrible state of mud and water, deep enough to render promenading almost impossible. However, with my young subaltern, Lieutenant Preston,[6] I took refuge occasionally in an empty magazine, which gave us good shelter. Here, seated upon sandbags, the weary hours of night flitted by— broken by frequent visits to my sentries—and we hailed with delight my sergeant's welcome intelligence at half-past five a.m.: "Av ye plase, sir, the reliefs comin'."

The huts were gradually springing up in camp, and we had four erected already.

One day, wishing to set my watch, I sent my servant to ascertain the correct time from the sergeant-major. Upon his return he informed me that it wanted *six minutes to three* when he left the sergeant-major's

6. Killed in the trenches, April 14, 1855.

tent, and, as he had been *two minutes coming*, it must then want *eight minutes to three*; and, moreover, Paddy persisted he was right.

Sir George Brown returned to the front on the 12th, but did not assume the command of the division for a few days.

On the 14th I was busy all day superintending the boarding of the floor of my company's tents. This kept my men from the damp ground, and was, of course, much cleaner also than the bare earth. As my company was now partly in huts and partly in boarded tents, the men were very comfortable and protected against wet weather, for the climate was most changeable. If all this could have been done *before*, instead of *after*, the worst parts of the cold and wet weather, much sickness would have been averted, and many a life saved. Well might the question be asked at this time in the House of Commons—"If out of the 54.000 men which have left the shores of England only 14,000 remain—and they, too, crippled by sickness—where are the 40.000 to complete?" Our cemeteries, our battlefields, and our hospitals afforded the only reply.

About this time all kinds of eatables and drinkables were sent out by the *Times* Fund, to be sold at cost price; the articles were placed in lots and drawn for on the 15th, proving very acceptable; my share was two bottles of brandy, one of claret, a jar of butter, and a bottle of pickles—rather a mixed allowance, I must confess. I was on picket all day on the 16th, which passed off quietly. The duties now were very much lighter than they had been, and we went on picket for twelve instead of for twenty-four hours. This change made us pass our days in comparative ease, reading and writing, or riding when weather permitted, for the climate had become quite spring-like. During this month the French commenced making a battery for us in the Right Attack; it was afterwards called the 8-gun battery, situate in the Second Parallel; this battery was supposed to cover the advance of the French upon the Malakhoff.

On the 17th I received a parcel from home, containing, among other useful things, some knives and forks, besides an *old great coat* of mine, the first sight of which was like *meeting an old friend* after a lengthened separation. From among the things I took up a small box, marked outside, "Rimmels pure Florence Oil Soap;" it felt very light, and I remarked, " Ha! it is evidently some new and good kind of soap." I opened it and found to my amusement, as well as surprise, that it contained some *balls of worsted for mending socks*—a very useful present from my thoughtful mother. A waterproof coat was also among the things, but, as I already had one, I handed it over to my brother who had none.

On the night of the 19th I was in the advanced trench, engaged with my company in working at the new battery, commenced by the French. The night was very dark, but mild, with drizzling rain. In the middle of the night the wind suddenly changed; it rained, hailed, and then snowed, freezing intensely. It was bitterly cold, but, having a hood over my head, I managed to keep dry and warm. My pony was generally brought down to meet me on my return from picket or trenches. This morning I passed him, thinking, in the fog and darkness, that the animal was *grey*, and the groom in *white*, so thickly were they covered with snow and icicles.

The 20th was a bitterly cold day, blowing and snowing incessantly; I kept close to my tent, voting it night; unfortunately fuel was now scarce and I had a bad fire.

Our duty-strength now was 270; and at most we could bring into the field 350 bayonets; our officers mustered, two field-officers, six captains, and eight subalterns.

To kill spare time I amused myself making a map for my father of the position of the allied forces, and all the morning of the 22nd I was sitting in my friend Major Hallewell's tent, who kindly placed paper, paints, and pencils at my service, and where I drew and gathered information.

The navvies at Balaklava were progressing with the railway at this time, and promised to be of great service, but the road to Balaklava was far from complete. The casualties at this time were happily few; we had one man, Private John M'Gindley, severely wounded on the 23rd.

About three a.m. on the 24th, we were roused from our slumbers by heavy firing in front of the French position at Inkermann; the Russian yells and the firing lasted about two hours; it was the French attacking some newly erected works which the Russians had thrown up near the French position.[7] The French were repulsed with a loss of 150 men and 11 officers; the *Zouaves* engaged were much incensed with their marine infantry, whom they accused of having bolted at a critical moment. It was also said that the Russian officers adopted the somewhat questionable stratagem of calling out, *"Par-ici les Zouaves,"* which the latter, in the dark, mistook for the order of their own officers, and thus fell into a trap.

---

7. Called by the French *"Les ouvrages blancs,"* from the earth excavated being almost as white as chalk.

On the 24th a draft, with two officers, joined the I regiment, and we were very glad to receive this reinforcement to our ranks. Now that the distresses of the miserable winter had become fully known in England, innumerable presents of warm clothing, &c., continued to pour in from various sources, public and private: the gentry and tradespeople of Bury, in Lancashire, sent all kinds of warm clothing *for the whole regiment*.[8] A shoemaker whom I employed when at Bury sent me two very useful things—a pair of socks and some boot-laces, with a very warm-hearted letter of good wishes—a genuine expression of kindly feeling which I shall never forget; and the clergyman's family (friends of mine) there most kindly sent me a knitted comforter, a pair of *muffetees*, a bottle of cayenne pepper, and a toasting-fork.

In addition to these and other presents, came two larger boxes, addressed to the regiment, thus: "From the Housemaids of London to the 88th Regiment"They contained 800 packages, of which each held a short clay pipe and half a pound of good tobacco in the middle of one box was a pound of tobacco, "a present from the poor packer." How on earth our Paddies, who had never been quartered in or near London, gained the esteem of these *patriotic damsels* I cannot say; but the contents were most acceptable and highly appreciated. As the chests did not contain any address, or names of the senders, the colonel acknowledged their receipt in the *Times*. A gentleman (Captain T.) formerly in the 88th, most kindly sent each officer one dozen of pale ale, a very acceptable present.

Among other presents to the regiment from strangers, was one from Dr. C, Rector of St Stephen's, Walbrook, who very kindly sent the colonel a frying-pan and a coffee-roaster, two exceedingly useful presents. Government also issued at this time most comfortable tweed coats, very light, and lined with rabbit or fox-skin, &c.; they were exceedingly warm, and, being loose, they could be easily worn over uniform.

Postage-stamps at one time were very scarce, and my servant used to borrow from me occasionally; he told me that his friends were sending some out to him, and when the mail arrived one day, I asked if he had received the promised stamps; he replied that sure enough

---

8. The regiment had been twice quartered in Bury—first, the *depôt*, in 1850-1, and the headquarters in 1853-4, when the officers experienced much hospitality, and the men, from their continuous good conduct, were most popular with the inhabitants. After the war we sent to the mayor and people of Bury several Russian drums, helmets, rifles, &c., which, I believe, are now (1878) in the town hall of that place.

he had, but, he added, "they were all put *outside* the letter, *and every mother's son of them is tattooed*." I was in the Middle Ravine picket all day on the 26th; I amused myself watching the Russians very busy at the battery, which the French had unsuccessfully attacked on the 24th; they were as thick as ants on an anthill. We had a few casualties at this time; Private Frederick Molton was killed on the 25th, and Private Daniel Cockerry was severely wounded on the 27th; we also had twenty-two deaths in our hospital during the month.[9]

I laughed very much at M's costume as he started for the trenches on the evening of the 1st; he was got up in a pea-coat, pistol round his waist, waterproof leggings over his long boots, and (to crown all) a scarlet comforter converted into a cap and drawn over his forage-cap and ears. I somewhat disturbed his dignity by saying that he looked more like a French fisherman than a British officer; the fact was that our uniforms being ill-suited for the requirements of campaigning and such-like rough work, it was no wonder that both officers and men took many liberties in the matter of dress, adopting the most comfortable style. I often wished that I had my warm and comfortable Canadian uniform.

Our brigadier (Buller) returned at this time and our colonel (Shirley) had to relinquish the temporary command of the brigade, and to resume his trench duties.

The weather continued snowy and wintry, but the nights were beautiful, bright moonlight and very cold I passed the night of the 2nd on picket; my party consisted of 100 men and two subalterns; we had a very good fire, and spent the time between reading, chatting, and visiting sentries. This was my last tour of duty on the Middle Ravine picket, where I had passed many an anxious hour; the 97th joined our brigade during the month, and we discontinued furnishing the picket; this gave all ranks an extra night off duty. No more attempts had been made by the French upon the new Russian batteries; since the recent attack the Russians had been very busy constructing a battery in front

---

9. Privates—February 1st, No. 2657, William Fee. 2nd, No. 2757, Patrick McNamara. 4th, No. 2825, Edward O'Connell. 5th, No. 2453, James Mullens and No. 3090 James Whitaker. 6th, No. 2914, Michael McCarthy and No. 1670, Patrick Rielly. 8th, No. 3338, Charles Cook. 10th, No. 3236, Patrick Mannion and No. 3293 Patrick Barry. 12th, No. 3049, James Ryan. 13th, No. 3486, Daniel Reid. 16th, No. 2117, John Mannion. 17th, No. 3283, Joshua Levery. 18th, No. 3121, Denis McMahon and No. 2855, Maurice Cahill. 20th, No. 3251, James Jenkinson, No. 2562, Jeremiah McCauliffe and No. 2934, John McMahon. 21st, No. 3545, George Glass. 24th, No. 3614, George Hersey.

of them, so indefatigable were they now in throwing up new works. At this time our commanding officer received orders to complete the men with all clothing, &c., necessary for service in the field early in the spring; this raised our hopes and expectations, for we longed for a change from the monotony of siege duties.

A story was current in camp, that a lady had written to a British officer with the injunction that when Menschikoff was taken prisoner, she would like a button off his coat as a memento; meanwhile her friend had been taken prisoner, and the lady's letter, being forwarded, passed through the hands of this Russian general, who, as is customary, read its contents; Menschikoff, thereupon, very politely cut off one of his buttons, requesting that it might be delivered to the fair lady with a message, that he had no intention of being made prisoner, but, anticipating the lady's wish, begged to send her one of his buttons.[10]

I was in the advance work all day on the 6th. The enemy fired some round shot and shell at us; one of the latter bounded over the parapet, struck the ground close to me, as I reclined lazily reading some very entertaining novel, and passed along, bursting harmlessly. The Russian sharpshooters kept up a brisk fire at us all day, but we fortunately had no casualties; at night the Russians troubled us but little, confining their attentions almost exclusively to the French, who, in return, showered rockets into the town all night.

On the 7th Lord Raglan heard from Lord John Russell, at Berlin, of the death of the Russian emperor. A flag of truce, with the news, was sent into the town, but the Russians would not believe the report. It was said that the Russian general in command (Osten Sacken) observed that if it were true he would not fire another shot.

One part of the connecting trench, or left *boyau*, between the advance work and Gordon's battery, had become completely enfiladed by the Russian sharpshooters, who seemed to play a kind of game of chess with our engineers as regards the relative positions of our trenches and the rifle-pits.

We now enjoyed most lovely spring days. On the 9th I was sitting with my tent-door wide open, and no fire lighted, and the sun was very warm. Now that the wintry weather was over, of course

10. Singularly enough, when dining at the house of the Hon. H. B. (whose son was in the 88th), in August, 1856, I met the lady who had made the request She corroborated the anecdote as I have related it, but added that, much to her annoyance, she had never received the said button, as it had been lost by the officer to whom it had been entrusted for conveyance to England.

the warm clothing was gradually arriving, so we reasonably expected summer clothing about November. The country around us abounded in yellow crocuses, and I picked one growing in one of the gabions of the parapet in our advanced work.

On the 10th I rode into Balaklava, with my friend E. H. M. and my brother, to market The place was beginning to look quite English, The railway had progressed rapidly; fat horses and jolly-looking carters thronged the streets, reminding us of Old England; a "restaurant" had been established, at which we dined. We boarded a brigantine, called *Norma*, when I was much astonished to meet a friend, Captain L. W., formerly 24th Regiment; he had come out on "spec" with a mixed cargo.

I purchased a chair one day at Balaklava, and found it most comfortable, not having sat in one for many months.

On the night of the 11th we were suddenly ordered out on a working party. Great was the excitement, as we fancied that we were going to have a brush with the Russians. The party, consisting of 600 of the Light Division, proceeded, laden with gabions, pick-axes, &c., to the advanced work, from the right of which they commenced throwing up a trench towards the round tower, as far as some caves from which the Russians used to fire into our batteries, and joining the French trenches in the ravine; a covering party of 1000 men, under Colonel Shirley, was posted in the ravine. There was a false alarm during the night, and some regiment in the advanced work behind us commenced firing into us, fortunately without causing any casualty; the Russians fired occasionally at us, but we continued our work, without casualties, until three the next morning.

Our artillery also fired shell from the 21-gun battery during the night, but nearly all the shells burst in the air, sending splinters amongst us; so that what with this fact, and that of the vagaries of the trench party behind us, we had more to fear from our friends than our foes. The night was very dark. On the 13th I was on a working party during the day; in the afternoon. Captain Craigie, R.E., was killed by the splinter of a shell while returning to camp along the middle ravine; it took place some way from the trenches, and where he might reasonably have expected to be safe from shot or even shell; but it appeared that the shell exploded when very high up in the air, and consequently the splinters were scattered a long way; he had been ordered off to Corfu, and it was his last day in the trenches; little did he think, poor fellow, that it was his last day in this world. I knew him very well, when I was with the Engineers, I attended his funeral on the 14th.

On the 15th I rode with W. to the monastery of St. George, near the village of Karani; we heard that picnics here were all the fashion for the ladies of Sebastopol last year; now they had to find another Crimean Shanklin Chine, there to discuss "those, horrid Allies." After cantering along the downs, above lofty cliffs, reminding us of the south coast of the Isle of Wight, we came suddenly upon a rocky gorge, opening upon the calm sea; here was situate a little church and monastery, besides a few other houses; below these, and reaching to the beach, were neglected gardens in terraces, and a hut in which lived a hermit The view was very pretty, but much spoilt by nearly all the trees having been cut down for fuel; all looked calm and peaceful, a contrast to the scene daily before us m the front; seventeen monks, some Greek families, and the late Governor of Balaklava, were prisoners here, under surveillance.

Commencing on this day we had twenty-four hours instead of twelve hours' duty in the trenches. The days were very fine, like an English spring; the nights were, however, very dark and favourable to sorties. On the evening of the 17th we were turned out by firing on our right, which proved to be nothing.

As a diversion from the usual monotony of our present camp life, horse races were frequently got up, and this month we had several meetings; one at Karani, near Balaklava, a small village, inhabited by several Greek families. These races used to be well attended by French and English of all ranks, and afforded considerable amusement; Lord Raglan and other bigwigs were frequently present.

On the 18th I passed the day in the 21-gun battery, where I commenced a letter home, but I found writing in the open air very cold work for the fingers. At this time the Russians were remarkably quiet but very busy, and had constructed many new rifle-pits, from which their sharpshooters caused numerous casualties in the new trench, which we had constructed on the night of the 11th; and on the morning of the 19th there were two men killed and four wounded in this trench; these pits were thrown up about one hundred yards in front of the French trenches on our right; they attempted to take them three several times, but failed.

The French batteries fired showers upon showers of shells upon the town all night (18th and 19th), and our practice during the day was very good, but the Russians did not return a single shot. We could make out a strong force of Russians marching into the town during the day. Rumour said that Lord Raglan was very sanguine in his expectations respecting the prospect of peace; a steamer was now kept lying at Varna ready to convey any message sent by Lord John Russell from Vienna.

Our batteries were now very quiet, no symptoms of reopening fire, although great exertions were being made to bring up shot and shell from Balaklava; but this quiet state of things was considerably disturbed on the morning of the 22nd, when the French attacked some rifle-pits in front of their works under the Mamelon, but failed in retaining them. The following night the Russians made a vigorous sortie upon the French trenches under the Mamelon. and, at the same time, upon our advanced trench, Right Attack; they seemed to make a feint upon the left of our trench, which induced the officer in command of the trench-guard to draw off some of the covering-party from the left to reinforce the right. Meanwhile the enemy came over the parapet into the mortar battery, which had nobody in it: they were headed by an Albanian chief, and, advancing up our trench, soon encountered a party of the 7th Fusiliers; the Albanian attacked and killed Captain Cavendish Browne of that regiment, and then tried to explode the magazine, when he was quickly despatched by many bayonets.

The loss on our side was eight officers and thirty men killed and wounded, amongst whom were Colonel Kelly (34th). wounded in the hand by a bayonet and taken prisoner, and Captain Gordon, R.E., wounded: Captain Browne (7th), Captain Jordan (34th), and Captain Vicars (97th), killed. The French loss was very severe. A detachment of the 88th was in the trenches at the same time, under Captain Bayley; they were not engaged, but Captain B. very judiciously pushed them forward in support The men implored their captain to "let them go at the Rooshians." We had only one casualty—a sergeant slightly wounded. The same night a slight sortie was made upon the Left Attack, when Captain Montague, R. E. was taken prisoner.

Lord Raglan was round our camp at an early hour on the morning of the 23rd, visiting the wounded officers and men, and inquiring about the sortie, which seemed to have been of a most determined character. Night attacks are always unsatisfactory things; great confusion necessarily ensues, and many valuable lives are sacrificed, without any advantageous results. Our men (88th) got great praise for their steadiness on this occasion, when we had many recruits in the ranks with only a sprinkling of old hands.

On the morning of the 24th we were under arms until two a.m., having been roused at eleven the previous night. I turned in very tired, but at four a.m. we were again under arms; all, however, passed off quietly, and I was very glad to sleep until breakfast time. The French fired a good deal during the night, but still the indefatigable Russians contrived to increase their rifle-pits. Soon after mid-day on the 24th a flag of truce was hoisted to enable both sides to collect the dead; no sooner were the white flags fluttering over the parapets than swarms of English, French, and Russian soldiers, carrying stretchers, were seen advancing towards each other. Several of us walked down the middle ravine and went in front of the French trenches, among the Russian rifle-pits; the ground was as thickly covered with dead as on the field of Inkermann. I recollect one French sergeant exclaiming with apparent emotion, on discovering the body of a French officer, "*Ah! mon pauvre Capitaine.*"

We afterwards went across to our trenches, and saw the Albanian chief, leader of the sortie, carried away; he was dressed in Greek costume, with pistol and *yataghan*, and a Russian grey coat over all; he was a very fine man.

In front of our trenches was a crowd of English officers and men, mingled with the Russian officers and escort, who had brought out the flag of truce; the officers chatted away in French and one in English; they were very gentlemanly men. The conversation was carried on very warmly, as if the greatest, friends; while the privates, who five minutes before had been firing away at each other, might now be seen smoking together, exchanging tobacco and drinking rum, with the usual compliments of "*Bono Inglis,*" &c. It was a singular sight. At length, on reference to watches, it was found that the time allowed—*viz.*, two hours—was almost up, so both parties gradually retired to their respective works, after shaking hands and somebody saying, "*au revoir,*" five minutes afterwards firing commenced as if nothing had happened. The French did not fraternise, but seemed to regard the Russians with supreme contempt.

Our morning parade now took place every day at half-past four a.m., when we remained under arms until daylight; the regiment began to be much healthier, and our number on parade gradually increased.

On the 25th I rode to Inkermann with our quartermaster and W.; the place was much changed, being entirely cleared of the thick brushwood, which had covered the ground on the memorable 5th of November. Dismounting, we scanned the surrounding country with our glasses; we could distinguish where we crossed the river Tchernaya at the Traktir bridge, September 25th, 1854, and that the Russians had erected works there; the ground over which we now passed was covered with crocuses, and violets abounded in all the ravines; the weather was very warm.

On the 29th General Duller inspected us, and in the evening I went to the trenches, where I remained for twenty-four hours in the advanced work; it rained and was very cold; in fact, the weather was too changeable for winter clothing to be left off. The camp abounded in peaceable "shaves," and we awaited news of the conference at Vienna; all ranks were getting very tired of their present monotonous kind of life.

Our losses by sickness somewhat decreased during this month, only five of our men having died in hospital;[11] our casualties also were very few during the previous month, only five slightly wounded.[12]

---

11. Privates—March 2nd, No. 1897, James Stack. 3rd, No. 3314, William Harker. 10th, No. 3237, Robert Andrews. 19th, No. 3528, Michael McMahon. 24th, No. 1788, James Gready. 12. Privates—3rd March, Martin Noffin, 12th, Daniel Quinn, 14th, John Hough and William Huntley, 28th, Lieutenant and Adjutant Little.

CHAPTER 6

April 1st to June 30th

The hardships of the winter of 1854-55 were now numbered among the things of the past, and the advent of spring had considerably ameliorated the health of the army; before, however, resuming the thread of my story. I will recapitulate some of the principal causes which led to the miserable condition of the British army generally, and the 88th in particular, during the previous months of November, December, and January; a period which can never be forgotten by those who underwent and fortunately survived the miseries then experienced; these causes may be classified under the following heads:—

1st *Overwork.*—The severe and constant work which arose from having some six to seven miles of front to defend, and the works of two attacks to throw up, with a greatly reduced and daily decreasing army, was the principal cause of all our misery; as the men had neither time nor strength to perform the duties of a camp, nor to obtain fuel and cook their rations.

2nd. *Want of proper cooking utensils to enable the system of company messes to be maintained.*—It was said that our men brought this want upon themselves by throwing away their camp-kettles at the Alma and on the subsequent marches; but the truth is that none had been issued since we left Scutari in the previous May; and as those then issued were fairly worn out, the numbers of course decreased, and each draft brought only their own complement

3rd. *Want of clothing.*—For many weeks our men were in rags, and not until December did they get a few articles of clothing, procured at Balaklava by our colonel; the men gladly paid for these things, but, as they were of bad texture, they soon wore out.

4th. *Insufficiency of tents.*—A double tent was I found to be a better protection than a hut I lived in one throughout the siege, and found it comparatively warm and dry; had all the companies been provided with extra tents to put over the others, much misery and sickness might have been averted.

5th. *Want of transport.*—This terrible defect might have been remedied, as there were plenty of horses and mules at Varna, which could have been brought over.

6th. *Want of pickaxes and billhooks.*—We had scarcely any of these necessary articles for many weeks; pickaxes were then issued, but we did not get any bill-hooks until the brushwood had nearly all disappeared, and we therefore had no use for them.

7th. *The faulty system of requisitions.*—This was another great cause of misery; much time and labour were uselessly expended in getting them properly signed; besides which, we seldom knew, except accidentally, what articles could be obtained; and, when we did know, the articles were often gone before we (in the front) could get a requisition signed, and then send to the stores. It was not until nearly spring that we were informed what description of articles was in store: more frequently our quartermaster found out privately.

8th. *The impossibility of getting our kits and some tents from the "Orient," in spite of strong representations on the part of our commanding officers.*—Even when these things did arrive we could with difficulty send to Balaklava for them; the men being so overworked, and our ponies being few, only a portion of the knapsacks could be brought up at first; and *as there was no store-hut in Balaklava, the remainder of the knapsacks were left piled in the street*, and were consequently robbed of the few things which the crew of the *Orient* had considerately (!) left in each.

9th. *Want of fresh meat and bread instead of salt meat and biscuit.*—It was considered that fresh meat might easily have been obtained if some of our men-of-war, which were lying useless off the harbour, had been employed in fetching cattle, as was done subsequently by the French and Sardinians; the animals could have been driven up to camp more easily, and with less fatigue to all parties, than salt meat was conveyed from Balaklava to the front.

10th. *Green coffee and no vegetables.*—*Green coffee was issued without any means of roasting it*; this deplorable blunder, and also the absence of vegetables, induced much sickness, and, as previously stated, when a cargo of cabbages was sent up from Constantinople, red tapeism would not issue them to the troops.

The causes which led to the terrible disasters of the previous winter were investigated by a committee, consisting of Sir John MacNeill and Colonel Tulloch, which assembled in the Crimea in February (1855).[1]

It was a custom with some of us to walk up to the picket-house almost every day, to take a look round and to see what was going on; a stray shot or shell occasionally came near us; but our usual afternoon stroll was now forbidden, in consequence of the Russians having taken to firing at groups of men, or even at one individual.

We had two men wounded in the trenches on the 4th—*viz.*, Donald Munro, slightly; and James Lysaght, severely.

On the night of the 5th we were all turned out under arms by heavy firing in our Right Attack; it appeared that the Russians had made a sortie upon our trenches, but were completely driven back by the steady fire of the trench-guard; the firing was very severe, and the casualties on our side were numerous. Some of our men were there, and were highly praised for their steadiness; they had fortunately no casualties, but one of our men (Corporal John Downie) was slightly wounded in the morning. In these alarms we (in camp) used to march up the hill to an "alarm-post" near the picket-house, and, as on numerous occasions, we merely marched up to return at once, the result reminded us of the lines—

King Pippin and his valiant men
Marched up the hill and down again.

The 6th being Good Friday we had the usual Divine Service. Our duties were now confined to the trenches only, and the middle ravine picket was among the things of the past, the place being occupied by French troops.

---

1. It subsequently transpired that this committee arrived at a decision which led to the commissary-general being recalled, and that they also threw great blame upon certain superior officers in the Crimean army, from which, however, they were entirely exonerated by the military commission which assembled at Chelsea in 1856.

Our paymaster (Belfield) went away for a short time to Smyrna at the beginning of the month, and I was made acting-paymaster, but still continued to do all other duties.

Great preparations were now being made for reopening fire. Ammunition was brought up daily by railway in large quantities, and the batteries were rapidly armed.

At the first streak of dawn on the 9th the Allied batteries opened the second bombardment upon the town; and the roar of shells bursting and of round shot rushing through the air continued for hours. It poured with rain all day, and the fog was very thick; the platforms became so slippery that the artillerymen could hardly stand to work the guns and mortars; a good many of the latter were mounted by this time. Our artillery firing was said to have been very good. The Russians replied but little during the day; hence arose the usual diversity of opinion as to the cause; perhaps want of ammunition, perhaps want of gunners, perhaps—anything. The 2nd Division were on duty in the Right Attack today. When coming off trench duty the day before the bombardment began, I expected my batman (named Geoghegan) to meet me with my pony near the trenches, but as he did not appear I had to walk to camp; shortly after my return, while discussing my dinner, G. appeared at my tent-door, and said in true Hibernian accent:—

"Shure I took the little baste to the middle ravine, and while lading him up to the battery he got scared by a shell, and away he wint, and this is all the tidins I got of him," producing a stirrup-iron, which he had clutched in the vain attempt to stop the pony. It was next to impossible to keep from laughing at the long face of the man peering through the tent-door, with the sole remains of my pony in his hand; to say nothing of my still longer face and M.'s suppressed smile at the absurdity of nothing being left of the pony except a stirrup-iron; meanwhile the pony wisely returned to his stable.

The bombardment continued (night and day) for the first three days, and gradually slackened until the 17th, when all firing ceased. The Russians throughout this second bombardment used to fire five guns to our one, and knocked our batteries about our ears, disabling many guns. On the 11th they nearly silenced Gordon's Battery. Some days the firing, on both sides, was very heavy, and the casualties in our trenches necessarily severe. When off duty I used to walk up to some commanding spot, to see how the bombardment progressed.

The weather continued very fine, and the number of sick in hospital considerably decreased.

My poultry-yard became very flourishing; I had new-laid eggs every morning, and only wanted a cow to complete my establishment with milk, a luxury I had not tasted since the previous August (nine months).

About this time some of Omar Pashas fighting Turks arrived at Kamiesch; a camp-shave said that they were intended to replace the French on our right, who were going to attack (in strong force) the Russians on the Tchernaya.

On the 14th my subaltern, Lieutenant Preston, was shot by one of the Russian riflemen when in the advanced work: he was in the act of looking over the parapet, through an opening between some sand-bags, when he was hit, and died half an hour afterwards, while being carried home. Poor little fellow, he was but sixteen, and very young-looking for his age; he had joined us only a few weeks previously, and was a clever, promising lad, always ready and willing at his duty.[2] On the same day we had the following casualties:—

Sergeant William Hopkins slightly wounded, Privates Thomas Carter dangerously, and John Cullinane, severely.

And on the following day we had one man (Private Richard Nelson) dangerously wounded. In the evening I was in the 21-gun battery, where I remained all night; it rained and was very cold. I was in the caves, above the Woronzoff road, all the following day, a safe and snug place. At this time the caves had been converted into magazines, and in one was established an electric telegraph office, from which messages were transmitted to headquarters, and also to Sir George Brown, so as to enable reinforcements to be sent down in case of a sortie.

We had at this time erected a hut, and fitted it up with tables and chairs, as a kind of mess-room, and it had the good effect of bringing us more together. Here many of us breakfasted every morning, a pleasant change from eating under canvas, and eventually we used to bring our dinners and dine at the same hour, thus forming a scratch mess. The furniture consisted of a long table down the centre, where we placed our newspapers, &c., *pro bono publico*, forms on each side, two small tables in the corner, and two easy-chairs; walls covered with white serge. The hut was generally full every evening, some playing

---

2. Upon my return to England I found that Preston was a nephew of my father's old 20th friend, Colonel Hogge. The men of the company showed some good feeling at young Preston's death; and I heard some remark that it was a sin to send out such a child to be murdered as they called it.

at whist, others talking or reading, and nearly all smoking, under the light of three lamps.

Captain M. having been appointed to the post of "Officer on the Lookout," was struck off all duty, and used to take up his position in a place erected in front of the picket-house; here he remained for six hours every day, provided with a good glass, watching the enemy's movements, and made a daily report to Sir George Brown. The 10th Hussars and 12th Lancers arrived at N. Balaklava from India on the 15th.

The Crimean Army Fund continued to supply us with various articles at a very cheap rate; some received *gratis*: among these I got a compact cooking apparatus, by means of which I used to cook my breakfast in the trenches. The Duke of Portland also sent some Welbeck ale. Port and sherry were issued one day to the men, and 1200 pints of ale were given, as a present, among the men, on returning from the trenches on the 14th.

The artillery received orders on the 16th to slacken fire. During the 16th and 17th we had three men wounded; Private John MacGuire, severely (16th); Privates Eugene O'Sullivan, dangerously, and James Connors, slightly (17th).

The Russians had established rifle-pits within a stone's-throw of an advanced position of our second parallel; these pits interfered with the further progress of our works in the Right Attack, and it was therefore necessary that they should be taken; this intention had been delayed from time to time, but it was finally determined that the attack should be made on the evening of the 19th. The strength of the covering parties was considerably increased, and I went down to the trenches at half-past five p.m., with four officers and 224 men under my command; among the former my friend, J. W. We fancied at the time that it was to be our lot to take the pits, but subsequently found that the 77th Regiment had been told off to do so. My party occupied the right trench adjoining the French; the rifle-pits were in front of the left of the advanced work (second parallel), a few hundred yards in front of us.

In marching down to the advanced trench, which we had been told to occupy, I was—through a blunder on the part of the field officer in charge—ordered to take my party through the 21-gun battery, and along the various trenches, instead of proceeding along the middle ravine direct to our position, as was always customary when going to this advanced part of the trenches during daylight, so as to avoid casualties. The consequence was that, as soon as we appeared at the cutting where the second parallel joined the trench we had to occupy, we became very distinct marks for the enemy's riflemen, who opened a sharp fire upon us, and two of my sergeants (Charles Cunniffe and Andrew Liddell) were severely wounded alongside me. The officer in question had not been in the Right Attack, since the erection of new approaches and batteries, and consequently did not know its numerous intricacies; nevertheless I could not convince him of his error, although I, of course, was well acquainted with every nook and comer of the now extensive labyrinth of trenches.

About eight o'clock we were all on the *qui vive*, when we heard musketry on our left and knew it was the attack; then came the well-known British cheer, and we were sure that the pits had been captured: after a lull the heavy firing was renewed, which we concluded was caused by the Russians attempting to recover the pits. It appeared that our attacking force, consisting of a party of the 77th Regiment, supported by part of the 33rd, advanced upon the pits and carried them at the point of the bayonet, headed by their gallant chief, Lieutenant-Colonel Egerton, a fine, tall, and powerful man. The Russians returned in force and made several ineffectual attempts to recover the pits during the night. The loss on our side was severe; sixty men and seven officers killed and wounded; Lieutenant-Colonel Egerton and Captain Lemprière of the 77th were killed. Captain L. was a very young man and had just got his company; he was a great favourite with the colonel who called him "his child."

Poor young Lemprière was killed at the first attack, and Colonel E., although wounded, carried him to the rear, declaring that the enemy should never take his child. The colonel shortly afterwards fell mortally wounded. The 77th and 88th, situated in adjoining camps, were very intimate, and Colonel Egerton used to always to call his regiment our second battalion. Two Engineer officers were also severely wounded on this occasion; one of them, named Baynes, whom I knew very well, died afterwards; he was a particularly nice fellow.

On the 19th a "reconnaissance" was made by some Turkish infantry, with French and English cavalry and artillery, in the vale of Balaklava towards the village of Tchorgoum. This force was under the command of Omar Pasha. I walked out with M. and saw the troops return; it was a very pretty sight, as we looked down from our heights upon the various regiments retiring across the plain, covered by cavalry skirmishers. Colonel Egerton, Captain Lemprière. and four privates

(77th), killed on the 19th, were buried on the 21st Lord Raglan and a large assemblage of officer, including myself, were present It was a sad scene; we all knew Colonel Egerton very well, and he was deservedly popular.

On the 23rd the early parades were discontinued, much to our delight When in Balaklava with my brother today we found that the 2nd Battalion Royals and 48th Regiment had arrived; the 10th Hussars had also landed, and we rode through their camp. When the weather permitted and we were off duty, we had drills in the afternoon. We had two men severely wounded in the trenches today—*viz.*, Lance-Corporal Henry Hulston and Private Patrick Foley.

On the 24th we had completed twelve months under canvas. Fifteen medals for distinguished conduct and one medal, with an annuity of 20*l.*, had been awarded to the regiment; to the former a gratuity was added—viz., *15l.* for each sergeant, 10/. for each corporal, 5*l.* for each private. The following non-commissioned officers and privates having been selected, the presentation, to such as were present with the regiment was made by Colonel Shirley on the 25th:—

Medal and Annuity of 20l.

Colour-Sergeant George McNally. (He had been discharged, having lost a leg at the Battle of the Alma.)

Distinguished Conduct Medals.

Sergeant-Major Patrick Cooney. (Lost a leg at the attack on the Redan, 8th September, and afterwards died in our camp hospital.)

Corporal Hourigan. (Died of wounds received at the attack on the Redan, September 8th.)

Corporal Thomas Champ. (Sent home sick.)

Corporal (afterwards Sergeant) Savage. (Killed in the trenches, June 7th.)

Corporal (afterwards Sergeant) Price.[3]

Private (afterwards Sergeant) Michael Wrenn. (Killed September 8th.)

---

3. This brave fellow was recommended a second time for gallant conduct at the attack on the Quarries, June 7th, having been observed by two officers of other regiments. On the 8th September, although wounded in the trenches before the attack on the Redan, he nevertheless took part in the assault, and was killed.

Private Michael Dempsey. (Killed in the trenches.)

Corporal J. Connolly. (Lost an arm in the attack on the Redan, September 8th, and died in hospital.)

Private Pat. Duffy. (Died in hospital of sickness.)

„ John Burke. (At home, sick.)

„ Pat Scheal (*Ditto*)

„ William Mills. (*Ditto*, wounded severely, September 8th, in the attack on the Redan.)

„ Pat. O'Rourke. (*Ditto* slightly.)

„ John Connell. (*Ditto*)

„ Jas. Burke. (At home sick.)

On the 26th all of us (officers) went up to the picket-house to be photographed in a group by a Mr. Fenton, who had come out to take views of the siege, &c.; the result was pretty successful, but, as the as the colonel's horse moved, his likeness was unfortunately a failure.[4]

In the afternoon I rode out to see 40,000 French troops reviewed by Canrobert. Strong columns of artillery, cavalry, and infantry were drawn up to receive him. About two p.m. he made his appearance, followed by a large and brilliant staff, and galloped down the line, being received by each regiment, successively, with the usual honours, flourish of trumpets, &c. Following the French general and staff was a motley crew of English officers in every variety of costume, from the orthodox uniform to the Balaklava marketing style, presenting a sadly ludicrous contrast to the showy appearance of the smartly dressed French officers. Such an exhibition made us, who were correctly dressed, much ashamed of our comrades.

The whole force afterwards marched past, and, as each regiment passed the general, the colonel waved his sword, shouting "*Vive l'Empereur*," which was repeated by the men. The *Zouaves* looked the most soldierlike of any, being good-looking fellows, favoured of course by their picturesque uniform. To our ideas the marching was very indifferent, little or no attention being paid to dressing or keep-

---

4. The following are the names of those who formed the group on this occasion:—
Colonel Shirley. Lieutenant-Colonel G.V. Maxwell. Major Norton. Captains Bayley, Maxwell, Corbeit, Steevens, Gore, Wray, Browne (G. R.); Lieutenants Beresford, Webb, Pearson, Vernor, Perceval; Ensigns Kenny and Grier; Surgeon Dunlop; Lieutenant and Adjutant Little; Quartermaster Moore. Corporals Price, Hourigan, Connolly, Wrenn. Privates J. Connors and Grennan.

ing step. After the review was over Canrobert assembled the officers and addressed them in the usually flowery style of French military speeches, concluding by saying (in allusion to the difficulties attending the capture of Sebastopol), "If we cannot get in at the door, we must get in at the window."

The weather now was very wet and foggy. On the 27th I had a touch of ague, which made me keep to my tent all day.

The railway from Balaklava was rapidly progressing towards the camp. More regiments continued to arrive almost daily. The artillery were very busy arming our batteries with heavy guns. We had plenty of heavy mortars, of which we seemed to make no use, not being allowed (apparently) to fire into the town and knock it to pieces. Meanwhile the Russians were, as usual, far from being idle, and had thrown up a new battery near Careening Bay, not far from the works which the French had unsuccessfully attacked in the previous February.

Our duties came round about once a week throughout the previous month. During April, eleven of our men died in the hospital.[5]

On the 3rd I had a delightful ride to Kamiesch with my friend W., returning to camp about seven p.m.; I met my brother there. While at Kamiesch we saw French troops embarking, but could not ascertain their destination. Private Thomas Doulan was slightly wounded in the trenches today.

On the 4th an expedition, under the command of Sir George Brown, sailed for some place then un known to us,[6] to do something of which we had no idea; the force consisted of the Highland brigade and some French troops; we secretly wished that our division might have gone—anything to relieve the monotony of trench duty. On the night of the 1st the French captured a Russian mortar battery and some rifle-pits, when both sides suffered severely; the following day the Russians made a sortie on the French trenches about three p.m., but were signally repulsed.

On the evening of the 6th I went into the trenches; it was very mild, and the night passed off quietly. From our advanced works we threw a fireball (carcass) into the Russian works during the night, and caused much bugling and stir among the enemy, as they fancied, no

---

5. Privates—April 3rd, No. 1494, William Houlihan; 6th, No. 1430, Maurice Glannon; 10th, No. 1725, Martin Rielly, No. 3431, George Moore and No. 3378, Richard Condon; 14th, No. 2922, Patrick Murphy.;18th, No. 3009, Eugene Sullivan; 25th, No. 3177, Henry Huston; 26th, No. 2611, William Daley; 27th, No. 3634, Owen Flynn; 30th, No. 3438, Patrick Stevens.
6. It proved to be Kertch.

doubt, that we meditated an attack. I passed the following day in the 21-gun battery, and found it exceedingly hot; we had one man (Private William John Kennedy) killed today. On the 9th our casualties were—

Privates John Griffin severely wounded, Patrick Claherty slightly and James Smith dangerously.

On the morning of the 10th the division was turned out about one a.m. by heavy firing and great cheering in our Right Attack which lasted about an hour. It appeared that the Russians attempted a sortie, but, owing to the alertness and steady fire of the trench guard, they were forced to retire. We had 230 men there, two of whom were killed, and four were badly wounded,[7] but none of the enemy succeeded in getting into our trenches. The 10th was a thoroughly wet day; the camp was one vast puddle of mud and water; few human beings were to be seen in locomotion except mounted orderlies, and occasionally some staff officer; indiarubber-clad figures might sometimes be seen flitting about, to pay dodging visits and to compare discomforts with a damp neighbour.

Everything went on the same way from day to day; our life in camp was *ditto* repeated. I frequently rode into Balaklava on paymasters duty, and when I returned to camp (sometimes alone) towards dusk, with several hundred sovereigns in my saddle-bags, I must confess that I did not always feel at my ease; some vagabond of a camp-follower might, I fancied, smell the money.

At this time we began to look up our band, which by dint of trying circumstances had almost ceased to exist. The instruments were more or less damaged, and many of the bandsmen dead or invalided; a first attempt, with passable results, was made on the 5th; but it was a sorry display compared with the fine band of the French 25th of the Line, which still continued to play every day in their camp, immediately behind us.

The expedition under Sir George Brown unexpectedly returned, as by instructions received from Paris, Canrobert recalled the French fleet, and consequently all came back, much to the disgust, it was said, of Lord Raglan and Sir George Brown.

The regiment was now gradually becoming stronger; we mustered upwards of 300 duty men, and could turn out, all hands, to the num-

7. Corporal John Downey and Private Thomas Dowd, killed; and the following men wounded:—
Privates—James Connors, dangerously: afterwards died. John Donohue, slightly. William Connors, dangerously. Michael Cummins, slightly.

ber of 400. The total strength of the French guard at this time was 1800 in each Attack.

The Allied Armies were gradually being augmented by the arrival of fresh troops: 5000 Sardinians arrived at Balaklava; the 71st Highlanders marched up to the front on the 9th; the 12th Lancers also disembarked from India. As soon as regiments arrived rumour was very busy in saying that a 5th Division was to be formed; we therefore hoped that these arrangements might give our colonel (Shirley) a permanent brigade command, as he was one of the senior colonels in the Crimea, and had gone through everything; we should, however, have much regretted losing so good and kind a chief.

During this month the 2nd Zouaves got up amateur theatricals in their camp, not far from us, for the benefit of their comrades who were prisoners in the hands of the Russians. A performance named for the 10th was postponed on account of the wet weather, for it must be borne in mind that the audience was not under cover.

I heard today that it was intended to extend our line of outposts to the Tchernaya, in case the supply of water in camp should fail. On the 10th a Mr. Joly, a lieutenant in H.M. 32nd Regiment,[8] joined us as a volunteer, being on two years' leave from India: he was attached to my company. Mr. J. was a French Canadian.[9]

The Russians continued very busy repairing their old works and erecting new ones; and on the evening of 11th they opened a heavy fire upon the Right Attack. I was in the trenches on the night of the 12th; the rain was incessant, and the mud and water, in some places, almost knee-deep. There was a good deal of firing, but no sortie was attempted. The dreadful cholera again made its appearance amongst us on the 13th, and two of our men died.

The 14th, promising to be a fine warm day, I rode to Balaklava with my friend W. for the purpose of foraging; on the way we passed the camp of Omar Pasha's Turks, and saw them at drill; they were fine-looking men, and manoeuvred well. We lunched on board the *Europa* steamer with Captain Leitch, who brought us out in the *Niagara*; there were Sardinian troops on board. I saw some of them land—very soldierlike, smart-looking men; their cavalry, of course, looked better horsed than the French, as they had not roughed it as yet. I had a chat with some of the officers—pleasant gentlemanly men.

---

8. In which my eldest brother was then a captain; he, poor fellow, was killed in action at Chinhut, June 30th, 1857, during the siege of Lucknow.
9. Lieutenant Joly was killed at Lucknow during the Indian Mutiny.

The uniform of their riflemen (Bersaglieri), upon which they somewhat prided themselves, was picturesque, though, according to our ideas, decidedly theatrical-looking, consisting of a dark-coloured tunic, with a black wide-awake and plume of green feathers as a head-dress. The Sardinian troops seemed to be very complete in everything necessary for an army in the field, even to a field postal service, the head of which department was a tall and very stout individual, clad in a dark tunic covered with broad gold lace across the front "at open intervals." When this important personage appeared in the streets of Balaklava, a Jack Tar close to me observed to a comrade, "I say. Bill, whoever is this stout old party with a gold ladder up his body?"

Every day it seemed to us that Sebastopol was becoming more impregnable, so busy were the Russians in strengthening their various positions. We were now ordered to furnish ourselves with the regulated number of *bât*-ponies. Each captain was allowed two; so I completed my stable by purchasing one from the commissariat, but he unfortunately died shortly afterwards.

On the evening of the 16th I went to the trenches, and passed a quiet night in the advanced left sap; it was the nearest point to the most advanced Russian works, some of which were not more than fifty yards from us. The following day was excessively hot, without a breath of wind, and the glare from the bare ground was very trying to the eyes. I managed to erect a kind of shade, under which I was glad to have a doze, as my night had of course been sleepless. I passed the day in Egerton's pits,[10] and we were relieved about nine p.m.

The 18th was another very hot day, the thermometer in our mess-hut being 87°; it was almost the coolest place in camp, for our tents were like ovens.

This afternoon we (the Light Division) were inspected by Sir George Brown, which of course gave rise to the usual camp "shaves" that we were going off somewhere to do something. I had a visit today from my brother, who brought me some strawberries and cherries, a present from Constantinople—a great treat. One of our trench guard (Private John Hagerty) was slightly wounded on the 19th.

On the morning of the 20th one of our majors (poor Norton) died of cholera, after a few hours' illness, and was buried in the evening; the same day we also lost three men from this dreadful disease, which was very prevalent in camp at this time. In the evening I was in the 21-gun battery.

---

10. Those captured April 19th, 1855.

I passed the following day in the left part of the advanced sap; the day was intensely hot, but having taken the precaution to bring a patrol-tent, my subaltern (Joly) and I occupied it, and there, cross-legged, I wrote a letter home, with bullets whizzing over our heads, and an occasional shell, to keep us alert; during the previous night we heard the Russians very busy strengthening their works.

Much to the delight of all ranks the stock now ceased to be worn, being superseded by a black neckerchief.

General Canrobert was at this time succeeded by General Pelissier in the command of the French army, but we did not hear the cause of this change. Rumour—busy as usual—said that the Sardinian troops were to occupy the redoubts in Balaklava Plain, captured from the Turks on the morning of the 25th October, 1854, and thus to extend our position. Our paymaster (Belfield) having returned from leave, I was relieved from doing his duty. Nearly all the Turks, with a few French troops, had left for Eupatoria. This, coupled with the change in the command of the French army, led us to hope that we should now have a little more action and less inaction.

Tentes d'abri, like those used by the French, were now issued to our troops for use in the trenches, where the heat was very trying and cool breezes were conspicuous by their absence.

All had been very quiet in our trenches for many nights; but not so with the French, who made vigorous attempts one night to take some Russian intrenchments near the *"Bastion du Mât,"* and partly succeeded—not, however, without heavy losses. The enemy endeavoured to retake them the following morning, but failed. The slaughter on both sides, as described to me by an eye-witness, equalled that on the field of Inkermann.

On the 24th (the queen's birthday) I rode to Karani to see our cavalry and artillery reviewed before Omar Pasha and Pelissier. It was a very hot day. The artillery looked remarkably well, having been recently re-horsed.

On the morning of the 25th the plan of extending; our lines upon the Tchernaya as far as Tchorgoum. was carried out before daylight. A force, composed of French, Sardinian, and Turkish troops, advanced upon the Tchernaya, where it was expected that the Russians would make a stand. I was up betimes, and with my friend W., gazing upon the stirring scene, glass in hand. It was a beautiful summer morning, and very calm. We sat upon the heights near the field of Inkermann, and looked down upon the plain below. Before us the river Tchernaya, winding up to the bridge (Traktir Bridge), which we crossed on the evening of the fatiguing flank march, September 25th, 1854; to our right lay the plain of Balaklava, the scene of the memorable, though fatal, cavalry charge, October 25th, 1854.

Every hill around seemed glistening with bayonets— one crowned by the red-trousered French, another by the picturesque-looking Sardinians, or the much (though wrongly) abused Turks—each severally supported by their cavalry and artillery. There were several works erected near the bridge, but they proved to be unarmed. About five a.m. the troops advanced towards the river, and, after exchanging a few shots with some retreating Cossacks, took possession of the heights[11] above it, without experiencing any opposition. It was certainly a beautiful sight.

In the afternoon I rode with several others to see what had been done. Winding down the hitherto prohibited Woronzoff Road, leading from our plateau to the plain of Balaklava, we soon found ourselves in the valley below, surrounded by long grass, which abounded in every kind of wild flower, occasionally growing in bright-coloured patches; the sight of the grass was as refreshing to us as it was to our ponies, which seemed quite mad with delight and capered about. It was a most agreeable change to us after the barren scene by which we were surrounded in camp. Passing along the ground where the cavalry charge had taken place on the 25th October, 1854, and occasionally seeing some sad vestige of that eventful day, we forded the river Tchernaya, near Tchorgoum, and proceeded as far as an advanced post, held by the Sardinians, on a conical hill; as the village was said to be in the hands of Cossacks, we deemed it prudent to keep aloof from it, and did not go beyond the Sardinian sentries.

We afterwards found that a brother officer (Lieutenant P.) went into the village the same day that we had gone near it, found several things in one of the houses, and came away laden with a small table: he had, however, a narrow escape from being captured by Cossacks, some of whom entered one end of the village as he (table included) was galloping out of the other; among other things, he found some music, which I copied. It was a very fine day; the green view around us was varied by the brilliant hues of innumerable wild flowers. The hills above us were covered with French tents, below which the shallow river rippled placidly along. It seemed to me like a pleasant dream, and I could scarcely fancy that I was soon to return to my tent and all its

11. Called the Fedukhine Heights.

surrounding barrenness.

As we rode back to camp in the cool of the evening we visited the spot where we bivouacked on the 23rd September, 1854, and we fancied we saw the traces of the fire before which my captain and I had, eight months previously, stretched our weary limbs, after the long and fatiguing march by Mackenzie's Farm. We reached camp about eight p.m., after a most delightful day, very hungry and tired. The visit to our old bivouac was of great interest to us, though it was sad to reflect upon all the changes which had occurred among us since that day. Private John O'Hara was severely wounded on the 26th.

As no parades were, at this time, allowed to take place after eight a.m., we consequently paraded every morning at seven. The expedition to Kertch sailed on the 22nd, and we heard afterwards that the place was captured on the queen's birthday. On the 25th the various successes which had attended our navy, in the Sea of Azoph and elsewhere,[12] were made known to the generals of division, who ordered the brigadiers to assemble their brigades and to read the news, receiving it with three cheers, of the good old English description; our brigadier (Buller) having been invalided to England, the command of the brigade had devolved upon our colonel (Shirley), who assembled us all at twelve o'clock on the 27th, and proclaimed the news; it was received with vociferous shouts, and the noise frightened all the mounted officers' horses, which danced and pranced about; our brigadier was softly deposited on the ground, and our acting adjutant (the orderly officer) was to be seen rapidly disappearing in the distance, still zealously waving his cap—his pony having carried him away from the column altogether.

On the afternoon of the 27th we had a heavy thunderstorm; we did not get very much of it, as it broke principally over the distant mountains; in the evening I went to the trenches, and passed a quiet night in the advanced parallel; with my night-glass I could distinguish the Russians at work, but the nights now were too moonlight for sorties; the days in the trenches continued to be intolerably hot, with a plague of flies and mosquitoes. Private Geo. Smith was slightly wounded on the 29th.

---

12. Yenikale, as well as Kertch, seemed to have been captured without any loss on our side. Fifty guns, of heavy calibre, were taken, besides 100 prisoners. The Russians blew up their steamers, as well as some stores containing many thousand sacks of corn. One of the enemy's steamers escaped into the Sea of Azoph; it was said to contain a *grandee*, on a visit to Kertch from Sebastopol, and some of our small steamers were reported to have gone off in chase.

On the 31st the generals of division were assembled by Lord Raglan, which made us fancy that *something* was to be done soon.

About this time the regiment was getting very healthy, and the the number of sick in hospital was rapidly decreasing. During the past month eight of our men died in our camp hospital;[13] seven from sickness, one from wounds. Every day brought us some fresh intelligence of our successes in the Sea of Azoph, which made us all long to be there, and to get away from the wearying life of camp and trench duty; we felt somewhat grumpy that Sir G. Brown had not taken some of his own Division to gain a few laurels at Kertch, &c.

The 1st of June was a very hot day, reminding us of the heat which we had experienced in Bulgaria during the previous summer. I went to the trenches in the evening, with Mr. Joly (32nd) as my subaltern; we occupied the extreme left advance, where we were pretty well peppered by the Russians the next day; they killed two of my men (one named Michael Sherlock), and wounded a third severely. This poor fellow was struck when standing close to me; I was giving J. a light for a cigar, and, in doing so, we no doubt exposed ourselves to the enemy's sharpshooters, for a shot was fired at us, and it must have passed very near to our faces, as it struck this man, who was standing close behind us.

In this particular spot we were always obliged to lie very snug, as the least appearance of a forage-cap brought down a fire from the enemy, who had numerous riflemen posted on some rising ground (called the Quarries),[14] not far from us, which gave them the advantage of a commanding fire. Today many men in our trenches were wounded by our own shells, which burst sometimes too soon, a by no means unfrequent occurrence during the siege; during the night our batteries threw carcasses into the town.

The weather continuing very hot we paraded every morning at five a.m. On the 4th, one of our captains (Maynard) arrived at Balaklava with a draft of fifty men. Our casualties today were—Corporal Maurice Sullivan, slightly wounded; Private Michael Connolly, severely wounded.

---

13. privates—May 1st, No. 3300, Patrick Duffy. 8th, No. 3638, John Moffitt. 11th, No. 2047. James Connors. 14th, No. 1058 Martin Hogarty and No. 3439 Thomas Duffy. 16th, No. 3759, James Smith; (of wounds, 9th May). 20th, No. 3402, John Lay. 26th, No. 3606, Michael Hughes.
14. According to the plans in the *Journal of Royal Engineers* concerning the siege, the Quarries were about 200 yards from the trench we occupied, and no feet above it

On the 5th I had a delightful ride with my friend Captain Wray as far as Traktir Bridge, where we remained some time and watered our ponies in the river Tchernaya. We started about six p.m., and it was a beautiful calm summer evening. Little did I think at the time that this was my *last* ride with my constant companion J, W. As he, poor fellow, was killed two days afterwards; we chatted away about our prospects of returning to England, and he was longing to get home, but it was ordained otherwise; we rode back across the Fedukhine Heights, through the French camp, and reached our lines about ten p.m.

The news of the success of the Kertch Expedition was published in Orders today, telling of the capture of Genitch, with an immense quantity of provisions, corn, &c., besides that of Berdiansk and of ninety vessels; also that we had taken four men-of-war steamers, 246 merchantmen, 150,000*l.* worth of corn, besides four months' rations for 100,000 men, and 100 prisoners.

The nights now were bright moonlight and no dew. The costume of an officer for trench duty at this time, though comfortable, was decidedly peculiar in appearance: it generally consisted of a shell-jacket, over which was worn a short tweed coat, lined with fur;[15] a revolver was carried on one side and a field-glass on the other, boots up to the knee, and a seedy forage-cap completed the dress, which gave the wearer the appearance of First Ruffian in some Strolling Player's sensational tragedy.

Hitherto M. and I had occupied one tent together; he now removed to another tent, which was a much more comfortable arrangement for both of us.

At this time we calculated that, since we embarked at Liverpool, in April, 1854, 911 strong, we had lost—killed in action, died of sickness, wounds, &c., and invalided—about 800 of all ranks, making us almost a new regiment

On the 6th, the third bombardment opened in the afternoon, and continued all night for the first time; I walked up to the picket-house and saw it commence; at a given signal all the batteries opened from right to left, and a brisk fire was kept up upon the various Russian works, but the enemy were not to be caught napping, and their batteries replied very warmly.[16]

The enemy's guns in the "Mamelon" were fired all together in sal-

---

15. These coats I have already mentioned as being a present from Government.
16. A gunner was killed in the battery today, whose name, by a singular coincidence, was *Nathaniel Stevens.*

vos, at certain intervals, indicative, it was said, that the Russians were short of gunners; our shelling during the night was very heavy, and considerably hindered the enemy from repairing damages. The firing continued throughout the 7th, and we were all confined to camp after one p.m.

As the time had now arrived for the works of our Right Attack to be extended towards the town, it was decided to storm the rifle-pits and trenches which the enemy had thrown up in front of our intrenchments, and which not only impeded the progress of our siege works, but from which also they maintained such a continuous musketry fire upon our trenches as to cause numerous casualties among our covering-parties. That part of the Russian works which was immediately opposite the extreme left of our most advanced trench[17] we called the "Quarries;" it was an "ambuscade" which the enemy had constructed by strongly intrenching a quarry, which, as already stated, was situated on rising ground, about 110 feet above our nearest trench, and not more than 600 feet from it. The elevated position and close proximity of this ambuscade gave the Russians the advantage of a commanding fire, of which they persistently availed themselves with very harassing effect; many of our brave fellows here lost their lives, by incautiously exposing little more than their heads to the unerring aim of the ever-vigilant Russian marksmen.

It was therefore arranged that the attack upon the Quarries and adjoining Russian trenches should take place on the evening of the 7th June, at the same time that the French—on our right—stormed the Russian intrenched position on a hill in their front.[18] For this attack upon the Quarries, &c., a force of 1000 British troops were told off, under the command of our colonel (Shirley), who, on this day, was acting general officer in charge of the Trench Guard Right Attack: this storming party was divided as follows:—400 men, under Lieutenant-Colonel Campbell (90th Regiment), consisting of—

100 men (7th Fusiliers), under Major Mills (7th Fusiliers).

200 men (49th Regiment), under Major Armstrong (49th Regiment).

100 men (88th Regiment), under Major Bayley (88th Regiment).

This portion was to attack the Quarries.

Also 300 men, under the command of Lieutenant-Colonel Simp-

17. Called No. 2 Left Demi-parallel.
18. The French called this position "*Le Mamelon vert*," and with the Russians it was known as "*Lunetta Kamschatka*."

son, 34th Regiment—*viz.*, 200 men 34th Regiment, and 100 men of the 88th Regiment, commanded by Captain Corbett; this latter party was told off to attack the trenches and rifle-pits which adjoined the Quarries.

With the 200 men of the 88th Regiment, engaged on this occasion, were the following officers:—

Major Bayley, Captains Corbett, Maynard and Wray, Lieutenants Beresford,[19] Webb, Pearson, Kenny and Grier.

Colonel Shirley was accompanied by his *aide-de camp*. Captain Day (88th Regiment).

300 men, under the command of Major Urquhart (1st Royals), were in reserve; and two working parties were told off (to accompany the attacking forces), composed of detachments of the 7th and 77th Regiments, under Major Grant (49th Regiment), and also of the Royals and 55th Regiment.

The attacking force was thus distributed:—Lieutenant-Colonel Campbell's party was placed in the most advanced portion of our trenches on the left of our Right Attack,[20] with Lieutenant-Colonel Simpson's men on their right. The assault took place about eight p.m., on a preconcerted signal being given from a spot in rear of Chapman's Battery, Left Attack. The 400 men under Lieutenant Campbell advanced to the attack in two divisions, one on each flank of the Quarries; the 100 men of the 88th, under Major Bayley, being sent out to the front, assaulted the enemy's intrenchment, supported by the remainder of the 400 men under Major Armstrong; meanwhile, the 300 men under Lieutenant-Colonel Simpson attacked the trenches and rifle-pits adjoining the Quarries, aided by the working party of the Royals and 55th, who had been ordered to lay down their tools and to assist this portion of the attacking force.

Major Bayley and his party having gallantly carried the enemy's position in the Quarries—at the first rush and without much loss—pushed rapidly on and joined their comrades under Captain Corbett, who had meanwhile driven the enemy out of their trenches and rifle-pits, and had pursued them to the furthest part of their works.

As soon as our force had succeeded in establishing themselves in the Quarries, the working party, under Major Grant, advanced with gabions, and commenced reversing the parapet and constructing a

19. Lieutenant Beresford had been gazetted Captain on the 21st May, but the official notification of his promotion had not been received at this time.
20. Called No. a Left Demi-parallel.

covered way—from Egerton's Pit to the Quarries—under the superintendence of Colonel Tylden, R. E.

Shortly after it was dark the Russians, having rallied, advanced in great numbers—under cover of showers of grape—vigorously assailed our force, and succeeded in driving back into the Quarries those who were placed in advance; Colonel Shirley then sent in the reserve of 300 men, and the enemy was repulsed with heavy loss; he also telegraphed for reinforcements, which soon arrived and rendered the greatest assistance.

The enemy renewed their attacks no less than *six* times during the night, and the 88th, with the 7th and 34th, repeatedly advanced and retired, fighting gallantly and stubbornly, across the ground occupied by the Russian trenches; not, however, without experiencing severe losses, for many a brave fellow fell in repelling these persevering and violent assaults. The last attack made by the enemy took place about three a.m.; shortly before this Colonel Shirley, when looking out over the parapet of the Quarries, observed the flat cap of a Russian soldier, who was creeping stealthily along so close to him, that the gallant colonel could easily have hit him over the head with the stick he habitually carried; an alarm being raised, the intruder was quickly disposed of. Notwithstanding the persistent attempts made by the enemy to retake their lost intrenchments, our force successfully repulsed all the attacks, and finally succeeded in keeping possession of all the works, so gallantly, though so dearly, captured.

The 88th Regiment suffered severe losses on this occasion. Out of a strength of 9 officers and 200 men engaged, they had the following casualties:—

KILLED

3 officers—*viz* Captain's Corbett and Wray, and Lieutenant Webb;[21] 1 sergeant and 17 rank and file.

WOUNDED

4 officers—*viz* Major Bayley,[22] mortally:
Captain Maynard, severely in the arm;,

---

21. Lieutenant Webb was returned as "missing," and we did not know whether he had been killed or taken prisoner until the 9th June, when his body was found, far in advance, with seven wounds. He. poor fellow, had been frequently conspicuous for his gallantry when in charge of our regimental sharpshooters at the beginning of the siege.
22. Major Bayley died in camp early the following morning.

Lieut. Kenny, ditto in the instep;

Lieut. Grier, slightly; and

4 sergeants, 1 drummer, and 48 rank and file. Total casualties—7 officers, 5 sergeants, 1 drummer. and 62 rank and file—more than one-third of the number engaged.[23]

Lieutenants Beresford and Pearson were the only officers not wounded; Colonel Shirley and his *aide-de-camp* (Day) also came out of action untouched. The total casualties in the attacking force were 34 officers and 635 men, killed and wounded.

About eight p.m. I went down to the trenches, in reserve, with 100 men under the command of Major Welsford (97th Regiment); my company, being the last for duty, was the only one left in camp. As I passed through the Middle Ravine I met Maynard returning, wounded severely in the arm, and I also heard from him some of the sad losses we had then sustained. The sight I witnessed in the ravine was truly appalling, and never to be forgotten; crowds of wounded of all ranks, some being carried, and others hobbling along. Frenchmen helping Englishmen, and *vice versa*. I met a French officer, apparently badly wounded; he was a fine tall man, and as he limped past me I spoke to him; he gave me to understand that he had had a personal encounter with a Russian officer and had been badly wounded, but at the same time he remarked that although his antagonist had succeeded in wounding him, he had killed him—pointing to his bloodstained sword.

The French had, for the occasion, established hospital tents in the Middle Ravine, round which lay numbers of poor wounded fellows awaiting their turn, and also surgeons rushing about without their coats and with upturned sleeves, busy in amputations, &c. It was a truly horrible sight, to which the dim and flickering light of several candles added a repulsive appearance. As I proceeded with my party along the left *boyau*, some of us had a narrow escape; one of the numerous attacks upon our troops in the Quarries was then going on, and we were all crowded together in the trench, sheltering ourselves behind traverses, and parapet from the shell and shot which showered about us; one shell fell and remained about *two yards* from the spot where several of us, including Lieutenants V., B., and myself, were sitting; we at once threw ourselves down, and lay in a heap, as close as we could to our mother earth, and in almost breathless suspense, while the fuse

---

23. *Vide* Appendix A.

of the shell was fizzing away like a squib; at last it burst, covered with dust and stones, but, marvellous to say nobody was injured![24]

I returned from the trenches with my party about five a.m. on the 8th, at which time the Quarries were in our possession, and the French also firmly established in the Mamelon. I found that one of our poor fellows (Major Bayley) had died of his wound just before I reached our camp.

On the 8th we buried three of our brave fellows (Bayley, Corbett, and Wray) who had fallen on the previous day. As all the officers, except B. (the paymaster) and myself, were away on duty, we had to superintend the funeral arrangements. It was indeed a heart-rending sight, never to be forgotten; we had to deplore the loss not only of esteemed friends, but also of tried and valuable officers, and a sad and irreparable blank was therefore created in our accustomed daily social gatherings in the mess-hut. Poor Wray had been my constant companion at home and abroad, and, as we were like brothers, I felt his death most deeply; he was a truly kind and warm-hearted friend.

The Mamelon was easily captured by the French on the 7th June, but some of their soldiers, in their excitement, pushed on towards the Malakhoff, where they found a wide ditch to stop them, and, under a heavy fire from the Russians, they were repulsed with loss. The Russians attempted to retake the Mamelon, but failed, and the French captured Russian prisoners, to the number of three officers and fifty men. M. from his "lookout post" saw the French troops attack the Mamelon; the French advanced in a somewhat broken, though compact, formation; and, headed by an officer well to the front waving his sword (and doubtless shouting "*Vive l'Empereur*"), scrambled into the enemy's work like a pack of hounds; the Russians could be seen running out on the other side, but, soon rallying, they returned and as easily drove out the French, who, in their turn, were reinforced, and finally held the Mamelon.

On the 9th there was a flag of truce, to collect and bury those who had been killed; it lasted five hours. The Russians, it was thought, took advantage of this cessation of hostilities, to bring fresh guns into the

---

24. The Commanding Royal Engineer (Sir H. Jones), in his report to Lord Raglan respecting the attack on the Quarries, observed;—"The mode in which Colonel Shirley conducted this arduous service, and carried out the orders he received, entitles him to the greatest credit"

Lord Raglan, in his despatch about this attack, also wrote:—"The mode in which Colonel Shirley conducted this very arduous service, and carried out his orders, entitles him to my highest commendation."

Redan and Malakhoff, for when it was over they opened a heavier fire than ever from these two places, which *it was supposed* had previously been *nearly silenced* by our batteries.[25] Poor Webb's body was brought in about three p.m. today, and buried in the evening. One of our men (No. 4247, Private Callaghan) killed today.

At this time the Russians used to fire round shot into the various camps at an immense range; one fell near the hospital tent of the 23rd Fusiliers; these random shots, however, seldom did any harm, and it was amusing to see amusing to see the men running after a ball, to pick it up when spent, as if playing at cricket.

On the evening of the 10th all firing ceased; the third bombardment was now over; the Russians were busy repairing their damaged works; and thus, after an enormous sacrifice of life, the British and French troops found themselves pretty much in the position *in which they ought to have been last October, when the Russians were not in possession of the Quarries or Mamelon, and had no works (to speak of) where the Redan afterwards was, and none round the Malakhoff.*

On the evening of the 11th I went into the trenches with a covering party, on reserve, and we occupied the right *boyau* and rifle-pit; the Russian trenches taken on the 7th were now occupied by our trench parties, and as Major Welsford (97th) was conducting a party there this evening, they walked over a *fougasse*,[26] and strange to say, it was not until nearly the last man had passed by, that the *fougasse* exploded, killing two men and wounding six. I was watching this party when the occurrence took place, as they passed close to where I was standing. We had a fine night and the Russians were remarkably quiet.

We had one man killed, and two men wounded on the 12th and 13th.[27]

The number of our officers being very much reduced, M. joined us from the "lookout," which gave us four captains for duty, so that I used to be on trench duty now about every third day.

---

25. I used often to think that we were inclined to overrate the effect of our artillery fire upon the Russian batteries, and that frequently, when the Russians did not return the fire, it was not because they were silenced, but because they withdrew their guns from the embrasures, retired to their bomb-proofs, and allowed our guns to pound away at them; and, as soon as our fire became slack, the; reopened fire as briskly as before.

26. A small mine, placed in a box, and sunk in the ground, which exploded if struck by anybody walking over it

27. Private Martin Connors was killed on the 12th; and, on the 13th, were wounded—Private James Murray, dangerously, and Private Matthew Smith, severely.

At this time the days were very hot and oppressive, especially from six to nine a.m., after which a breeze generally sprang up, and rendered the evenings very pleasant, but the flies, both *in* and *out* of the trenches, were a perfect plague. The majority of the army still continued in tents. Little firing went on now, although the Russians caused many casualties by shelling the reliefs.

The Kertch Expedition having returned, Sir George Brown resumed the command of the Light Division.

A draft of fifty men, with Lieutenants P. and H., joined us on the 15th.

Late on the evening of the 16th, we received information that a grand attack was to be made upon Sebastopol at daylight on the following morning. The Redan was to be assaulted, and our 1st Brigade (7th, 23rd, 33rd, 34th, and Rifle Brigade) was to form the attacking party and supports, and our brigade (19th, 77th, 88th, 90th, 97th) was to be in reserve.

The fourth bombardment commenced at three a.m. on the 17th, and continued heavily all day; the French opened fire from a battery of twenty-four guns in the Mamelon; most of the 88th were in the trenches today. This morning about twenty of us assembled in a hut and received the Sacrament from our chaplain, Mr. Wallace.

About two a.m. on the 18th the remainder of the regiment in camp marched down to the trenches under Captain M., together with similar parties from our brigade; we all went to the 3rd Parallel—under the command of Colonel Campbell (90th)—as support to the columns told off to assault the Redan. The attack was to be made at daylight, but the Russians were evidently aware of our plans, as they made a determined sortie upon the Mamelon about dawn; they were, however, repulsed and followed up by the French columns, which proceeded to attack the Malakhoff. It was an anxious and exciting scene; I witnessed it all; the Russians behaved nobly, *standing upon* the parapet of the Malakhoff, and firing down upon the French with terrific effect; the French bravely held their ground for some time, but were at last repulsed with heavy loss.

Meanwhile our gallant troops attempted to storm the Redan, but such a murderous fire of grape-shot and bullets was opened upon them that they were forced to retire, leaving the ground thickly covered with many a poor dead and wounded fellow; the ladder party, composed of the plucky blue-jackets, were all shot down, and none reached the ditch of the Redan. The s total loss in this unsuccessful attack was fourteen officers killed, seventy-one wounded, and one taken prisoner, 1440 rank and file killed and wounded. Many valuable lives were sacrificed in this terrible failure, among them Colonels Sir John Campbell (38th), Yea (7th), and Shadforth (57th), each in command of one of the columns of attack, and Lieutenant Hobson, Adjutant 7th Fusiliers.

Captain Forman of the Rifle Brigade was also killed; he had previously served in the 88th Regiment, and one of the men of my Company (No. 2), named John Dempsey (who had belonged to Captain F.'s Company in the 88th) volunteered to bring in the body of his old captain; this brave soldier attempted to reach Captain F. by crawling along and pushing a gabion before him as a protection, but he was quickly observed by the enemy, and the gallant fellow was soon killed.

After the attempted assault our trenches presented an appalling scene, being choke full of dead and dying. One of our captains (G. R. Browne) had his right arm carried off by a round-shot when standing in the 8-gun battery.[28] Lord Raglan was in the trenches and had been standing in this very battery, a most exposed and dangerous situation. A friend of mine (Lieutenant H. 20th Regiment) was carried past me on a stretcher, wounded. As the assault upon the Redan had failed, my party returned to camp about eight a.m.[29]

On the 19th the flag of truce for the burial of the killed; as we had a general parade we were all confined to camp. I had a slight touch of ague in the evening which made me rather weak.

I was in the trenches with M. on the evening of the 20th; it was a fine night, without dew, and we could hear the Russians busily repairing their batteries. We had moonlight until midnight; this was a delightful change from the long and tedious nights experienced during the winter; those who have not passed a night in the open air, in *total* darkness, for more than fourteen hours, have little idea of the wearisome and de pressing effect thus produced; never was the arrival of dawn more anxiously and eagerly awaited. As we now sat star-gazing in the trenches the otherwise continuous silence was broken by a concert of innumerable crickets.

---

28. The same shot killed and wounded several artillerymen standing near him.
29. The casualties in the 88th Regiment today were:—Private John Dempsey, killed in attempting to recover Captain Forman's body. Captain G. R. Browne, severely wounded; lost right arm. Privates Patrick Conroy and Denis Killaher, dangerously wounded, No. 1651 James Farrell, slightly.

The Brigades of Guards and Highlanders having at this time come up to the front, the duties for the men were thus considerably lightened; but as we (88th) had only three captains for duty, I was still very frequently in the trenches.

The dust in camp and trenches was disagreeable beyond description, and very trying to the eyes, and I used to envy anyone who was fortunate enough to possess a pair of wire spectacles.

On the evening of the 21st I went to the trenches with M. The night was very stormy, plenty of thunder and lightning, but no rain with us; we heard afterwards that heavy rain, the same night, had flooded Balaklava, causing much damage, and carrying away the railway in some places. The following day was dreadfully hot and dusty, and I was very glad to be relieved at seven p.m. after a very tedious twenty- four hours, completely *saturated* (so to speak) with dust. On the 23rd we had one man (private Patrick Duhig) severely wounded.

But little seemed to be going on now, as regarded siege operations, except that we were busy throwing up new batteries in advance of the old ones. Sir George Brown having gone on board ship ill, the temporary command of the Light Division devolved upon our Colonel (Shirley); General Escourt, adjutant-general, died on the 24th, and Lord Raglan was very ill; General Pennefather had been invalided on the 22nd; thus, singularly enough, we seemed to be losing all our senior officers.

On the 25th I had a very warm ride to Balaklava, on a housekeeping, foraging excursion, returning to camp in the cool of the evening, laden with geese and fowls, the results of my marketing.

On the same day our colonel attended a court of inquiry upon our commissariat department. He was examined as a witness, when, absolving that department from all blame for the defective commissariat arrangements during the past winter, he attributed all the disasters, which then resulted, entirely to the negligence and mismanagement of the quartermaster-general's department; so much so that the court would not accept his evidence. We had one man (Private William-Knowles) killed on the 25th.

I commenced at this time making a military sketch of the camp, trenches, &c., and I used to roam about at an early hour, armed with a prismatic compass.

One of the regiments (34th) in our 1st Brigade had suffered so much on the 7th and 18th June, that they were reduced to the commanding officer and four subalterns.

On the 27th we had some heavy rain, which laid the dust, much to our comfort.

The following day I went out to the trenches and spent the night in the old advanced work; the clear moonlight made it almost as light as day; the next morning I had a touch of ague while in the trenches.

Captain G. R. Browne's parents came up from Therapia to attend upon their wounded son, who was still in camp, Mrs, B. lived in a tent, and was attended by one of our soldiers' wives.

On the 29th Lord Raglan died; the failure of the attack upon the Redan on the 18th inst, had, it was said, preyed upon his mind, and he never recovered it. The command of the army now devolved upon General Simpson.

In anticipation of future active operations in the field, I received today (29th) a pair of bullock-trunks from England, in which my thoughtful parents had packed many useful things for my brother and myself.[30]

During the month of June 12 of our men died in camp, 10 from sickness and 2 from wounds.[31]

---

30. Our casualties on the 29th were:—Private Thomas Cummins, killed. Corporal John Fitzgerald, severely wounded. Privates Patrick Connelly and Harry Holland, slightly wounded.

31. Died from Sickness.—Privates—June 1st, No. 3209, Edward Mansfield. 2nd, No. 3416, Alexander Brown. 8th, No. 3786, Michael Donovan. 15th, No. 3694, Edward Wilson. 22nd, No. 3578, James McCarron, No. 3617 John Quinn and No. 2769, Daniel Kelly. 24th, No. 2930, Timothy McCarthy. 27th No. 3404, Edward Cassidy. 29th, No. 3753, Patrick Reddington.

Died from Wounds.—June 8th, Sergeant John Savage and Private Patrick McMahon, wounded, 7th.

CHAPTER 7

July 1st to September 9th

The weather at this time was showery, and occasional rain considerably cooled the atmosphere, and rendered: the trenches more agreeable (?). I continued very busy completing my plan of the trenches and neighbourhood, and I was out early every morning sketching ground, &c., with the assistance of one of my sergeants (Hubert Kelly).

We were all very glad to hear, about this time, that our colonel (Shirley) had been awarded a good service pension of *100l. per annum.* At this time I used to be in the trenches about once a week.

On the 2nd a telegraphic message arrived from England, expressing the Queen's profound grief at the death of Lord Raglan.

On the 5th[1] I rode to the monastery of St George with my brother and M. We took provisions with us, and had a kind of picnic; since my last visit the trees had come forth in full leaf, adding considerably to the beauty of this picturesque spot; the peaceful scene broke suddenly upon the view after the eye had become wearied with the sight of the innumerable tents, barren downs, and stony ravines, through which we passed *en route.* Leaving our ponies in charge of a Tartar, we entered the monastery grounds, and, descending to one of the terraces, took up our position near a fountain of icy-cold water, which, while it cooled our wine, enlivened us with the musical sound of its rippling stream.

It was delightful to find ourselves in this cool retreat, reminding us of quiet scenes at home, and we felt quite a relief to get away from the din of war, and to plunge suddenly into a peaceful spot like this. The

---

1. Our casualties began gradually to increase, and on the 4th and 5th they were as follows:—Private Robert Lynch, killed, 4th. *Wounded*—Privates—Thomas Wilson, Thomas Baker severely, and John Griffin, dangerously, on the 4th. Hugh Campbell, dangerously, John Waters, severely and George Vershaw, slightly on the 5th.

rocks beneath us sloped towards the sea; a cool breeze was blowing through the acacias and other trees; birds were singing undisturbed, and little else but the occasional tread of some bearded monk, coming to the fountain, broke the perfect stillness in this secluded place. In the afternoon the musical sound of the chapel bells summoned the monks to celebrate vespers. We went into the little chapel and listened for some time to the monks singing; it was very good, and the music, although harmonious, had nevertheless a wild sound, well suited to the surrounding scene. We returned to camp in time for a late dinner.

It had been determined at this time to construct an 8-gun battery on the left of our Second Parallel; the ground was selected, and the work commenced, when it was discovered that the site was too low, and that any guns so placed would fire into a bank, so it had to be converted into a mortar battery.

Captain Grogan[2] joined us again at the beginning of this month, after his leave to England on very urgent affairs, and Lieutenant Joly (32nd) left us for Canada. I was very glad to welcome back my old chum G.

The hot weather had now returned, and with it the plague of flies in the trenches, as well as in camp. Our mess hut proved a great boon to us (officers), and was a comparatively cool retreat during the hot days. All ranks were very healthy at this time.

The 13th Light Infantry arrived at Balaklava at the beginning of the month.

Our casualties in the trenches increased very much as we neared the Redan, and at this time the shelling upon our works became much heavier; the enemy used to worry us in this way considerably during the night.

On the night of the 7th we had a working party in the trenches, under the command of Lieutenant Vernor, which was employed in an advanced situation, very much exposed to a harassing fire from the enemy. Our men worked, nevertheless, so persistently, as to merit the commendation of the Engineer officer in charge, who made

1855.

---

2. Some months previously Captain Grogan had applied for leave to England, where his presence was absolutely necessary for the arrangement of family affairs. Lord Raglan at first was firm in his refusal to let him quit the Crimea, even under such urgent circumstances; but at last consented, on the earnest solicitation of Lieutenant- Colonel M., who knew what an honourable fellow Captain G. was, and that he could place implicit reliance on his promise to return to the regiment by a certain date. True to his word, Captain G. rejoined the regiment *almost upon the very day* on which he had promised to return; he was, poor fellow, killed on the 8th September.

a special report of their conduct to the general commanding, and the following letter was communicated to the officer commanding the 88th:—

Headquarters, 8th July, 1855.

Sir,—I am directed by the Lieutenant-General Commanding to inform you that he has received, with much satisfaction, a report from the Engineer officer in charge, stating the admirable manner in which a working party of the 88th Regiment, under the command of Lieutenant Vernor, performed their duty last night under a heavy fire from the enemy.

The Lieutenant-General Commanding begs to express to Lieutenant Vernor and the soldiers of the party under his command the pleasure he feels in acknowledging their good service. &c. &c. (Signed)

W. L. Pakenham,
Lieutenant-Colonel, A.A.G.

By order of the Lieutenant-General Commanding.
To Major-General Codrington, Commanding Light Division.

When in the trenches on the 8th two men of my company (Privates John Hanley and Edward Montague) were both killed by a shell while on day sentry-duty in the advanced *boyau*; one of my sergeants (Goggins) went to visit them, when he found both the poor fellows lying dead, evidently killed simultaneously by the bursting of a shell between them. I was very sorry indeed to hear of their sad fate, for they were two of the most cheery and willing men in my company, and had weathered the hardships of the and the dangers of the siege without a grumble. Three men were also wounded today.

On the afternoon of the 9th I rode, with a brother officer, across the plain of Balaklava to Kadikoi, and then extended our ride to the Tchernaya; we also went to the village of Kamara, the encampment of Sardinians; here we heard their excellent band, which was such a great treat, that the following day four us dined at Kadikoi, and afterwards galloped across the Balaklava plain to Kamara, where we again listened to the band, which played some very nice operatic selections. After a chat with some of the Sardinian officers, we returned in the cool of the evening, reaching camp about ten p.m. The following day we had a violent thunderstorm, which cooled the atmosphere considerably.

On the 13th a draft from Malta joined us, with Captain B. B. M., and Lieutenant M. Our casualties during the preceding week had been very heavy.[3]

At this time the regiment was drilled every morning at five a.m., for an hour. Sir George Brown having gone to England, General Codrington assumed the command of the Light Division.

Our division had daily working-parties, which were employed in strengthening our old works, and also in converting into trenches those captured from the Russians on the 7th June; in this way we constructed another parallel, in front of the Quarries, which brought us within 300 yards of the Redan. The enemy now shelled the trenches terribly, and caused many casualties.

On the 14th, Captain Browne left for England, accompanied by his parents, who had remained in camp to nurse him, since he lost his arm on the 18th June. I went down to Balaklava with them, and saw them off. In the evening the Russians made a sortie upon the French trenches, between the Mamelon and Malakhoff, and drove out the French; but they returned the compliment, and captured some arms and accoutrements, left behind by the Russian working-party, which had commenced destroying the French works. The French lost one officer, and twenty men.

The duties of the Right Attack were now taken by a division at a time, instead of each division furnishing a portion of the trench-guard every day.

On the 15th, we (88th) had 300 men in the trenches, and although there was a great deal of firing, we fortunately had no casualties. Today M. heard of his promotion to Major (*vice* Bayly, killed 7th June).

St Swithin kept up his reputation for rain, favoured us with a wet day on the 15th.

On the 18th, we had four men wounded in the trenches.[4]

I went to the trenches on the evening of the 19th for twenty-four hours; of my party I had one man (Private John Jones) killed, and two men wounded (one named Private John Noone slightly); the following day was very hot, and the Russians shelled us a good deal; during the night they had been pretty quiet, favouring us with a few shells only. We passed our turn of duty in the trenches in front of the

3. Killed—Privates John Hanky and Edward Montague, 8th.
Wounded—Privates Michael Keenan, severely, Joseph Nayle, and John Burke slightly, 8th. Andrew Clarke, dangerously, Edward Rielly, Charles McNamara and Charles Blackwell slightly, 9th. Edward Malone, dangerously, James Quinn, John Collins and Charles O'Callaghan, slightly, 12th.
4. Wounded—Privates Thomas McKeogh, severely, and John Cullinane, George McLoughlin and Thomas Murphy, slightly.

Quarries. Generals Simpson and Jones (R.E.) visited this spot during the day.

At this time my friend Hallewell wanted me to assist him in his survey of the valley of Baidar, but, unfortunately, I could not be spared from the regiment

On the evening of the 21st I was again in the trenches, and occupied a portion of our most advanced works; when occupying the same post on a previous night I deemed it advisable to place a corporal and file in a small ravine, which ran up towards our trench from the Russian side, and which, being a weak point, required watching. With Sergeant Goggins, a corporal, and two men I proceeded down this ravine, and had progressed but a short distance, when several Russians jumped up from the long grass close in front of us and bolted. Soon afterwards we heard a rustling in the grass, and could just discern some figures moving at the end of the ravine, and we could hear the sound of fixing bayonets; some shots were fired at us, but nobody was touched; they seem to have retired after this, and my sentries kept their ground and were not molested afterwards. I had one man killed, and five men wounded today.[5]

We were now enabled to give 400 men for duty, but we had only five captains; and, as the parties in the trenches were increased in strength and frequently required more than one captain with them, the duty for captains came round very often.

About six a.m., on the 23rd, in company with our paymaster, surgeon, and M., I started for a ride to the valley of Baidar; our saddlebags were laden with sundry cold fowls, &c., to say nothing of bottles of beer. Our road lay across the celebrated field of the battle of Balaklava, where, here and there, a few round shot and remnants of uniform, were the sole remaining vestiges of that memorable engagement Ascending the hills on the opposite side of the plain we reached the village of Kamara, with its green-roofed church; here we passed by the encampment of the Sardinians, were at once struck with its neatness and cleanliness; being surrounded by trees the Sardinians had added bowers to their tents, as we used to do Bulgaria.

At length we came suddenly upon a change of scene; from a bare and uninteresting country found ourselves in a deep woody ravine, bounded by bold, lofty hills, almost mountains; wending our way

---

5. Killed—Private Thomas White. Wounded—Sergeant John Flaherty, severely. Privates James Murray, dangerously, Edwin Pollard and James Neville, severely, William Brown, slightly.

along a shady path and crossing the bed of a mountain torrent, we at last reached the Woronzoff Road, along which we took it quietly. Our road wound round the base of the high rugged hills; below us lay the precipitous ravine; the morning was intensely hot. We continued along the road for some miles, until the valley opened out upon the beautiful and extensive vale of Baidar, now dotted with Turkish tents, as well as those of some of our cavalry.

As we progressed the trees became larger, and it is difficult to express the pleasure we experienced in finding ourselves once more among fine shady trees and running streams, after a long and monotonous camp-life

After riding about twelve miles we reached a house, called "Count Peroffsky's Villa," prettily situated in the midst of trees, and commanding an extensive view of hill, dale, mountains, and woods. Here we picketed our ponies, and proceeded to explore the house; outwardly it appeared large, but it disappointed our curiosity, being divided into small rooms, in which there was barely space to swing a cat. Being built in the *pagoda*-style of architecture, outward appearance and not internal comfort seemed to have been the builder's object; the house, surmounted by a green dome, had been completely gutted, little being left but the bare walls.

As there was no water to be found near the house we explored the wood, and soon came upon a well of icy-cold water; here we divested ourselves of our coats, swords, &c., took the saddles and bridles off the ponies, tethered them to the trees, and gave them *their dinner* (which we had brought with us), while we put our bottles of beer to *ice* in the well; we then laid our viands upon the grass, and then our hot selves, under the delightful shade of the thick trees. It was true enjoyment; away from the wearying sound of guns and perpetual sight of soldiers—besides being unmolested by flies—we almost fancied ourselves in Old England, until the illusion was considerably disturbed by the appearance (at the well) of a French soldier from a neighbouring picket, and was utterly dispelled by the worst feature in the case—*i.e., that we had to return to camp.*

The ponies seemed to enjoy themselves as much as their masters, discussing their picnic of oats and rolling on the shady grass. We remained here until four p.m., when we returned through the vale of Baidar, passing by the village of Vernutka, and a Turkish camp. A winding road brought us to the top of a mountain, commanding a fine view of Balaklava harbour. We passed through the Sardinian camp, too late, however, for the band, and, crossing Balaklava plain, we reached camp about eight p.m., hungry and tired.[6]

On the 27th we were very glad to hear that our colonel (Shirley). and also Lieutenant-Colonel G.V. Maxwell, had been made Companions of the Bath.

On the evening of the 28th I was in the trenches in charge of a working party of 100 men; we were employed in the Quarries. The Russians fired at us a good deal with every kind of disagreeable missile, but although the fire was heavier than any I had previously experienced in the trenches, no one was touched except myself. I was slightly wounded; a round shot struck the top of the parapet close to me, and sent a stone with great force into my face; It knocked me down, and caused me to bleed profusely from the nose; and mouth; as it did not necessitate my immediate return to camp, I remained to bring back my party in the morning. I was now obliged to keep my tent for a few days, as my face was much bruised and swollen.

A Russian deserter came over to us the evening I was wounded; a fine tall man, and apparently well fed, not as if from a garrison bearing the reputation of being half-starved. At this time the weather was very rainy, which cleansed the camp, and increased the supply of water, which was beginning to run short, so that some of us were obliged to send our ponies to water in the Tchernaya. During the month of July we lost three men in hospital—two from sickness, and one from wounds.[7]

On the night of the 2nd the Russians made a demonstration upon the Quarries, and at the same time they came out in great numbers upon the Woronzoff Road, carrying off some of the *chevaux-de-frise*, placed across the road, which divided our two Attacks. The shelling was very heavy, and an officer of the 77th[8] lost his leg by a shell bursting in the trench. A party of the 88th, placed on the left of the Right Attack, rendered valuable assistance by keeping up a heavy fire upon the enemy during their sortie in the Woronzoff Road; but in General Simpson's despatch respecting this affair no mention was made that a trench party of the Rangers had fired into the enemy, but only that some of the Royals and 89th had done so from the right of the Left Attack.

---

6. Our casualties on the 25th and 27th were—On the 25th, killed, Privates Alexander Gordon and Philip Gilligan; John Allman, slightly wounded, on the 27th.

7. From Sickness—July 16th, No. 3040, Private Hugh McGuire. July 17th, No. 3748, Private Thomas Stanwell. From Wounds—July 13th, No. 3070, Private J. Byrne, wounded 7th June.

8. Lieutenant Fosberry.

Captain H. rejoined us today with six subalterns. Such an influx of new faces made us appear like a new regiment, and it was sad to reflect how many of our old hands were now no more, and how changed the regiment had become, both in officers and men, since we embarked at Liverpool in April, 1854.

It struck us as very singular that the only one in the regiment with a Crimean medal was H., who had been away for some time invalided; ours had not yet arrived.

The heavy rain we now had tested the huts, and the "tents proved the driest of the two; the hot weather soon returned.

As any exertion brought on violent bleeding in my nose, I remained on the sick-list until the 6th, when I resumed my duties. I was very glad, however, that my tour of duty in the trenches had not, meanwhile, come round; having hitherto not missed a turn since the commencement of the siege, I was very anxious to have no break. The only effect produced by my contused wound was that it considerably lessened my sense of smell—a result, however, which was more advantageous than inconvenient in camp and trenches during hot weather.

The mice, which abounded in our camp, having extensively undermined the sides of my dugout tent, I busied myself on the 6th with executing sundry repairs and improvements, so as to defy the persistent ravages of my enemies, which had held illegal and riotous meetings in various parts of my tent every evening, devouring my sugar, &c., and filling my boots with dust and stones. I afterwards strolled towards the picket-house; it was a beautiful evening, the sun just setting; the white curling smoke from occasional guns indicated the position of the various batteries, as it was too misty to distinguish anything distant.

On the 8th I went to the trenches, where we occupied the Fifth Parallel, our extreme advance; the night was very dark, and, although the shelling was heavy, our casualties were but slight,[9]

There was a false alarm in the French trenches near the Mamelon, which caused us to stand to our arms.

The following day was overpoweringly hot in the trenches, in spite of a heavy thunderstorm, which deluged us with rain. Notwithstanding the excessive heat at this time all in camp continued very healthy. We had five of our men wounded on the 11th.[10]

---

9. Two men wounded—Privates Samuel Provens, severely, and Pat Hurtney, slightly.
10. Privates Edward Murray, severely, James Mullins, Michael Mulcahy, James Quin, and George Smith, slightly.

On the 12th information was given by some Russian deserters, said to have been an officer and a boat's crew, that the Russians, having recently received reinforcements, intended to attack us in front and rear on the 13th. Consequent upon this report all the division were ordered to sleep fully accoutred, ready to turn out at a moment's notice. We paraded at two a.m. on the 13th, and remained under arms until broad daylight, when we returned to camp unattacked. We were also warned to be prepared for an attack the following evening. The camp at this time was very dull in news, not even a good "shave" stirring.

On the 14th Colonel Shirley, having been appointed a Brigadier-General, resigned the command of the Rangers to Lieutenant-Colonel G.V. Maxwell. Colonel S. had commanded the regiment for many years and was beloved by all; upon this occasion the following order was issued by him:—

August 14th, 1855

The General Commanding-in-Chief having been pleased to confer on me the local rank of Brigadier-General, I now resign, with sincere regret, the command of the 88th Regiment. It is now more than twenty-one years since I joined the Rangers, and a more happy twenty-one years no man ever passed; the cordiality and good feeling of the officers to each other, and the attachment and ready obedience of the non-commissioned officers and men to their officers, has been frequently remarked by officers of all ranks throughout the army, and has caused us to be the envy of many.

I have now commanded the regiment for more than seven years, and I feel confident that no commanding officer ever commanded a regiment, for so long a period, with fewer occasions of annoyance than I have had.

Many of you are, I suppose, aware that Her Majesty has lately been pleased to confer on me the Order of the Bath, as well as a grant of 100*l.* a-year; these honours and rewards have been gained for me by the Rangers: it is to your gallantry, your bravery, and your patience under the severe trials of last winter, that I am indebted for these honours and rewards, and most sincerely do I thank you for them.

The old soldiers will recollect that I felt confident that the Rangers of the present day would prove equal to the Rangers of the Peninsula, and most nobly have they answered my expectations.

In giving up the command of the regiment, I have the satisfaction of feeling that I hand it over to one who is worthy of it—*viz*., Lieutenant-Colonel Maxwell—who has shared all your dangers, and is most capable of performing the duties to the satisfaction of everyone and I have little doubt that you will shortly gain for him the honours you have already earned for me

I have also the very great satisfaction of knowing that I am not to be entirely separated from my old regiment, but am appointed to command the same brigade; and, should I be mercifully spared to receive further honours, they will still be gained by my old regiment, in conjunction with our brave friends and comrades on the right and left—the 19th and 77th.

      (Signed)   H. Shirley, Brigadier-General.

On the evening of the 14th, I was in the trenches, when one of my men. Private Thomas Handley, Grenadier Company, behaved very well. I had always considered him a most trustworthy man on sentry duty, and when I visited the various posts in front of our trench, I found H. collaring his young fellow-sentry, a new arrival, and threatening to "bate the brains out of him if he stirred," for the young fellow seemed disposed to retire; the heavy fire of grape &c., kept up every night, at this time, rendered the duty of sentry a very hazardous one, and on this night Handley, by his courageous behaviour, prevented many of the young sentries from quitting their posts; he was subsequently awarded the French war medal.[11] The Russians shelled us very heavily during the night, and we had several severe casualties;[12] I returned to camp on the evening of the 15th.

On the morning of the 16th we were aroused by heavy firing in the direction of the Traktir Bridge we were all confined to camp ready to turn out. It appeared that the Russians, coming down in a large force from the Mackenzie Heights; had made a vigorous attack upon the French and Sardinian positions near the Tchernaya; some of

---

11. *Vide* Appendix B.— French war medal.

12. Wounded— Corporal Tim Fahey, Patrick Murphy, Patrick Toole and Pat. Murphy dangerously. Privates William Whitehead and Michael Russell slightly. Thomas Flatten and James Quinn severely. These casualties were caused by one shell, which lighted in the midst of a knot of men, and burst before they had time to get out of its way.

the enemy forced the Traktir Bridge and penetrated into the French camp on the Fedukhine Heights; but, after a desperate struggle of several hours, the Russians were finally repulsed with heavy loss in killed and wounded, besides several hundred prisoners; their killed alone, including the General Commanding (Read) and many officers, numbered 1500.

Some of us being allowed to leave camp, I rode off with Captain B. B. M., to the field of action; the scene carried me back to the bloody fields of Alma and Inkermann; the ground was thickly covered with dead and dying Russians and many French, but in comparison with the former the French loss seemed small. The chief struggle appeared to have been at the bridge.

It was indeed a field of horrors; we crossed the river and rode all over the ground; we observed that across the aqueduct[13] the enemy had here and there placed small wooden foot-bridges, evidently constructed so as to be carried easily by a couple or so of men.

The Russian troops engaged had (we heard) all recently arrived in the Crimea, and report said that Prince Gortschakoff witnessed their defeat from the neighbouring heights. Upon the body of the Russian general (Read) was found the plan of attack; it appeared that 20,000 men were told off to attack the Sardinians, and 40,000 men to engage the French; and, if they succeeded in forcing these positions, they were then to form-up on the Fedukhine Heights, and here await the reserve under Prince Gortschakoff; if, again, this were carried out they were then to divide their force, one portion proceeding to attack Balaklava while the remainder assailed our rear on the plateau; these attacks were to be the signal for a general sortie from Sebastopol upon the English and French trenches.

This agreed with the information supplied by the Russian deserters which I have already mentioned. All the *ifs* however failed, and, although the Russians considerably outnumbered their opponents.[14] the indomitable pluck of the French and Sardinian troops compelled them to retire with enormous loss.[15] The Sardinian troops behaved very gallantly; this was their first action with the Russians, and they

13. This aqueduct ran along the Tchernaya valley (to Sebastopol), between the river and the French position.

14. Numbers engaged—Russians 35,500, French and Sardinians 23,600

15. The killed and wounded were: *Officers*—French 62, Sardinians 10, Russians 112. *Men*—French 1335, Sardinians 197, Russians 8114. *Total.*—French 1957, Sardinians 207, (2164), Russians 8226.

had a general severely wounded, and many other casualties.

On the morning of the 17th the fifth bombardment opened upon the town; it took us all by surprise, as we had not previously heard anything about it.

A portion of the regiment at this time always remained confined to camp, ready for any duty, and on the first day (17th) of the bombardment the whole regiment paraded for trench guard. We had several casualties on the 17th and 18th.[16] The firing slackened considerably every day, and ceased altogether on the 24th. On the 19th we had seven guns dismounted in the Left Attack. The Malakhoff was very silent—at their old tricks—for when the fire of our batteries became very severe, the Russians used to draw back their guns and retire into their bomb-proofs, leading us to suppose that they were silenced.

A rumour was afloat that another attack was to be made in the Tchernaya Valley, as it was said that the Emperor of Russia had ordered that the Fedukhine Heights were to be recovered at any sacrifice; this report was not disregarded by our general commanding, for we used frequently to parade before daylight, in case of any attack.

At this time the British Army was ordered to be formed into six divisions, each division to have two brigades, and each brigade four regiments, as far as practicable.

The trench duty for captains came round now about once a week, and for subalterns less often. I was in the trenches on the 19th, and again on the 24th.

The bombardment had now entirely ceased, and we gradually subsided into a comparatively quiet state of things, with a shell here and a shot there to remind us that we were really still at war.

The indefatigable Russians were, at this time, very busy in constructing a floating bridge from Fort Nicholas to Fort Michael on the opposite side of the harbour, and it was nearly completed; unfortunately it was beyond the reach of our guns.

We were all getting heartily tired of our life of comparative inaction, and used sometimes to indulge in speculative surmises as to the siege being ended and the prospect of returning to England, wonder-

16. 17th, Private John O'Brien, slightly wounded. 18th, Privates Peter Fegan and John Hough, killed, Drummer Michael McCann, severely wounded, (Drummer McCann suffered amputation of a leg. He was quite a lad, and when lying in our camp hospital, his leg having just been amputated, he remarked to a comrade alongside him: "If I lose my leg I will get 1*s*. a day pension," *not being then aware that his leg was off*.) Privates John Dacey, slightly wounded, Michael Foley, dangerously, Henry Purcell and Michael Garry, severely.

ing if it would ever happen; sometimes in the middle of one of these reveries, a sergeant would thrust his head into my tent, saying, "As you plase, Sir, yer for the trinches tonight," which rapidly destroyed my castle in the air, and brought me back from the realms of fancy to the regions of fact.

Our casualties in the trenches were now very severe, as the Russians shelled our works incessantly; it was calculated that the losses in our army, at this time, were 1500 monthly. As we were comparatively close to the Redan, the enemy used to fire frequently what we called "bouquet-shells," which were about a dozen small shells (hand-grenades) fired out of a mortar; showers of these were sent nightly into our trenches, but I do not think that they had as much effect, or created the same feeling of dread, as the ordinary shell.[17]

The sailors in our Right Attack adopted the Russian plan of sinking, in a hole or trench, a gun which had become disabled by the loss of one or both of its trunnions; in this way they obtained a long range; they used guns which, for the above reason, could not be fired on carriages, but with a considerably increased elevation sent a shot an enormous distance. I saw several shots fired, in this way, at the enemy's ships and bridge; some fell in rear of, and some beyond, the mark, as accuracy could not be obtained. In the same way the Russians used to send round shot into some of our camps. About the 27th the Russian bridge was completed, and we therefore expected that an attack might be made upon us. The 56th Regiment marched into camp on the 26th, and encamped in rear of the 4th Division. At this time we had several casualties among our men on trench guard.[18]

On the 27th Lord Stratford de Redcliffe arrived from Constantinople and invested, with the Order of the Bath, the various generals, admirals, &c., who had been made K.C.B.'s. This day twelvemonth we marched from our camp at Monastir, Bulgaria, to embark for the Crimea. What sad changes had taken place among us since then! many old faces gone, and new ones arrived.

I was in the trenches on the night of the 29th, and about one a.m. on the 30th I was employed with a working party in the 5-gun battery, 2nd parallel, when a French magazine exploded in the Mamelon.

17. Casualties—Privates—24th, John Fury, slightly wounded. 25th, John McMullen killed and Richard Hyth severely wounded.
18. *Wounded*—26th, Corporal John Reilly, severely. Privates Thomas McManus, Edward Farrell and John Low, dangerously (3132). Pat Sheehan, Robert McKeon, Thomas McLoughlin and Edward Quinlan slightly. *Killed*—27th, Private John Roberts. 28th, Privates Michael O'Connor and John Henry.

The report and shock was something awful; the air became filled with fragments of stones, gun-carriages, &c., which showered down upon our trenches, and injured several of the men.

The Russians cheered, but a heavy fire was opened from our Right Attack, to aid the French, who had suffered severely; various were the conjectures and rumours as to what had really occurred, and anything but the true facts was summarised; a dark black cloud hung over the Mamelon, like a huge canopy, for more than an hour afterwards.

On the morning of the 31st the Russians made a sortie upon our Right Attack, where we were pushing new works towards the Redan. Several officers and men were killed and wounded. We had a working party near the place attacked, but had no casualties.

Rumours of a Russian attack were now afloat; spies had brought information, it was said, that some of the Imperial Guard— 60,000 strong—had reached Sebastopol; but we did not feel at all nervous in consequence; we, however, received orders of readiness to turn out at a moment's notice.

Our brigadier (Shirley), not being well, went on board the *St. Jean d'Acre* about this time—she lay off Kamiesch. We had 11 deaths in hospital during August—5 from sickness and 6 from wounds.[19]

Our casualties now continued to be very numerous among our trench guards, so incessant was the shelling and firing of grape-shot, which the enemy kept up every night.[20]

On the 5th, the sixth and final bombardment opened upon Sebastopol at daylight; it was kept up, day and night, until the 8th.[21] I was in the trenches all day on the 6th and previous night; the fire from our batteries was the hottest I ever witnessed, but the Russian batteries were very silent As I sat in the 2nd parallel, I witnessed a most conspicuous act of bravery on the part of some artillerymen; the heavy fire from the Russian batteries had shut up one of the embrasures in our 21-gun battery, so that the gun could not be fired; some gun-

---

19. From Sickness—Privates—3rd, No. 3642, Joshua Hardy. 4th, No. 873, Edward Connors. 5th No. 3794 Henry Davis, 6th, No. 3900, John McAreavy. 10th, No. 3680, James Geary. From Wounds—Privates—2nd, James Murray, wounded June 13th. 14th, Patrick Higgins, wounded 7th June. 15th, Patrick Toole and Patrick Murphy, wounded 14th. 26th, Private John Rielly, wounded 25th. 18th, Corporal Timothy Fahey, wounded 14th.
20. Casualties—3rd September, Corporal B. Ward, severely wounded. Privates Peter Gavin and John McTag dangerously, Edward McCormick, Pat. Cottingham, James Cox, John Farrell, Michael Walsh and Thomas Brien severely. 4th, Private Edward Mahoney, killed. 21. Private Pat. Keoghan, slightly wounded on 5th.

ners, with shovels, at once came out to clear it; the enemy seemed to concentrate a fire upon them: round shot after round shot struck all about them, still they worked as coolly as if not under fire, finishing their work, and quietly strolling out the embrasures with their shovels over their shoulders we anxiously watched them with "bated breath." felt quite a relief when these brave fellows returned into the battery untouched.

About this time we read a paragraph in the *Times*, announcing that *Colonel Shirley's remains were "en route" to England;* his name had been confounded with that of Colonel Shearman (62nd Regiment), who had been killed on the 8th June; our brigadier (Shirley) wrote a very characteristic contradiction of this false report.

It was made known to us on the evening of the 7th that an assault upon the Redan would be made on the following day at noon. Well do I remember that evening; we all sat discussing the proposed plan of attack, and several officers of other regiments dropped in to say their say, among others, Colonel Unett, of the 19th Regiment, who, poor man, was killed the next day.

We all felt in high spirits at the prospect of getting into Sebastopol, although we did not altogether fed sanguine of success, when we found that the mode of attack was to be only a repetition of that, which had failed so signally on the 18th June. Attacking with a force composed of driblets of regiments, instead of with entire regiments, seemed to us a fatal mistake; the sequel will unfortunately show how far our surmises proved correct.

Our brigade paraded early on the morning of the 8th; all ranks seemed in great spirits at the thoughts of capturing the Redan, and of terminating the siege; our fellows, with their natural Irish vivacity, gave vent to their feelings in hearty cheers and yells, as soon as it was announced that we were to take part in the assault on the Redan; an ebullition of spirits which a somewhat excitable staff-officer in vain tried to suppress.

About seven a.m. we marched down to the trenches, and took up our position in the 4th Parallel; a strong wind prevailed at the time, accompanied with clouds of dust; each man carried three days' provisions. While in the trenches we had two men wounded, one was Sergeant Price; he would not, however, return to camp, but remained to take part with his comrades in the attack on the Redan, and he was killed, poor fellow, during the assault; he was a fine, brave soldier, and his loss was much regretted in the regiment, in which he was deservedly esteemed for his conspicuous gallantry throughout the siege.

We remained in the 4th Parallel all the morning, during which time our batteries kept up a murderous fire upon the Russian works, to which the enemy vigorously replied. Exactly at noon the French attacked the Malakhoff; it was an exciting scene to see the red-legged little Frenchmen pouring over the parapet in a continuous stream, for the French, having sapped close up to the ditch of the Malakhoff, had therefore no intervening space to cross before they placed the ladders, by which their men passed into the Russian work. (See note following). As far as we could observe, but few Russians seemed to be flying before them. The tricolour soon floated on the Malakhoff, and this was the signal for our troops to attack the Redan.[22]

Note:—When strolling in an inquisitive mood, about the camp, in an inquisitive mood, about a week before this, I happened to pass the French Engineer park, when I saw a party of French sappers engaged in practising an expeditious mode of crossing a ditch, such as the enemy had made in front of the Malakhoff and Redan. Having formed a parapet and ditch to represent a portion of the Malakhoff, they had a party of men lying down, not far from the counterscarp of the ditch, as if behind the parapet of an advanced sap. Part of these men had scaling ladders, each of which had a plank fastened along it; the remainder of the men were told off to carry long wooden rollers (about three feet long, I should say), supported at both ends on trestle,

22. I believe the truth to be that, at the time at which the French attacked the Malakhoff, there were only a few Russian sentries in it, and that the French *actually captured the work with a loss of one sergeant,* shot by a retreating sentry; and the losses, which they were *said* to have suffered at the assault, were sustained when the enemy endeavoured to recapture the Malakhoff on the afternoon of the same day. The fact of the Malakhoff being almost empty when attached by the French, was thus explained:—The Russians were aware that the allied forces were going to assault Sebastopol on the 8th, but expected the attack to be made at the usual time—*i.e.,* daybreak. As noon approached without any signs of the attack being made, it was regarded as postponed, and the Russians proceeded to relieve the parties in the various batteries, &c. To avoid casualties during the bombardment, which was then going on from our batteries, they had adopted the plan of allowing the party on duty in the Malakhoff to march down to their barracks (in rear of the Redan), leaving the work in charge of a few sentries, and the relieving guard did not march off until this party had reached the barrack. In this way they had only one party of men exposed to the severity of our fire. As good luck would have it, the French attacked the Malakhoff before the Russian relieving party had reached it; hence it fell easily into their hands.

so that each revolved easily.

At a given signal out rushed the roller men, closely followed by the ladder party; the former placed the rollers close together in a line near the edge of the counterscarp, while the latter pushed a ladder along each roller until its furthest end rested at the foot of the parapet on the other side of the ditch. In this way some half-dozen ladders were speedily placed across the ditch. To remove the rollers and to work the ladders close together was the work of a few moments, and thus was rapidly constructed bridge, broad enough and firm enough to support an advancing column of six men abreast.

It seemed an excellent plan, and I recollect mentioning it to some of our engineer officers, who considered that it was a capital idea; but I am not aware that it was ever adopted in our army. When visiting the Malakhoff after the siege, I observed that the French *had* crossed the ditch of the Malakhoff by a *bridge of planked ladders*—no doubt placed in the way which I have endeavoured to describe.

Our attacking party consisted of portions (300 men) of the 90th and 97th Regiments, supported by some of the 2nd Division; these parties dashed out of the trenches and made for the Redan; shortly afterwards the 19th and 88th were ordered up in support; at this time the Russians had opened a heavy fire upon our trenches, and the grapeshot fell thickly among us as we hurried along the narrow trenches. We rushed through the Quarries, where I recollect we encountered an obstacle in the shape of a lame civilian, who was hobbling along, and being terribly in our way at this critical moment, was speedily and roughly pushed aside.

We soon reached the 5th Parallel, where, under the superintendence of our brigadier,[23] each company, headed by its captain, dashed over the parapet—by means of a kind of wooden step—and made towards the Redan. We now had to pass through a murderous fire of round-shot, grape, and bullets, and the ground over which we passed was thickly covered with many gallant fellows, killed and wounded. Not far from our trenches we passed Colonel Unett (19th) lying mortally wounded. I went across with Major M., followed by my company; we had 280 yards to traverse before we reached the Redan, and

---

23. Our brigadier (Shirley), although ill on board ship, hurried up to the front as soon as he heard of the intended attack, and resumed command of our brigade.

our ranks became considerably thinned by the terrible fire through which we had to pass.

At the Redan we found a deep ditch with only two scaling-ladders on one side and *one* on the other side; to scramble down and struggle up the steep sides of the ditch was the work of a few moments, when we found ourselves among a densely crowded mass of officers and men of all regiments) crammed and jammed on the salient of the Redan. Meanwhile part of the regiment had been moved towards the right of the 5th Parallel, as it was reported that the Russians were threatening an attack upon our left flank. Finding that this was not the case, this portion of the 88th were ordered to advance over the parapet towards the right flank of the Redan, which they did most gallantly, but suffered severely from the heavy fire of grape, &c., from the enemy's works. In this advance poor Captain Grogan fell, mortally wounded by a grape-shot, saying to his subaltern (Hall) "It's all over with me."[24]

I felt his loss very much, for we had always been on terms of the greatest intimacy: his death was also universally regretted throughout the regiment. Part of those companies which crossed to the salient of the Redan did not go over the ditch, but were employed in keeping up a fire upon the flanks of the Redan, so as to silence, if possible, the galling fire to which the troops were here exposed; this, however, was not effected without severe loss on our side, and here many of our brave fellows were killed, and many of our officers severely wounded.

In the meanwhile the troops crowded on the salient, although not exposed to the murderous fire from the flanks of the Redan, suffered severely while firing over the parapet upon the enemy in the interior of the work, whence a brisk fusillade was returned by Russians behind the various traverses, as well as under cover of a breastwork across the gorge of the Redan; and where also they subsequently brought up some field pieces, which fired upon the interior of the salient, so as to render impossible any effectual entrance into that part of the work.

Each fresh arrival of troops upon the salient increased the terrible confusion which prevailed there, instead of coming as an effective re-inforcement; for not only had companies become partially broken up, but the men of different regiments, as well as of different brigades, became inextricably mixed together; and also, besides the hopeless con-

---

24. His death was doubly sad, for he had sent in his papers to sell. They had been accepted, and, on the very day that he fell, his name appeared in Orders to proceed to England.

fusion which thus ensued, there was no space on which any adequate body of troops could be collected, for a sudden rush into the Redan. All the unceasing efforts and daring exposure displayed by both officers and men proved of no avail for the restoration of order, and those upon the salient remained there an immovable mass for about an hour and a half All this time supplies of ammunition continued to be passed up to the men in front, who kept up a continuous fire into the interior of the Redan. Numbers were falling all around, and the salient, as well as the ground on the other side of the ditch, was thickly covered with numbers of killed and wounded men and officers, while in the ditch below lay many a gallant fellow.

At length the supply of ammunition began to decrease, and the enemy, apparently emboldened by the gradual slackness of our fire, crept up towards the salient, and threw hand-grenades among us, which, I believe, caused ugly wounds.

At last our ammunition became entirely exhausted, and our position became therefore untenable. The enemy, perceiving this, made a sudden rush upon the salient, which caused those in front to fall back, and never shall I forget the frightful scene that consequently ensued: the whole of us, *en masse*, were precipitated into the ditch upon the top of bayonets, ladders, and poor wounded fellows, who writhed in their agony under the crushing weight of us all; and the shouts and cries were fearful.

The Russians now stood upon the parapet, which we had just left, and pelted us with hand-grenades, stones, &c.; under a heavy shower of these missiles I found myself in the ditch, jammed under a ladder, a firelock between my legs with the bayonet through my trousers, while I was trodden upon by numerous feet. With no little difficulty I managed to extricate myself from this awkward predicament, and to clamber up the side of the ditch; and then what a gauntlet there was to run! Amid an almost worse fire than when we advanced, we all made the best of our way to the trenches; I was, however, providentially guarded in this hour of danger, and reached the left *boyau* untouched, save a few cuts from bayonets, and numerous bruises. When about half-way a bullet grazed the band of my forage-cap; it felt as if I had received a sharp rap with a knobbed stick, and the back of my head was bruised and tender for several days afterwards.

Our loss in this unfortunate attack was very heavy; we had one officer (Captain Grogan) killed, and eight officers wounded severely—*viz.*, Lieutenant-Colonel G.V. Maxwell; Captains Mauleverer and

Beresford; Lieutenants Lambert, Hopton, Scott, Watson, and Ensign Walker; also 2 sergeants and 30 rank and file killed; and 10 sergeants, 2 drummers, and 107 rank and file wounded. Total of all ranks, 160 killed and wounded.[25] Both my subalterns (Scott and Walker) were wounded, my colour-sergeant (Gilmore) was mortally wounded, and 15 men of my company were killed and wounded, out of a total strength of 40.

Shortly after we had retired from the Redan one of my sergeants did a very brave act; my poor colour-sergeant (Gilmore) was lying wounded about halfway between our trenches and the Redan, when Sergeant Sept. Hubert Kelly went out and carried him in *under a heavy fire.*[26]

My friend M. was, like the rest of us, carried into the ditch of the Redan, and was in the act of scrambling out of it with no little effort, when a sturdy officer of one of the regiments put his foot most inopportunely upon M.'s shoulder, and sent him back into the ditch. When he shortly afterwards met M. in the trenches, he made the *"amende"* by offering him a "refresher" out of his flask.

Immediately upon our reaching the trenches, after quitting the Redan, we received instructions to keep up a continuous fire upon the salient, and Russian accounts stated that this incessant fire caused many casualties among them. About five p.m. we were relieved by the 79th Highlanders, and marched back to camp, under the command of Major E. H. Maxwell, our ranks considerably thinned, having left behind us so many of our brave fellows, besides those who had been carried off wounded. It was a remarkable fact that almost, if not every, man of ours, in possession of a Distinguished-Conduct Medal, was either killed or wounded.[27]

---

25. *Vide* Appendix A.
26. For this act of bravery Sergeant Kelly was awarded the French war medal, and was promoted to be colour-sergeant. I have always thought that he ought to have received the Victoria Cross for this courageous conduct, especially as in this campaign, as well as during the Indian Mutiny, this decoration was conferred for precisely similar acts of bravery. I did my best to get the Cross for him, but I was unsuccessful. This gallant soldier was killed during the Indian Mutiny, 1857.
27. *Viz.*:—Sergeant-Major Cooney, wounded, lost a leg; Corporal Hourigan, wounded; Sergeant Price, killed; Sergeant Wrenn, killed; Corporal Connelly, wounded, lost an arm; Privates Mills, O'Rourke, and Connell, wounded; altogether, two killed and seven wounded, Fifteen men had been awarded the D.C. Medal in April, 1855; nine were present at the last attack on the Redan; and, of the remaining six, two had been killed in the trenches; one died of sickness, and three had been invalided.

One of these men (I think Private William Mills) was severely wounded in advancing to the Redan, and, thinking that he might not survive, he tore off his medal and gave it to a comrade (Corporal Hourigan), from the same town as himself, to be sent home to his friends. Corporal H. was afterwards dangerously wounded, a bullet striking his medal and causing a frightful wound, of which the poor fellow subsequently died in hospital; Mills survived, but his medal was lost, and our brigadier (Shirley) had no little difficulty in obtaining another.

There was much discussion as to which troops were first in the Redan. I believe that the attacking parties of Light Division and Buffs penetrated and fought inside the Redan, before Colonel Windham and his party (of 2nd Division) reached the edge of the ditch.

During the attack upon the Redan our brigadier (Shirley) was unfortunately placed *hors-de-combat* by a round-shot striking the parapet in front of him, and sending the gravel and sand, with much force, into his face; he was so completely blinded that he had to be led back to camp, and for many days his face was swollen and scratched, and he suffered much discomfort from the dust in his eyes.

Our drum-major (Beck) behaved remarkably well in removing the wounded from the scene of action under the heavy fire; among others he carried off the field our commanding-officer (G. V. Maxwell) Although he frequently crossed to and fro between the trenches and Redan, he escaped unhurt, though he had a very narrow escape, a bullet going through the top of his forage-cap.

A sort of gloom was cast over the camp that night; for besides having to lament the loss of so many of our gallant fellows, the fact that the British had been repulsed at the Redan, while the French held the Malakhoff, rankled in our minds.

Soundly did I sleep after the fatiguing and anxious day, never hearing the terrific explosions of magazines, &c., in the town, which shook the camp repeatedly during the night.

Early the next morning my servant roused me with the joyful intelligence that the Russians had evacuated Sebastopol; I could scarcely believe it until he bade me look out of my tent, when the dense clouds of black smoke rising from the town, and the frequent violent explosions, showed me that the memorable siege was ended at last

The Russians retreated across their bridge, to the north side of the harbour, about two a.m., having previously set fire to the buildings of Sebastopol, and blown up some of their works. They also sank all their ships-of-war, excepting a few steamers; Fort Paul was blown up on the 9th. We now saw that our attack upon the Redan had been quite unnecessary, and that all the consequent sacrifice of valuable lives had been made to no purpose; the loss of the Malakhoff, which was the key of the enemy's position, compelled the Russians to evacuate the town; and they only awaited the night in order to do so, having previously made a brave defence so as to prevent their retreat being cut off. The French, of course, were very glad that we did assault the Redan, as we thereby drew off a large force of the enemy from the Malakhoff.

CHAPTER 8

September 10th, 1855, to April 20th, 1856

No more duty in the trenches! How strange this seemed! We now sent pickets into Sebastopol to *prevent* our soldiers from entering the town, whereas during the previous eleven months *we had used our utmost endeavours to effect an entrance into it.*

On the 9th Lieutenant-General Codrington, commanding the Light Division, issued the following order:—

> The Lieutenant-General Commanding the Division must give his hearty thanks to those who so gallantly attempted the assault of the Redan; leaving a narrow trench they had to pass over 280 yards, to the edge of the ditch, crossed by fire of heavy artillery as well as musketry, on the open; and though many circumstances prevented the complete execution of orders, and interfered with that combined rush which would have insured success, yet the Lieutenant-General feels that efforts were made by non-commissioned officers and men, and by officers of all ranks and ages, which entitled them to win, and will ever be remembered by him with gratitude and affection.

Although I knew that my brother's regiment (the 20th) had not been engaged on the 8th, still I was naturally anxious to hear how he had fared on that day; he relieved my anxiety by coming to see me the following day, when it appeared that during the assault the 20th occupied a portion of the Right Attack and had a few casualties.

The British troops were prevented from entering the town at this time, but French soldiers were all over the place, and might be seen returning thence laden with a mixed cargo of coats, helmets, and cats, as well as crockery ware, which they sold in the various camps. I invested in some plates, dishes, and a soup tureen.

On the evening of the 9th I walked up to the picket-house to see Sebastopol in flames; it was a grand sight, and, as we looked on, continual explosions took place all over the town. On the 12th I rode down on an exploring excursion; never did I before see any place in such a state of ruins; handsome houses roofless and gutted, and every inch of ground ploughed up by the enormous fire of shot and shell, which had been poured into the town.

I visited the Redan, and was decidedly of opinion that, even if we had effected an entrance into the work, our force was far too small to hold it; the ditch was now partly filled up with the brave fellows who had fallen on the 8th. It seemed very strange to be riding unconcernedly about the trenches, where a short time before I did not dare to show even my cap. The death-like stillness, too, which now pervaded the trenches and deserted Russian works, was very remarkable. Our camp-life also, how different! we could now exult in comparative security, without night alarms, enjoying our slumbers undisturbed.

The Russians had now sunk the remainder of their vessels in the harbour, the masts of which could be distinctly seen above water. They also left many dead and wounded in some buildings, used as an hospital, in Dockyard Creek; these poor creatures were not discovered until the 10th, when the scene that presented itself is too horrible to describe; there was a flag of truce, and the Russian wounded were removed. Captain Hutton (97th Regiment) was found among the dead in this hospital, in an emaciated condition: and Captain Vaughan of the same regiment was discovered, badly wounded, trying to crawl downstairs to get water, being, poor fellow, quite delirious from privation and exhaustion, having been stripped of almost everything. He died in camp on the 13th.

Our paymaster having gone to England on sick-leave on the 14th, I became acting paymaster. On the 15th our Colonel (G.V. Maxwell), who had been severely wounded on the 8th, went home in the *Alma* steamer, and Major E. H. Maxwell assumed command of the regiment On the 20th, being the first anniversary of the Battle of the Alma, the Light Division was formed up in front of our camp to receive the Crimean medals; but, as the home authorities never could manage anything without some blunder, they were sent out without names engraved on them, and with only a *few* clasps; we ought to have received 130 medals, but only 26 were given.

In the evening we had a regimental dinner. With the assistance of a committee of taste I acted as caterer and *chef-de-cuisine*; we had champagne and a very good spread,[28] and the whole affair passed off very merrily. Such had been the changes among us since the action, that out of twenty-four, who dined on this occasion, only six (besides our brigadier) had been in the engagement.

At this time I was hard at work preparing for the future by building a winter residence; and, as we were now allowed access to the town, we used to send out parties, who procured windows, doors, and planks in abundance; nails were only to be obtained at Balaklava or Kamiesch—and very dear they were too.

I rode into Sebastopol with our quartermaster on the 24th, and visited the Malakhoff; it was the most wonderful work of the kind which I had ever seen. Every effort had been made to render it, as it proved to be, a work of great strength; enormous labour had been bestowed upon its massive traverses and bomb-proof magazines, &c., which were formed of layers of masts, sandbags, and earth, in comparison with which many of our engineering operations in the trenches appeared very paltry.

Although the Malakhoff was now no longer in the possession of the Russians, it was however very numerously occupied by another enemy—ycleped *fleas*—which made such a vigorous onslaught upon our ponies as well as ourselves, that we were very glad to beat a speedy retreat.

We also paid a visit to the Redan batteries; the massive construction of these works, and the enormous timbers used to form the numerous magazines and bomb-proofs, showed what immense labour must have been employed by the Russians in order to attain such perfect solidity. Mortar batteries were at this time being thrown up, by the French and ourselves, inside the town. The 3rd Buffs were quartered in the dockyard for some days; but the frequent firing from the batteries on the north side of the harbour rendered their residence rather a dangerous one, and they returned to camp with the loss of a few men. At this time the Russians were very busy intrenching themselves on the north side, and they also made a reconnaissance towards the Tchernaya.

One day a magazine exploded in the Redan, killing and wounding

28. Contrast this with our dinner on the field of Alma, a repast which consisted of a piece of salt-pork, flinty biscuit, and a glass of grog.

several soldiers and mules. I also heard of a singular occurrence, which might have proved serious; some men on guard in the Redan selected a *nice smooth* spot, upon which they lighted their fire and hung up the camp-kettle to boil the dinner; the *nice smooth* spot proved to be a *shell*, which soon blew up, pots and all, but the men, sitting round the fire, escaped injury. A fire broke out on the 29th in the White Buildings (barracks), near the dockyard, and destroyed a great deal of wood, temporarily stopping our plundering parties; but as my pony and a cart had only recently brought up a good supply of timber, I did not care, and my house now gradually progressed towards completion. The interior of the town daily presented a curious scene at this time; every house swarmed with men stripping off the roofs and floors, and all around resounded with the noise of incessant hammering, and the clatter of carts and horses.

Our wounded were now getting on very well, and all the officers but one (Lieutenant W.) had left for England; the number of sick also had considerably diminished. During the month four of our men died of wounds.[29]

An expedition to Kinburn started on the 4th of Oct October; my brother went there, in H.M.S. *Algiers*, with the 20th Regiment. The force consisted of 1 5,000 men, English and French; part of our 4th Division accompanied the expedition—*viz.*, the 17th, 20th, 21st, 57th, and 63rd Regiments.

Many regiments brought up bells from Sebastopol, hanging them up in front of their camps, where they were struck to indicate the hour. I got many useful things from the town—in the shape of chairs, tables, doors, windows, and a chimney-glass. It was very amusing to meet the numerous pillagers returning to camp, laden, sometimes, with the greatest rubbish, brought away from the simple love of appropriation. Some of the men of my regiment tried to bring up a piano; but, being prevented by the picket from bringing it to camp, they smashed it to pieces rather than let it fall into the hands of any French soldiers.

On the 5th the last of our wounded officers, one of my subalterns (Lieutenant G. W.), left for England in the *Niagara* steamer, and by him I sent to my parents my journal to the end of the siege. The Russians used to fire shell into the side of Sebastopol occupied by the French, but they seldom molested our portion, which was called the Kara-

---

29. Privates—Sept 5th, No. 3131, John Lowe, wounded 26th Aug. and No. 3482 Peter Gavin wounded 3rd; Sept. 7th No. 3494 John Joyce; Sept. 21st No. 3760 Thomas McLoughlin.

belnaia suburb, and was situated behind the Redan, Malakhoff, and adjoining works.

The arrival of the mail on the 8th brought us the comments upon General Simpson's despatch respecting the assault on the Redan, September 8th. We all thought that this despatch contained a very meagre description of that memorable day. General S. did not mention that while for some hours previously our Right Attack batteries had rendered great assistance to the French by keeping up a heavy fire *upon the Malakhoff*, they had gradually *slackened* their fire *upon the Redan, because it was thought that its guns were silenced*: whereas the Redan batteries, though *silent*, were *very far from being silenced*, as we afterwards found to our heavy cost

General Simpson said in his despatch that the trenches were in too crowded a state for a *second* assault to be organised; but we never thought that our trenches were so constructed as to admit of our *first* assault being *effectively* organised. The French, I understood, levelled some of their trenches near the Malakhoff, so as to form a kind of "*place d'armes*," of open space, where a body of troops could be formed up for attack; we could not (at any rate did not) attempt anything of the kind. After the assault the trenches became so obstructed, by parties of men bearing away wounded, that it was next to impossible to move about troops and, at the same time, to keep them under cover, a very material object; one man borne on a stretcher, through the narrow trenches, was sufficient to arrest the progress of a whole regiment.

Our wounded at this time were getting on very well, and the troops generally were very healthy. On the morning of the 12th, in company with our brigadier (Shirley) and some brother officers, I visited several of our wounded men, who were lying in the general hospital about a mile from our camp. Some were progressing very well; others, poor fellows, were rapidly sinking under the severity of their wounds. They were truly delighted to see their kind old chief, some grasping his hand, too ill to otherwise express their joy; it was a very painful scene. After the 8th of September the number of our wounded was so great, that they were distributed throughout the various hospitals, and some days elapsed before we had any clue to the whereabouts of many of our wounded fellows. Our sergeant-major (Cooney) was lying in our regimental hospital, and I used often to visit him. He had one leg amputated, and subsequently died.

I rode into the town with a brother officer on the afternoon of the

12th. Parties were busy everywhere, as usual, stripping the houses of wood, &c. The Russians fired a few shells into the part occupied by the French, but they did not honour our side of the town while we were there.

We now had beautiful autumnal weather, very favourable for building our house, which progressed rapidly. We were also very busy getting on the roof and erecting the chimneys, for which we had procured quantities of bricks from the dockyard. These bricks were English manufacture, and stamped "*Stourbridge.*" My *bât*-man (Geoghegan), a mason by trade, did the building part, and another man the carpenter's work, assisted by myself. M.'s *bât*-man (Cullen) was invaluable in making daily trips to the town, whence he brought up loads of various useful things upon our ponies' backs.

Major Vesey Browne arrived from Malta on the 13th, with Ensign D., and assumed the command of the regiment, being senior to Major Maxwell. Interchanges of civility, in the shape of shot and shell, took place daily between our batteries in the town and those of the Russians on the north side of the harbour. On the 14th they fired very viciously, as the French had opened a new mortar battery.

Besides building a house, I now commenced forming a small farmyard, which I stocked with fowls, geese, turkeys, &c. Such cackling, quacking, and gobbling as there was early every morning! Unfortunately there was no pond for the ducks and geese,

I dined with General Codrington on the 15th, and we had a very pleasant dinner party.

It was very interesting at this time to read the various opinions concerning the cause of our failure to take the Redan, as set forth in the *Times* and other papers; in which also a speech of Sir George Brown, at Leamington, was much cut up, because he said that our soldiers required leading. To our minds, very unjust aspersions were cast upon the conduct of the men at the recent assault. It was said that, in spite of efforts on the part of the officers, they would not come on; and that, having been, so to speak, bred in the trenches, they kept behind cover whenever and wherever they found it; and General Markham was reported to have said that with a corps composed of 200 officers he could have carried the Redan.

Any apparent hesitation on the part of the men—crowded upon the salient of the Redan—to quit the shelter of the parapet and to advance, did not, in my humble opinion, arise from any reluctance to leave their temporary shelter, because, for so many months, they had been trained to fight behind intrenchments; but because, in action, soldiers very naturally look to being associated with *the men of their own regiment or company, under the guidance of their own officers*; whereas on this occasion the troops on the salient had, from regiments and companies being separated and intermingled, become a confused assemblage, as before described; officers looking for their men, and men for their officers. All ranks seemed most eager to advance, but, as previously mentioned, there was not space enough for reorganising such a mixed and densely packed body of men; if they had all belonged to the same regiment they *would*, I felt convinced, *have rushed into the Redan to a man.*

The failure of this assault seemed, to those on the spot, to have principally arisen through the insufficiency as well as the defective organisation of our attacking force, coupled with the fact that the successful assault upon the Malakhoff having taken place *before* we advanced upon the Redan, the Russians were thus forewarned, and were quite ready for our attack.

The assault upon the Redan seemed, from the outset, destined to be unsuccessful; besides our attacking force, as I have already said, being of insufficient strength, and moreover composed of portions of regiments instead of entire regiments, these troops had also to file through the narrow trenches, which caused the ranks to open out; then there was no place in which to assemble, so as to recover their formation, preparatory to advancing to the attack; and also the wooden steps, erected over the parapet of our last trench, being quite inadequate for the passage of a body of men in compact formation, they had to scramble over them in any way they could; hence the opening out of the ranks became still more increased.

Under such conditions the attacking force had to advance towards the Redan, across an open space of fully 280 yards exposed to a murderous fire, reaching at length a broad and deep ditch, to be crossed as best they could, through the scarcity (I might almost say absence) of scaling-ladders. In like manner the supports—at best a scanty number—became still more scanty when they had crossed the same ground. Thus regiments became inevitably divided and mixed together; a state of confusion which resulted, as we have seen, in the troops on the salient becoming a body of soldiers without any cohesion.

How different were the circumstances which attended the attack upon the Malakhoff! The French, having sapped close up to the edge of the ditch, had no open space to cross, neither had they any crossfire upon them. Besides these favourable conditions, they were also enabled to bring up all their supports, &c., close to the place, *under cover*,—and, to crown all, they found the Malakhoff almost, if not quite, undefended.

On the 19th we heard of the success of the expedition to Kinburn, and that the Russian general (Kokonowitch) and garrison—13,000 men and seventy guns—had capitulated. It appeared to have been an almost bloodless affair.

Rumours of an intended attack upon the Allied forces caused early parades—before daylight—to be resumed at this time.

The French, in rear of us, shifted their ground towards Inkermann during this month; we missed their beautiful bands very much, and now heard only their bugles and drums, which used to keep up an incessant noise from sunrise to sunset I went to Balaklava almost daily on marketing excursions, and, among other luxuries, I used sometimes to buy Black Sea turbot, a very delicious fish, and quite as good as those purchased in England; some of them were very large, varying in price from five to ten shillings. Fowls, ducks, &c., could now be purchased in Turkish vessels; not very cheap, but then nothing was cheap, thanks to the sutlers—robbers, and spies too, as they were—who made a good harvest out of our pockets. Camp continued very dull, no good shaves stirring, no nothing. The arrival of the mail (now regularly) each week was the only excitement; and the only change seemed to be in the weather, which was gradually breaking up and getting colder.

Our Engineers were very busy throwing up a 10-gun battery near the ruins of Fort Paul; a heavy fire from the Russian batteries (on the north side) could have been concentrated upon this spot, and the general opinion was that this battery would therefore be useless.[30] On the 26th we gave a farewell dinner to our brigadier and late commanding officer (Colonel

Shirley), who left us for England on the 27th, going to Constantinople in the *Emperor* steamer. We were all most sorry to lose him, both as our colonel as well as our brigadier, and much wished that he had never left us. Colonel Lysons (23rd Fusiliers) was appointed our brigadier.

I moved into my house on the 27th, and was not sorry to be once more under a roof, having resided in a bell tent for the previous eighteen months, passing through the ordeal of a severe winter. The

---

30. This battery, although finished, was never armed.

room of my house (or rather hut) was ten feet square, whitewashed, with a fireplace and two windows. My next door neighbour M. had a separate entrance, our rooms being divided by a wooden partition. I lined my side of the partition with white serge, and boxes built into the walls formed my bookcase and cupboards. My chimney, of course, smoked at first, but that defect was speedily cured without the aid of a professed chimney doctor.

The early parades having ceased, the troops were now employed in constructing roads. The weather was like summer, and therefore very favourable for finishing a good road between Balaklava and the camp. *Sirocco* winds, and dust penetrating everything, were of frequent occurrence, and most unpleasant they were too. During October five of our men died in the camp hospital. [31]

Sunday (the 4th) being appointed for a general Thanksgiving Day, we had a very appropriate sermon from our chaplain (Wallace), and the Sacrament was afterwards administered, at which many of us attended.

On the afternoon of the 5th our band played before our messhut; this was their first appearance for many months. Today being the first anniversary of the Battle of Inkermann, great were the rejoicings throughout the various camps; innumerable bonfires were lighted, and repeated shouts of merriment resounded through the air. Report said that the Russians were certain that the Allies were *all drunk* on the anniversary of the Battle of the Alma; and, taking it for granted that we should all be in the same condition tonight, that they meditated an attack.

Being desirous of seeing my brother, who was off Kamiesch in the *Algiers*, I rode there on the morning of the 7th, in company with a brother officer (Lieutenant W. B.). The day being very calm we obtained a boat and went on board the *St. Jean d'Acre*, as B. wished to see his brother, a naval officer on board. I found that the *Algiers* was much further out to sea, and our boatman—a sulky Maltese—would not go on. so I gave up my intended visit; however, the first lieutenant of the *St. Jean d'Acre* most kindly sent me on board the *Algiers* in one of their boats, so that after all I had the pleasure of seeing my brother. The 20th had been off Kamiesch for a week. I dined on board, and returned to camp in the evening.

About this time I applied for leave to England for a short time, but

31. Privates—October 9th, No. 3869, James McCarte; 19th No. 3889 G. Lenox and No. 4013 M. Carroll; 30th No. 3368 Edward Pollard and No. 4103 John Kearns.

it was refused because we had too few officers with the regiment.

Sir William Coddrington was now appointed to the command of the army, and commenced his duties on the 11th, publishing a farewell order to the Light Division. He was succeeded by Major-General Lord William Paulet

During this month our men were busy erecting a new description of hut, double boarded, easily put together or taken asunder, and capable of containing fifty men. I built a very comfortable stable for my ponies, but building materials were now becoming very scarce.

As far as we could judge, the Russians seemed to have no intention of retiring from the north side, where they had recently increased the number of their intrenchments.

On the afternoon of the 15th, about three o'clock, a terrific explosion took place close in rear of our division, in the British and French siege parks. I was standing in my hut reading a letter, when I was startled by a most violent noise like the discharge of hundreds of guns, which lasted many seconds with a deafening roar; ground trembled under my feet, my windows were smashed to atoms, and I was nearly knocked down by the terrible concussion of the air. I rushed to my door, and never did I before witness such a scene as presented itself. The sky over the camp was thick with bursting shells; showers of splinters, round-shot, grape, &c., were falling all around; men and loose horses flying from the scene; poor patients, who had rushed from their beds in the hospitals just as they were, were running away in all directions; and everything and everybody seemed in a state of confusion. Surgeons and ambulance wagons, &c., were quickly on the spot to attend to the many injured and to collect the dead. Our hospital sheltered many wounded men. It was like a scene after an action.

As we were not far from the scene of the explosion, most of the splinters, &c., seemed to pass over our regiment, and we had only two men injured, Sergeant John M'Hugh and Private Christopher M'Dermott, one of whom (M'Dermott) suffered amputation of a leg. In one of the hospital huts *ten pieces of shell came through the roof*, but, marvellous to relate, none of the patients were touched. The same evening a French officer died in our hospital from injuries received. The French had nineteen officers, and the English nearly 150 men, killed and wounded; one British officer (Mr. Yellon, Dep.-Asst.-Commissary-General) was killed. It was a melancholy sight to witness the numerous funerals which passed out of camp on the following day.

The conflagration which ensued after the explosion destroyed many huts, tents, gun-carriages, &c. In the windmill, close by the explosion, were hundreds of tons of gunpowder, and the sparks showered around it Fearing that the powder might explode, every regiment in the Light Division was at once marched away from camp to the high ground near the old picket-house, and there formed into brigades. On the Sunday following our chaplain preached a very impressive sermon in allusion to the recent fatal catastrophe. We now had afternoon service every Sunday in a hut in the 90th lines, and it was well attended by all ranks.

On the 16th we received the news of the brevet promotions for services during the war, and I was much rejoiced at finding myself a brevet major, and also my brother and E. H. M. brevet lieutenant-colonels.

The roads being nearly all finished, the regiments were employed in improving the camps, in repairing their huts and in erecting new ones. On the 18th, M. and I gave our servants a dinner to celebrate our promotion, and several of us dined at a neighbouring restaurant, which, with many others, had sprung up in the vicinity of the camps. Kadikoi was rapidly becoming a town of wooden huts, with all kinds of shops; it was our principal market, and named "Vanity Fair." In Balaklava now there were no shops. Behind the 4th Division was a small village of huts, called "Donnybrook," from being a noisy locality; and in rear of our division was the French bazaar, called "*La Petite Kamiesch,*" where everything was sold at the most exorbitant prices.

The French troops seemed to be doing little towards hutting themselves; they hutted their *stores*, but not *their men.* The railway at Balaklava was now in full force, and it was very singular to see an engine puffing away, and to hear the whistle resounding through the valleys, reminding us of home scenes.

Heavy showers of rain having proved that the roof of my house was rather leaky, I purchased some canvas at Kadikoi, stretched it over the roof, and then pitched it. After a deluge of rain visitors used frequently to pop in to compare notes as to the waterproof qualities of each other's residences, returning to their respective establishments with great inward satisfaction if it happened that *my* house leaked, but *theirs did not.* On the 26th we had our first cold wintry day, and the ground was covered with snow. Afterwards the weather changed to rain, so I occupied myself daily by carpentering in my hut. All the huts in our camp were not yet erected, but were gradually rising up. An officers hut was in course of erection, capable of containing sixteen occupants.

At this time our mess-hut was also thoroughly done up and made very comfortable, Sebastopol windows being put in. Here we all assembled every evening, some for whist, others to smoke, read, or chat During the month of November five of our men died in the camp hospital;[32] and in the months of September. October, and November many of our poor fellows died of wounds received on the 8th September.[33]

The weather at the beginning of December was very wet and stormy, and the camp was in a terrible state of mud and water, offering little inducement to stir out. We had only one death in hospital this month—*viz.*, No. 3331, Private John Conway, who died on the 2nd, of sickness.

A grand military steeple-chase came off on the 3rd, but I was unable to go there. On the 10th I rode to Balaklava with my brother. I never saw the bazaar at Kadikoi in such a state; it was a sea of mud. The road from camp was a great improvement to what it had been last winter, though it required to be often repaired from the constant traffic upon it. Road police were established to prevent irregularities.

It poured with rain on the evening of the 12th, and I was rejoicing at my hut having proved quite watertight, when the stupidity of our servants caused us to be flooded; we had placed tubs outside the hut to catch the rainwater; these not having been duly emptied, overflowed, and put us into a sorry plight

The tents of the Light Division were now gradually disappearing, and huts were springing up in all directions; as we became more comfortable we almost forgot the existence of the Russians.

I had a great laugh at my brother for being taken in by a French soldier. He bought what he supposed to be a bag of Sebastopol coal, and put some on the fire when I was paying him a visit; it made a great blaze and smoke, and then melted away, turning out to be nothing but lumps of pitch! The 17th was a bitterly cold frosty day, and I found the air very cutting when riding to Balaklava; the ground was covered with snow. The winter had now regularly set in; the surrounding country was one vast white expanse, and the camps looked cold and cheerless.

All ranks seemed, however, to enjoy the severe weather; desperate snow ball encounters took place between the officers; and the men,

---

32. Privates—November 3rd, No. 4198, Private M. Dacey; 11th No. 3910 Michael Fealey; 13th No. 4056 John McIntyre; 16th No. 4176 James Foley; 18th No. 3204, Sergeant James Prescott.
33. *Vide* list of wounded 8th September, Appendix A.

following their example, erected a snow redoubt, and a terrific battle ensued between our right and left wings. It was a great pleasure to see the men in such high spirits, and the tumbling and scuffling was very amusing. How different to the miseries of the previous winter, when all were too hard worked to think of amusement! Being then half-starved, ill-clothed, and sickly, few had the heart—not to say the strength—to do anything beyond struggling through their arduous duties. All this was now, happily, numbered among the "bygones." During this cold weather I found my hut very snug and warm. Occasionally you might see officers driving about camp in a sleigh captured in Sebastopol.

The brigade used to march out very frequently during the winter; the regiments were very healthy and had very few men in hospital—colds, coughs, and frostbites being the only maladies. On the 18th our regiment was inspected by our brigadier (Lysons), who expressed himself highly satisfied with us.

The first amateur theatrical performance took place in the Fourth Division on the 23rd, and it was very amusing.

The mails used to arrive most irregularly at this time. This was very disappointing, as we looked forward to the arrival of letters and newspapers, which always created a pleasant break in our daily monotonous life. Our Christmas party went off very well and merrily; we sat down twenty-six, and the amateur plum-puddings were pronounced excellent.

The duties were very light during this winter, consisting of a few guards in Sebastopol and a picket at Fort Paul; altogether the men had a very comfortable time of it; comparatively little to do, plenty to eat, too much to drink, and well-housed; consequently they looked the picture of health, and the hospitals were very empty. We now had parades twice a day and plenty of drill, as the recruits from England were frequently a comparatively rough set, and required much brushing up. During the month Lieutenant W. joined us with a draft. As for the Russians, we seldom used to talk or even think of them.

Continued falls of snow made the camp look very dreary; frequent snow-battles took place between our two brigades, causing much merriment. The combatants (about 3000) were sometimes headed by officers; many prisoners were taken, and both sides suffered heavy losses—of breath. About the 11th the wintry weather entirely disappeared, and was succeeded by calm, mild, showery days, and therefore plenty of mud The changes of temperature were very frequent, and a mild night was often followed by a cold snowy morning. I used frequently to go to the 4th Division Amateur Theatricals; the plays were exceedingly well got up and afforded much amusement The actors were officers, and the female characters were sustained by young and smooth-faced "sons of Mars."

The 14th was bitterly cold, hard frost and snow; the following day my brother paid me a visit, and as it was our good father's birthday, we drank his health in a bumper of champagne.

Through the exertions of our indefatigable chaplain (Mr. Wallace) a church was opened in the brigade; it was formed of two huts joined together, and was capable of containing about 200. There was a weekday service, with a lecture every Friday afternoon, and there was always a very good attendance. Mr. W. also established a library for the use of the officers and men, and anyone might take a book and keep it for a fortnight. Readings and lectures upon various subjects were also given by Mr. W., assisted by volunteers, every Tuesday and Friday. They were intended for the non-commissioned officers and privates, but some of us used to look in occasionally. The first evening he gave Readings in Shakspeare.

My regiment at this time mustered about 500, and we had only twenty-seven men in hospital. All the British troops looked healthy and robust—a great contrast to the French soldiers, who were very sickly at this time, and looked haggard and half-starved. In the French hospitals the patients were lying upon straw *palliasses placed on the ground*; our sick men had bedsteads and sheets, with every comfort to alleviate suffering.

The mails continued to arrive very irregularly during the winter. We were all full of hopeful surmises about our future movements, which the rumours of peace rather upset.

On the 29th a Rangers was on picket at the ruins of Fort Paul under Captain H., when the Russians opened a tremendous fire. Round-shot, shell &c., roared through the air, and this heavy bombardment lasted for some time from *all* their batteries on the north side, from right to left. Fortunately none of the Rangers were touched, and this was the last time they were under fire in the Crimea.

The real cause of this heavy firing was never satisfactorily ascertained; our sentries said they saw boats on our side the harbour,[34] and, although the British sentry in the Crimea was noted for seeing

34. As the Allies had guard-boats in the harbour, the appearance of boats on this
night did not engage particular attention.

wonders at night, still the Russian account of this affair corroborated the statement of our men, and said that on this night a boat of theirs penetrated as far as the Shears' Point (Dockyard Creek), where they saw a British guard sitting round a fire. It appeared also that they afterwards landed near the Admiralty buildings (French side), and then returned to the north side.

The mail received (31st) mentioned that peace was almost certain, but the papers warned John Bull against being too sanguine in his expectations, and not to fancy that the only thing now remaining to be done was ringing the bells, lighting bonfires, and paying the money.

The regiments were constantly out at brigade drills under our indefatigable brigadier, and they sometimes marched out

On the 3rd of February I was appointed a town-major in the Kalabelnaia suburb (Sebastopol), being the part held by the British; so I handed over my quill-driving occupation of paymaster to Major E. G. M. I rode down to the town the same afternoon and reported myself to the Commandant, Colonel Turner (7th Fusiliers), and I found that Major C. (62nd Regiment), an old school-fellow of mine at the Cheltenham College, and Major D. (49th Regiment), were town-majors with me. On the 4th I moved from camp and took up my new quarters in the Dockyard, having handed over my hut to my subaltern. Lieutenant T. B. The town-majors lived in one house, near the docks, with separate bedrooms, and one sitting-room furnished with Russian tables, sofa, &c.

Our mess consisted of a very pleasant party of four, including the commandant. The sitting-room was about twenty-five feet square and twenty feet high, warmed by a Russian stove, with two large windows (overlooking the ruined docks), the glass of which was much shattered by the sundry explosions. Lofty double doors led into a broad high passage, on the other side of which was my dormitory, a spacious and very cold room, being plentifully ventilated by a large hole in the ceiling made by a round-shot during the siege. Behind our sitting-room was a large room where my brother town-majors slept.

My duties were not arduous: when on duty in the town I had to inspect the various Karabelnaia Guards, paraded in the Redan at ten a.m., afterwards remaining all day in the dockyard, visiting the sentries, &c. In the evening I had to post the first relief of the sentries at Fort Paul. The next day I had to go to our army headquarters for orders, and was off duty the following day: these were my principal duties. In case of any attack by the enemy we each had an alarm-post to which to repair, and to instruct the troops told off to assemble there.[35]

On the 4th Fort Nicholas was blown up by the French; it was a wonderful sight; a low, rumbling sound was heard, like distant thunder; then the fort became suddenly enveloped in smoke and dust; at the same time there was a rushing noise, like falling stones, and when the smoke and dust had cleared off, you beheld the once formidable battery a shapeless heap of ruins.

Our Engineers were very busy every day destroying the docks and blowing up the barracks (White Buildings, as we called them). Mr. Deane,[36] the diver, was also hard at work fishing up some Russian field-guns, thrown by the enemy into Dockyard Creek when 1856. evacuating the place, and succeeded in getting up two batteries, complete with limbers, &c. The Russians used occasionally to send a shell into the dockyard, but caused no damage to anyone. The docks were completely destroyed on the 8th, and Fort Alexander was blown up by the French on the 10th. Our every-day life was ditto repeated, but we had numerous visitors from camp. A detachment of the 48th Regiment was quartered near us; the officers were a particularly nice set of fellows, and frequently dined at our mess.

The weather was now very fine, though cold. I used on clear days to have a good look with my telescope at the north side of the harbour; the narrowest part (across from Fort Paul) was not more than 600 yards wide and I often watched the enemy's regiments at drill. On the 16th, being on duty, I took the opportunity of strolling about the town and works with my commandant; as this was my first visit to many of the places, I was much interested. We had a pretty good round to make, and our path frequently lay over very rough ground, paved with round-shot and shell splinters. Every wall, far into the town, was thickly pitted with the marks of our rifle bullets, especially the wall bounding the docks, and some way in rear of the Redan, showing what a *hot time* the Russians must have had in the town during the siege.

In the Redan, Malakhoff, and other works which we visited it was wonderful to observe the enormous amount of labour which had

---

35. When the town-majors returned from their alarm-posts on the night of the heavy bombardment before mentioned (January 29th), they found that the ceiling of their bedroom had been penetrated by a round-shot, which lay on the floor, and the room was filled with dust and rafters.

36. Mr. Deane was employed in 1838 in blowing up the remains of the wreck of the *Royal George* at Spithead.

been bestowed upon the construction of the different intrenchments. For the protection of those on duty in the batteries, &c, the Russians had constructed extensive chambers (cellars, so to speak) excavated some ten feet underground, with a massive bomb-proof roof, composed of masts and other timber, sandbags and earth, piled up to a thickness of fully twelve feet These chambers were capable of containing a large number of men, who were here perfectly secure from every kind of missile, and were moreover assembled close at hand, ready for any emergency. No wonder that private letters (found in Sebastopol) showed how rejoiced all ranks were when it was their turn for duty in the Redan, &c., where they were far better protected from danger than in the barracks or town.

Part of our duty as town-majors was to go out (in our garrison boat) with a flag of truce to the masts of the sunken *Vladamir*, halfway across the harbour, there to meet a Russian boat, and to deliver or receive letters. The Russian officers were very pleasant, gentlemanly men; some spoke French only, others English also. Those I generally met were Captains Scherrimetieff, Frankini, and Ÿevsky.

Both English and French were now busy removing guns, and such-like spoils of war, from the Russian works; blastings and other explosions took place all over the town; the bomb-proofs were being rapidly dismantled, the timber—sufficient to supply fuel to our army for many months—being split up and distributed as firewood among the divisions. The houses also in our part of the town were completely stripped of wood.

On the 18th I dined in camp, and went to the opening of the Fusilier Theatre, where I saw *The Unfinished Gentleman*, and *Grimshaw, Bagshaw, and Bradshaw*; it was a very successful entertainment.

On the 23rd, a soldier (a private in the 77th Regiment) was executed for the murder of a comrade when in hospital The execution took place not far from the old picket-house in front of our brigade, in the presence of detachments of various regiments. Our chaplain had to undergo the painful ordeal of preceding the cortege of prisoner and escort, and we felt much for him in this trying position.

On the 24th a review of the British infantry took place near the Guards' camp; the day was very fine. Six divisions—about 28,000 men—marched past Sir William Codrington; I never saw any body of soldiers looking better; the men were pictures of health, fit for any work. My brother marched past in command of the 20th Regiment.

On the 28th I attended a flag of truce; the Russian officer, in handing me a letter, said that it contained the terms of the armistice; the following day General Windham and the Russian chief of the staff met at Traktir Bridge and arranged the conditions. The same day a melancholy occurrence took place, when a portion of the White Buildings were blown up; Major Ranken, R.E.—who had weathered all the dangers of the siege and distinguished himself on the 8th September—was lighting one of the fuses to a mine, when an immediate explosion took place and he, poor fellow, was buried in the ruins; his death must have been instantaneous; his body was not recovered until the following morning.

On the 2nd of March, it was notified to the army that all firing would cease for the present, pending final arrangements for the establishment of an armistice; the lull and complete cessation from firing seemed very strange.

One of our men (No. 2974, Private Maurice Savage) died in hospital on the 2nd.

The Karabelnaia Guards were gradually reduced, but the Fort Paul picket was still continued.

Although the armistice was not yet officially announced, still it was virtually in force; we could go anywhere within the outposts, and consequently great fraternising took place between the soldiers of both armies, British and Russian, until the issue of some stringent order put a stop to it. I constantly explored the town; the scene of ruin and desolation was now rendered still more dreary by a heavy fall of snow on the night of the 4th. It was certainly a melancholy sight to look upon the once fine buildings and comfortable private residences, now changed into a shapeless heap of ruins, with protruding rafters and tottering walls; scarcely a sound to be heard nor a living creature to be seen; it was like a city of the dead. The weather was very changeable, on the 5th the snow turned into thaw and rain; it also blew very hard, and the Black Sea looked black indeed, and the breakers about Fort Constantine were very heavy.

Duty visits frequently passed between the French commandant of the Malakhoff portion of the Karabelnaia and the town-majors; his name was Captain Fabre of the 30th (French) Regiment; he was a very polite, obliging man.

On the 10th I was out in the harbour with a flag of truce, being the bearer of a letter to General Lüders; I met two Russian officers, who spoke French but not English; it was a beautiful day and I enjoyed my trip on the water. Sometimes I was the bearer of letters for the Russian Chief of the Staff, who rejoiced in the name of Niepolkhoitchitsky;[37] a Russian officer subsequently gave me a very simple way of pronouncing this formidable name, by dividing it into syllables, thus—Nee ep-olk-ho-it-chit-skee. Another day, when out with a flag of truce, I met a Captain Scherrimetieff, who spoke English very well; he asked my name, and said that I could not forget his if I thought of Sherry.

One afternoon I explored the Little Redan with Colonel Turner; this was the work unsuccessfully attacked by the French on the 8th September, 1855, when they suffered terrible losses; the place was covered with caps, coats, knapsacks, &c., the sole remains of that bloody fight. We afterwards continued our walk to Careening Bay, and thence to the three works[38] erected by the Russians in February, 1855, and where the French were repulsed on the 24th of that month.

On the 14th the armistice was signed at Traktir Bridge, and the line of demarcation was extended from the aqueduct to the left bank of the river Tchernaya. Crowds of Russian officers and men might now be seen on our side of the river. This evening my regiment furnished the picket for Fort Paul, under the command of Captain H. This was the last picket posted there.

I rode out with the commandant on the 17th, and explored the French side of Sebastopol. It was a bitterly bleak day and too cold to loiter, so we pushed on until we reached the ancient ruins of Cherson; little save a heap of stones remained to denote the site of this once proud city. The massive wall still stood in several places.

A draft from Malta joined the regiment on the 19th, with Captain R. and Ensigns M. and G.

I took a ride to the Tchernaya on the 22nd. Sentries were posted on the Russian side of the river. A carriage drawn by two shaggy ponies, containing an officer and two ladies, came down to the river side, escorted by a Cossack and some mounted officers; of course there was a general rush to see such a novelty, and had the fair ladies been some strange animals they not have been more stared at. As I returned to the dockyard I passed the place where the Russians retreated after the Battle of Inkermann; a few skeletons and other *débris* remained as the ghastly mementoes of at deadly fight

Colonel Turner and I went to see our races near the Tchernaya on the 24th. About 60,000 English, French, and Sardinians were present,

37. A name frequently mentioned during the Russo-Turkish war.
38. Called by the French "*Les ouvrages blancs.*"

and every kind of costume—naval, military, and civil—was here collected *en masse*. Many Russians came down to the river, but were not allowed to cross. Some French crossed over, and one of our sailors mounted a Cossack's horse and galloped about brandishing the lance. It was a beautiful day, and many ladies were present at the races. Some English and French bands played during the afternoon.

The French had a flag of truce on the 26th, when the Russian officer, in handing a letter, said that it contained the news that peace had been signed. The following day I went out with a flag of truce for the last time. The Russian officer spoke his own language only, so we parted, as we met, in solemn silence.

The news of the signing of peace having been received by telegraph our artillery fired a salute of 101 guns at two p.m. on the 2nd. The sudden termination of the war with the hasty conclusion of peace—brought about by the inability of France to continue the campaign—was regarded with feelings of dissatisfaction by the British army in the Crimea, and also (as we afterwards read) by the people of England. It was universally considered that, notwithstanding the noble though dearly bought achievements of the Allied forces, much more remained to be accomplished before the grasping ambition of Russia could be effectually humbled. While, however, the British troops—in the spring of 1856—were better prepared to take the field than they were in 1854, the French army, on the contrary, crippled by sickness and other causes, was at this time unfitted for the renewal of active operations; and, without the assistance of France, England could not undertake to resume hostilities.

Throughout the winter and spring we had frequent dinner-parties in the dockyard, which, with our pleasant *quartette* on other days, made our life in Sebastopol a very merry and agreeable one. On the 3rd I went to headquarters, and had the coldest ride I ever experienced. It blew hard and snowed in my face all the way (about three miles), and the atmosphere was so thick that I trusted entirely to the guidance of my pony. The camp was now overrun with Russian soldiers, and many officers came into the dockyard.

Now that we were at liberty to go anywhere, I started off on the 10th, with several others, up the Mackenzie Heights, and found the country about there much changed, the wood—through which we struggled on the 23rd September, 1854—being all cut down. Batteries had been thrown up in various directions near Mackenzie's Farm; we followed nearly the same route as that of our march in 1854, going towards the valley of the Belbek. The Russian troops on the "Heights" seemed very comfortable in mud huts.

On the 12th I had a long ride of nearly thirty miles with Colonel Turner; it was a very fine day; we crossed Traktir Bridge, ascended the Mackenzie Heights, and then proceeded some distance along the Bakhtschiserai road, until we looked down upon the valley of the Belbek and the village of Orta-Korales. We now turned off from the road and entered a narrow rocky pass, its precipitous sides being full of caves; here we passed the ruins of a small village, and a few grim-looking Cossacks eyed us as we went by, while some Russian dogs barked at our horses' heels, evidently regarding us as intruders; we at length came upon beautiful grass, covered with hyacinths and primroses, and also a spring to refresh our thirsty nags. As the day was getting on we retraced our steps, returning through a Russian camp, and, after continuing a winding route through ravines and gullies, we reached the Tchernaya, which we crossed at Inkermann over a bridge just erected by our engineers; the harbour was very calm and covered with wild ducks.

The following day I visited all the forts and batteries on the north side; the Russians were very civil and obliging; the casemate barracks in Fort Constantine seemed very comfortable, and both they and the various batteries were kept in beautiful order; the north side seemed covered with heavily armed works. As I stood on the parapet of Fort Constantine an English steamer passed in and entered dockyard Greek.

On the 15th a Russian officer, Captain Nicholas Ÿevsky, breakfasted with us, and afterwards accompanied Colonel Turner and myself to the French races near St. George's Monastery, and at which General Lüders and staff were present; here I met my friend Captain Scherrimetieff. The course presented a singular scene, being covered with a mixed assemblage of the allied troops with many Russians and Cossacks.

On the 17th there was a grand review of the French and English armies before General Lüders, the Russian commander-in-chief. General Lüders, accompanied by a large staff, crossed the Tchernya, early in the morning, at Traktir Bridge. At this time a company of the Connaught Rangers was on guard at the bridge, under the command of Lieutenant Woodard, who had the honour of being the first to receive the Russian general and to offer hospitality to him and his staff. The general rested in the officers' guard-tent for nearly two hours, before continuing his ride to the British headquarters.

At ten a.m. the French army was formed up in columns at *large intervals* (apparently to make their force look very numerous), extending from the Col de Balaklava to Kamiesch, a distance of five miles, and numbered about 80,000 men. A cloud of dust in the distance showed us that the generals had commenced the inspection; the brilliant cortege soon passed along, consisting of the three Allied generals and General Lüders, followed by their respective staffs, &c. The army took nearly three hours to march past, and almost smothered the generals in clouds of dust.

The generals and staffs afterwards lunched at the British headquarters; a squadron of the 8th Hussars formed two lines, between which the generals approached the house, where they were received by the generals of divisions and admirals; there was a great deal of bowing and elevating of cocked hats, and they all looked very dusty and, I concluded, thirsty also. In an adjoining hut there was lunch for humbler beings like myself, where I assisted in doing the honours to the Russian officers.

In the afternoon the British army—about 38,000 strong—was reviewed; soon after lunch the generals left headquarters, where the Highlanders formed a guard of honour in two lines facing inwards. Our different divisions marched past—the Light Division and Rifle Brigade with "trailed arms"—preceded by the artillery and engineers; the artillery horses looked in capital condition. All the men looked remarkably well and fit for any work; each brigade was preceded by the united bands of its different regiments; our brigade mustered one hundred performers and marched past to a well-known Irish air called "Katty Mooney." The review was not over until nearly seven p.m.

H.M. ships *Stromboli* (guardship) and *Gladiator* were now in the harbour. I crossed over to the north side on the 19th, and landed at Battery No. 24, where I met Captains Frankini and Yevsky, and delivered a letter from headquarters. The same day we lent our boat to Colonel D. (of the Guards) and his wife. Mrs. D. was the first lady I had spoken to for more than two years.

CHAPTER 9

April 21st to July 31st

Having obtained ten days' leave, I started on a tour round the south of the Crimea, in company with Lieutenant-Colonel B., Captain H., and Lieutenant T. B. (of the 88th) and F. H. (of the Militia). We left camp about ten a.m., taking with us a cart laden with our tents, besides sundry eatables and drinkables, and also accompanied by our servants, with one or two baggage- ponies to carry forage, &c.

We crossed the Tchernaya at Inkermann, where we were detained some time by the Russian guard, but at last proceeded. Passing through several Russian camps, we crossed the Belbeck at the same place as we did in September, 1854. We found the country much changed since then, being denuded of its trees. The day, which had been cold and threatening, here cleared up. About three p.m. we halted and lunched in an orchard, until a Russian clodhopper (his name must have been Warnusoff) warned us off, so we proceeded.

Passing along the woody valley of the Belbek, we reached the village of Duvankoi. The fair portion of the inhabitants presented a very ghost-like appearance in their long, white robes, and fled at our approach; but human nature is alike all the world over, and many black eyes could be seen peeping round corners. Our road afterwards lay through grassy fields and extensive orchards commencing to blossom, till we turned towards Bakhtschiserai, and wended our way along an uninteresting *steppe* country. About six p.m. we pitched our tents alongside a rippling stream, about four miles from Bakhtschiserai. We then set to work to cut fuel, made a fire, and, with the help of our three servants, cooked the dinner, after which we sat round the campfire, chatting and smoking, and turned in to our tents about nine p.m. We were up at daylight the next morning, and, with everything packed, started about seven.

We soon reached the town of Bakhtschiserai, a dirty Eastern-like place, prettily situated in a narrow valley; its ill-paved, muddy streets reminded us of Stamboul. A large building, once the palace of the *khans*, had been converted into a Russian hospital, and was now filled with wounded and sick. Riding through the town, we entered a narrow, rocky gorge leading to the village of Tchufut-Kaleh, inhabited by Koraite Jews. On each side of this narrow pass the rocks rose perpendicularly to an immense height, overhanging a Tartar village. Further on we came to the Monastery of the Assumption, situated about 200 feet above our heads, in chambers excavated in the solid rock. Dismounting, we ascended through galleries and up steps, cut out of the rock, till we reached the chapel. Service was going on, the congregation consisting of bearded monks, and white-capped nuns, rather *embonpoint*. We passed among them on tiptoe, our warlike costume, and our swords, forming a striking contrast to the peaceful scene around us.

Leaving this scene, we proceeded to the village of Tchufut-Kaleh, a small place situated above the valley, and inhabited by numerous Rabbi and snarling dogs. When descending the hill we were greeted by some Tartar music of tambourine and fiddle, to the tune of "I don't know what" As we returned through the Tartar village the children ran after us, offering bunches of violets. One very pretty little girl, about five years old, ran after my pony and gave me some flowers: with her long plaited black hair, hanging over her shoulders, and her picturesque dress, she looked a fit subject for a painter.

Leaving Bakhtschiserai, we had a long and monotonous ride towards Simpheropol, over flat *steppe* land, not a tree to be seen. *En route* we crossed the Katcha and Alma Rivers, whose woody banks and clear streams appeared like an oasis in the desert. While discussing bread and cheese in a shady spot on the banks of the Alma, a Russian infantry regiment passed us, on their way to Moscow, headed by a band making a noise very like penny trumpets, while the men sang. We did not again see any more Russian troops, with the exception of a few Cossacks at occasional guardhouses.

A few miles from Simpheropol we found a suitable spot, with plenty of wood and water, near a Russian generals house, where we at once commenced cutting wood, picketing our nags, and preparing dinner. The next morning we obtained bread and eggs from the farm adjoining the house. On the 24th we entered Simpheropol, a good-sized town, with ill-paved streets but well-built houses; these latter were now occupied chiefly by sick and wounded, while the dirty streets were filled with dirtier soldiers and stragglers. We made a few purchases at the bazaar, and about two p m. we continued our travels towards Aloushta. Following the course of the Salghir River, along which our road lay for about ten miles, we reached the small Tartar village of Mahmoud-Sultan, near which, on the banks of the river, we pitched our tents; it was a calm, warm evening.

The scenery around was beautiful: green fields and extensive orchards, enclosed by a range of lofty mountains, with birds singing and frogs croaking to complete the peaceful scene. The male portion of the village came to our camp, kissed our hands in token of welcome, and brought us eggs, milk, hay, wood, &c., until we had too much, and were forced to stop supplies. Throughout our trip the Tartars and Russians seemed glad to see us, and appeared an honest set. The former were very fine men, and the women seemed handsome, though they gave us but little opportunity of judging, for, like the Turkish women, they wore the *yashmâk* (veil).

This day was the commencement of fine, clear, hot weather, which continued throughout our tour. We left Mahmoud-Sultan early on the 25th. Before sunrise that day some of us had the courage to try a douche-bath under a cascade in a mountain stream. The water was *icy cold,* and had a fall of about twelve feet I leave my readers to imagine the *shocking* sensation of a first plunge. The scenery now became more magnificent day by day. Our road to Aloushta followed the direction of the Salghir River, which we frequently forded, and whose woody banks and clear stream wound along the valley.

Passing by orchards, cultivated fields, and Tartar villages, we struck into a beautiful valley. Above us were mountains, wooded to their summits: below us the Salghir, here a rapid torrent. On our right rose the Tchadir-Dagh. Or Trent Mountain—upwards of 4000 feet above the level of the sea—still capped with snow. The banks of the various streams which rushed down the mountains, forming waterfalls and cascades, were frequently quite golden with primroses; and as we rode along the air was perfumed with the scent of violets, which grew here in great abundance. Proceeding up a steep winding road we reached the highest point, about twelve miles from Aloushta, whence we looked down upon the sea; from this the road wound down the mountain side for ten miles. We fell in here with a fine-looking Cossack, who gave us to understand that he was a *Kasack Donsky*—i.e., Cossack of the Don. Here commenced the land of vineyards and snug little houses surrounded by gardens, but as the trees were not in leaf we lost much of the beauty of the scenery. We reached Aloushta—situated on the Black Sea—about seven p.m.; it consisted of a few houses only, and was said to be the resort of Russian fashionables in summer time We encamped outside the village on the bank of a river, and under an immense walnut-tree. The scenery around was magnificent; about two miles from the sea the mountains—with Tchadir-Dagh out-topping them all—rose up abruptly; from their base to the sea the ground sloped gradually down, intersected by ravines, with rapid streams occasionally broken into cascades.

At seven a.m. on the 26th we started for Yalta. The country along the coast abounded in trees, and was dotted here and there with private houses, gardens and lawns well kept, besides many Tartar villages with their flat-roofed houses. The day was exceedingly warm. We met several parties on the road, sightseers like ourselves. About six p.m. we reached Yalta, after a hot ride of nearly thirty miles. The town was beautifully situated in a woody valley facing the sea; behind it rose lofty, wooded mountains; in the neighbourhood were several comfortable-looking private residences, surrounded by nicely laid out gardens and vineyards. The town itself was small, English in style, with a pretty little Greek church.

It was, we were told, the fashionable resort of the Russians in summer. Here we met our surgeon with Lieutenant-Colonel H. (4th Regiment) and Major L. (28th Regiment), who joined our party for the remainder of the trip. We put up at the hotel, kept by an Englishwoman, married to a Frenchman; she came from Hampshire, and had lived fifteen years at Yalta. She made us take our tea *à la Russe*, in tumblers without milk and a slice of lemon in it. Here too I saw, for the first time, a Russian urn, called *samovar*, heated with charcoal. Next morning we started for Aloupka. On our way we passed the Palace of Orianda,[1] a very handsome-looking building in well laid-out grounds, with orange-groves and hot-houses. As it was Sunday the servants were away, and. unfortunately, we could not see the interior of the palace; the head-gardener, a German, informed us that even if we did find the servants they would most probably be *drunk*. We peeped through the windows, and the house seemed handsomely fitted up.

Continuing our travels through this land of mountains, vineyards, gardens, and luxuriant green fields sloping down to the sea, we reached Aloupka about four p.m., and there entered the courtyard of Prince

1. A favourite resort of the Russian Royal Family.

Woronzoff's palace, a large castellated building of granite, situate in extensive grounds overhanging the sea, which was now beautifully calm. This palace was fitted up with everything English, and built by an Englishman named Hunt. It was furnished in the old English style, oak furniture and floors; in the billiard-room was an English piano. The view from the upper rooms was very magnificent.

We encamped about six p.m. on a smooth grass plot near the village, which consisted of a few houses and an inn, where we met a Russian officer. At eight on the morning of the 28th we started towards home, and, after proceeding about four miles, found that the road had been carried away by a landslip, so we had to drag our cart up the steep hill on one side and lower it down into the road beyond. As the ground was very rough and precipitous, as well as marshy, this operation delayed us several hours; so we halted and pitched our tents at a place called Michailatka, near a deserted *château*, once a nice house, but completely emptied by *marauders*. The scenery here changed from wood and cultivated land to bold lofty rocks, evidently the remains of volcanic eruptions; on one side the mountains rising in perpendicular cliffs to a height of some hundreds of feet; below us heaps of enormous boulders of rock sloping towards the sea, close upon which were a few houses and other signs of life, though this wild part of the country seemed but little inhabited.

On the 29th at eight a.m. off we went; the mists of morning, having cleared away from the rocky mountains above us, still left the clouds below us, which obscured the sea and presented the appearance of an expanse of snow; whenever there was a small opening in the clouds—disclosing the sea and ships far below us—it had a very striking effect. After ascending a winding road of about six miles we reached the Phoros Pass, across which a gateway had been built. Here the scenery was very singular; on one side the gateway you looked down upon the sea from an immense height, the rocks perpendicular at your feet, and then sloping in enormous blocks to the water; on the other side (looking inland) the scene changed to the green and wooded vale of Baidar, through which we now wended our way and encamped near the village of Vernutka, fifteen miles from camp.

On the 30th we reached camp at eleven a.m., after a most delightful trip of nine days.[2] Upon my return I was very sorry to find that our commandant (Colonel Turner) was very ill. He was laid up for some time, and I used to sit with him every day.

---

2. One of our men, No. 4791, Private Michael Moran, died in hospital on the 23rd.

Active preparations were now being made for the embarkation of the British army to various destinations, and many regiments left the Crimea at this time. The French embarked troops on their side the town.

On the 2nd a particularly agreeable Russian officer dined with us; he was on the staff of General Lüders, and his name was Captain Alexander Mouravieff, nephew of the general (of the same name) who captured Kars. Captain M. spoke English fluently and without any foreign accent; he frankly discussed the war with us, and surprised us by singing an English comic song.

One of my brother town-majors, Major C. (62nd Regiment), embarked with his regiment on the 7th for Nova Scotia, and we were very sorry indeed to lose him. The harbour was now full of French and English merchant vessels, removing guns, stores, &c.; and a small Russian steamer was plying between Sebastopol and Odessa.

Everyone was busy parting with horses and ponies, which were generally sold at a great sacrifice.

The country about us began to look very green at this time, and grass was springing up in the trenches. One of the signs of peace was the fact of two swallows building a nest over the inside of our hall-door, near an old shot-hole, where they hatched several little ones; such chattering went on as they flew in and out during the day, when the door was always open! At night they were shut in, but were always up and flying about the hall at daylight, ready to be let out.

One day I adorned my table with some lilac, picked in the town, placing it in a pickle-bottle, which did duty for a vase. The camp and town were now constantly visited by Russians, and some fair Muscovites ventured across and drove about in their *drosky*. General Lüders having gone to Odessa, General Outschakoff commanded on the north side at this time.

On the 10th I went to see the Light Division reviewed by Sir William Codrington in the Balaklava Plain. The division looked remarkably well, and the regiments were very strong—the 88th mustered 700. The following day the 2nd Division was reviewed, but the weather, unfortunately, was very wet

As the Karabelnaia was nearly emptied of all its valuables (?), the duties of the town-majors were very light The divers commenced working at some of the sunken vessels in Dockyard Creek, and fished up rudders, &c. It was lamentable to observe the way in which John Bull seemed to be wasting money in the employment of civil labour

215

in the Crimea at this time; the fine sturdy fellows of the Army Works Corps might now be seen expending a vast amount of time and very little labour in repairing roads in the Karabelnaia; while the divers were equally diligent in fishing up rudders and similar useless things.

The Sardinian army had now nearly left, and our transports were arriving every day; the French troops had also come in from the outposts in and about Baidar, and were assembled near Kamiesch, ready for embarkation. One afternoon I went up the harbour in a boat, and landed at a place called Golandia, where there was a very nice house, once the residence of Admiral Nachimoff—killed, I believe, during the siege—and also a very good garden, where I gathered some flowers. Here I met a Russian officer who had been in the Redan during the greater part of the siege, and also when the last assault was made; he told me that out of twenty-four officers employed in the Redan, only he and another had escaped death or wounds; he was in the Marine Artillery.

Cricket and embarkations were now the order of the day. A cricket match was played between the staff and the army, in which the former were thoroughly beaten. The harbour at this time used to be full of boats sailing about, and an English schooner yacht anchored in Dockyard Creek on the 18th. In one of my rambles near the Malakhoff and Little Redan, I found a lark's nest, with eggs in it, curiously situated between two splinters of shell—a striking emblem of Peace and War. On the 24th, being the queen's birthday, there was a grand review of the whole army, but, thirteen regiments having left, it looked much reduced in numbers. On this occasion the French military war medals were distributed to each regiment: my regiment received ten medals.[3]

On the 28th the Light Division, under the command of Lord William Paulet, was reviewed in Balaklava Plain before General Wrangel, a Russian officer, I missed the best part, as my pony broke loose while I was dismounted and lying on the grass, but Lord W. P. very kindly sent off one of his orderlies (an 11th Hussar man), who had to ride to our camp before he could catch the little pony. I afterwards rode to Tchorgoum with Colonel B. (of my regiment), passing through deserted camps and scenes of many an outpost skirmish. It was a beautiful summers evening, and the grass around was quite brilliant with the hues of various wild flowers, while innumerable birds were singing merrily. We returned across the field of the hard-fought battle of the

3. *Vide* French War Medal, Appendix B.

Tchernaya (August 16th, 1855), where nothing but mounds, over the many slain, remained to mark the site of that bloody fight. Regiments continued to leave every week, and we were all anxiously awaiting the order for the Rangers to embark for Old England. One day when at headquarters a parcel from Odessa was handed to me; I was fairly puzzled, but found, upon opening it, that it came from Captain Mouravieff, who had sent me a Russian order of St. Ann (miniature), and a wooden and gilt cup made at Nijni-Novgorod, as souvenirs of a short but very pleasant acquaintance; together with a letter, written in excellent English, thanking the town-majors for their kindness to him.

During the month of May two of our men died in camp.[4]

On the 30th I took a long ride with Colonel Turner to Mangoup-Kaleh and the entrance to the Korales-Pass; it was an exceedingly warm day, but the luxuriant trees rendered the roads very shady. We passed through Tchouliou, Una, and several other Tartar villages, and, after discussing our lunch under Mangoup-Kaleh, returned in the cool of the evening. This was my last ride in the Crimea, and we went between twenty and thirty miles. Colonel T. was a most agreeable companion, and I had enjoyed many pleasant rides and walks with him.[5]

Lord Gough having arrived on the 4th, I went to see him confer the Orders of the Bath upon Pelissier, the French commander-in-chief, and some others.

All our troops were drawn up near the British headquarters; the bands of the different regiments played together, and the effect was very imposing when Lord Gough—in his uniform as Colonel of the Horse Guards—stood upon the rising ground, behind headquarters, helmet in hand, while the united bands played "St. Patrick's Day in the Morning." When the decoration was conferred upon Pelissier. he returned thanks in a complimentary, speech, addressing his lordship as "*Le conquérant du Punjab.*"

On the 7th we (town-majors) had a large dinner-party, and Colonel B., of my regiment, dined with us. Shortly after he returned to camp I had a short note from him, saying that the regiment was to embark the next morning in the sailing-frigate, *Belleisle*.

Early the following morning I left the dockyard and rejoined my

---

4. May 16th, No. 3487, Private Thade Donahoe, and 26th, No. 3668, Phelim Wallace.
5. Colonel Turner afterwards commanded the 97th Regiment, served during the Indian Mutiny, and was made a K.C.S.I. He subsequently commanded a brigade in Bengal, and died a few years ago, (as at time of first publication).

regiment; we were in the act of marching off when our departure was counter-ordered. Everything being packed up we passed a rather uncomfortable day. I dined with the general commanding our division (Lord W. P.), and slept in the hut of Major R. (41st Regiment).

At six a.m. on the 9th, we marched from camp to Kazatch, headed by the bands of different regiments. Just before we started I paid a last visit to the graves of our poor officers who had fallen during the siege. and gathered some of the wild flowers growing there, as a memento. My brother accompanied me to Kazatch, where I very reluctantly bade *adieu* to my faithful little pony, my constant companion during the campaign.

The day was very cool and we embarked about ten a.m.; a baggage-guard had preceded us, and a serious accident occurred on board just before the regiment reached the ship; through some carelessness on the part of one of the sailors in neglecting to check the capstan, it swung round, and the bars flew out in all directions; one of our men (Private John Burke, servant to Captain D.) was killed, and several injured, and Lieutenant-Colonel M. was severely cut in the face.

In the afternoon H.M.S. *Firebrand* towed us out of harbour, but the wind being fair we soon cast her off, and sailed away, the memorable Crimea rapidly fading from our view. During our voyage I shared a very comfortable cabin with our Surgeon (D.)

The following morning it blew fresh; the *Firebrand* kept with us all day, but we at last passed her, and she was out of sight by sunset On the 11th it still blew hard, accompanied by rain and fog; we made land in the morning, but could not find the entrance to the Bosphorus, so we cruised about off shore; there was plenty of motion, which considerably thinned our numbers at meals; no signs of the *Firebrand* today.

We entered the Bosphorus about daylight on the 12th; one of the men fell overboard, but was soon picked up. It was a lovely morning and on we went merrily, with a fair wind, until, opposite Buyukdere, *i.e.* most unfortunately ran upon a shoal and were soon hard and fast. Tug-steamers were sent from Constantinople to pull at us, but all to no purpose; the admiral came on board and also General (afterwards Sir Henry) Storks.

The next day we still remained fast aground, and it was very tantalising—when in this fix—to be passed by many regiments, of which we had several days' start. Various nautical appliances were resorted to in vain; at length, by the combined efforts of several steamers (after some of our cargo had been shifted into another vessel), the *Belleisle* was got off at mid-day amid loud cheers; we were then towed to Scutari, where we anchored off the barracks about six p.m.

The following day several of us landed at Scutari, and visited the tomb of our poor adjutant (Maule) in the cemetery; we afterwards crossed to Stamboul, and made sundry purchases in the bazaar. We sailed at five p.m. accompanied by the *Firebrand*. The weather low was very calm and warm, with bright moonlight nights.

On the morning of the 15th the *Firebrand* took us in tow, and, passing through the Dardanelles, we were off Tenedos in the evening.

On the 16th we went through the Doro passage between the islands of Negropont and Andros, and the strait between Zea and Makronisi.

Early on the morning of the 17th, off Cerigo, we were roused up by the cry of "a man overboard;" it proved to be one of our men (Kelly, No. 3 Company); he was picked up by one of the ship's cutters.[6]

At midnight on the 19th we made the light of St Elmo (Malta), and reached Malta about six the following morning, where we anchored off the naval hospital. Two of our officers (C. and B.) came on board; a few of us landed at Valetta for a short time, and we left Malta at nine p.m., with a fair wind, being towed by the *Firebrand*. Our progress was not very rapid, and we did not pass the island of Pantellaria until the evening of the 21st. We now began to lose our fair wind and fine weather, the sea also being rather rough; and on the 22nd the *Firebrand* cast us about, and did not make more headway than fifteen miles a day.

The following day saw us knocking about off Cape Bon, with a strong wind and rough sea. which was very trying to some of us landsmen. We did not see anything of the *Firebrand* until the 24th, when, after beating about off Tunis and Carthage for some hours, we saw her at anchor ahead of us. We anchored near her, about noon, to the west of the Gulf of Tunis, off a place called Porta Farina. As it still continued to blow hard the following day, we remained snugly at anchor. Some of us landed, and visited the miserable town of Farina, inhabited by Moors and Arabs. We were introduced to the commandant of the garrison, which consisted of 100 Tunisian soldiers.

The country seemed well cultivated in some places, and abounded in fruit-trees, palms, and the usual tropical vegetation. We found it very hot ashore, and had a fatiguing walk to our boats through deep

---

6. The fright, occasioned by being nearly drowned, seemed to have affected the man's mind, and, upon arrival at Portsmouth, he could not be induced to leave the ship, and had to be removed by force.

sand.

We weighed anchor at four a.m. on the 26th, and continued our voyage. The weather was now very warm and calm—too much so for sailing—and we did not make very much progress. We sighted the African coast, near Algiers, on the 29th, and reached Gibraltar on the 1st July. Some of us landed and explored the place. We left Gibraltar at five a.m. on the 3rd, with a strong head wind, towed by the *Firebrand*. Some of us dined today with our commander (Captain Hosken). We were off Cape St Vincent on the afternoon of the 5th, a strong breeze still blowing dead against us.

We passed many sailing vessels and steamers every day. The *Firebrand* having left us, we were beating about off Cape Espichell during the morning of the 7th; it blew a gale in the afternoon, which carried away our main and foretopsails, and split the driver. The same day we spoke H.M.S. *Brunswick*, with the 95th on board. The following morning we ran into Cascaes Bay, at the mouth of the Tagus. and anchored there. The *Brunswick* lay close to us, and I was much surprised at a visit from my brother, who, it appeared, was on board that ship, in command of a wing of the 20th Regiment. We landed at the clean but desolate-looking village of Cascaes, where I could not get any supplies for our mess.

The following day I sailed up the Tagus to Lisbon in one of our ship's cutters, but unfortunately could not land, because the cholera was raging there. I lunched on board the *Firebrand*, off Lisbon, and she brought us back to the *Belleisle*. The same evening we left the Bay, towed by the *Firebrand*. The wind still continued very strong, and, as the *Firebrand* went away altogether on the 12th, rather unexpectedly, we were now left to our own resources. The wind fell light, but there was still plenty of motion. We spoke H.M.S. *Majestic*, on the 13th, with the 18th Regiment on board. With a light but fair wind we now sailed away, all anxiety for the first glimpse of the shores of Old England. We spoke H.M.S. *Geyser* on the 17th, which signalled to us, "Prince (meaning Duke) of Cambridge, head of army"—the first intimation we had that the duke had succeeded Lord Hardinge in the command of the army.

We sighted the Isle of Wight about five p.m. on the 18th—the first view of our native shores—and anchored at Spithead at seven p.m.; it was a lovely evening, and several yachts escorted us, but the fast-sailing old *Belleisle* seemed to pass them all, covered as she was with a crowd of canvas. Captain the Hon. J. Spencer of the *Firebrand* came on board, and told us that their sudden departure on the 12th had been caused by an outbreak of cholera, which had carried off Captain Temple, who commanded some Royal Artillery on board the *Firebrand*; he also brought the news that some of us had been awarded the Legion of Honour. The following day I landed at Portsmouth with E. H, M., and put up at the George Hotel. Oh! the luxury of once more sleeping in a comfortable bed! a privilege I had not enjoyed for more than two years.

The regiment landed, in steamers, at the Portsmouth Dockyard at five a.m. on the 21st, and thence, amid the vociferous cheers of a few street urchins, proceeded by rail to Aldershot, where we took up our quarters in the south camp.

So numerous had been the changes in all ranks during the recent campaign, that we were almost a new regiment;[7] out of the thirty-four officers who had embarked at Liverpool in April, 1854, there were only four who now returned with the regiment, without having been absent from their duties throughout the campaign—*viz.*, Brevet Lieutenant-Colonel E. H. Maxwell, Captain Gore, Assistant-Surgeon Williams, and myself.

On the 30th the queen reviewed the troops in camp, on which occasion we marched past Her Majesty to the number of 2141, exclusive of officers, our ranks having been augmented by the addition of the *depôts* from Malta and at home.[8] On this occasion the queen appeared on horseback, dressed in the scarlet tunic and sash of a field-marshal, with a scarlet and white feather in a black wide-awake, and the corresponding horse-trappings. In this most becoming costume Her Majesty looked a queen indeed.

The following day the queen (in morning dress) came to inspect the medal-men of the regiment, who were drawn up to receive her—officers in front. Her Majesty, accompanied by the Prince Consort, walked down the line, speaking and bowing graciously to those offic-

7. *Vide* Appendix C.
8. Our strength was as follows:—

	Sergeants.	Band and Drummers.	Corporals.	Privates.
Service Cos. from Crimea	50	21	50	950
Depot from Malta	25	10	25	475
Depot at home	25	10	25	475
	100	41	100	1900

Grand Total   2141

ers and men, who were specially brought to her notice by our Colonel (G.V. Maxwell) as having throughout the campaign.

Several officers, non-commissioned officers, and privates of the regiment were awarded various decorations and medals, and eight officers received promotion by brevet for their services in the field during the Crimean Campaign.[9]

More than twenty years have now elapsed, (as at time of first publication), since the occurrence of the memorable events narrated in the preceding pages, and the political aspect of European affairs has, meanwhile undergone considerable change.

The irrepressible "Eastern Question" has again come to the surface; Russia—grown restless—has partly torn up the Treaty of 1856; vanquished Turkey lies prostrate under the foot of her old and ruthless enemy; Germany, and Austria—armed to the teeth—remain aloof, though not unconcerned; while Great Britain stands on her guard, fully determined to protect, if necessary, the interests of her vast empire against the encroachments of Russia's insatiable ambition.

The solution of this so-called "Eastern Question" is one of vital importance to our nation, and it therefore behoves us to be watchful, and ready for every contingency; thus prepared—strong in great resources and in the patriotic support of a united people—Great Britain can, come what may, calmly and confidently await the future.

---

9. *Vide* Appendix B.

Appendix A

Nominal List of Casualties at the Battles of Alma and Inkermann, Attack on the " Quarries," and Final Assault on the Redan.

Battle of Alma, 20th September, 1854.

KILLED.

P^{te} James Kernan.	P^{te.} Maurice Scanlon.
Patrick Lyons.	Edward Duffy.

WOUNDED.

Quar.-Master Moore.	P^{te} Maurice Tangney.
Col.-Serg. George McNally.	Patrick Farrell.
Serg. James Fallon.	Patrick Scheal.
P^{te.} Michael Grealy.	John Gallagher.
Daniel Gwynn.	Martin Day.
Peter McNab.	Alexander McClernan.
Peter Burke.	Constantine Smith.*
John Higgins.	Patrick Fegarty.
Thomas Shearman.	MISSING.
Thomas Killilea.	Hugh Cameron.

Battle of Inkermann, 5th November, 1854.

KILLED.

Serg.-Major R. O'Donnell.	P^{te} William Casey.
Serg. R. Clements.	George Connell.
Timothy Leary.	Patrick Connelly.
William Smith.	Thomas Murray.
Corp. William Segrave.	John Malone.
P^{te.} John Ferguson.	Daniel Bresnahan.
William Cassidy.	Martin Hartley.
Thomas Lowry.	John McMahon.
Patrick Walsh.	Patrick Connecan.

---

* Died of wounds.

P^{te.} Michael Connaughtin.
William Lewis.
Martin Faherty.
Thomas Joyce.
Matthew Keane.
Joseph Lyle.

P^{te.} Walter Nuttall.
John Nowlan.
Patrick O'Shaughnessy.
Coleman Nee.
Thomas O'Brien.

WOUNDED.

B^{t.}-Lt.-Colonel Jeffreys, slightly.
Captain Crosse, severely.
Lieut. Baynes   „
Cl.-Serg. Pat. Glyn, dangerously.*
        J. J. Holmes, severely.
Serg. Thomas Madden   „
        John Connors, slightly.
        Daniel Foley   „
        Patrick Moore   „
        James Carroll, severely.
        A. O'Flynn, slightly.
        M. Slattery   „
        F. Byrne   „
Corp. Michael Cregg „
        Thomas Conroy, severely.
        A. Gannon, slightly.*
        Patrick Lyons, severely.
        James O'Rourke, slightly.
        Michael Keegan,   „
        Thomas Kelly, severely.*
L.-Corp. S. Cunningham, slightly.
        Thomas Sullivan   „
Drum. Richard Grannon   „
P^{te.} Francis Bowles, slightly.
        Michael O'Neill, lost a leg.
        John Cohig, lost an arm.
        Thomas Fitzgerald, severely.
        Thomas Fitzgerald   „
        Charles Hogan   „
        Thomas Dillon, lost an arm.
        David Condon   „
        Patrick Cummins   „

P^{te.} John Fallon,   severely.
        John Mulholland   „
        Patrick Brennahan „
        Michael Flannagan „
        Patrick McCay, slightly.
        James Walsh, severely.
        Daniel McGregor*   „
        Michl. Holland, dangerously.
        John Dawson,   severely.
        Michael Spellman   „
        Thomas Finnecan   „
        Robert Neill, slightly.
        James Shea, dangerously.*
        James Hickey*   „
        John Enright, slightly.
        James Hannon,   severely.
        John Moore (2955)   „
        Dennis O'Brien   „
        Edward Lacey   „
        Dennis Kenny, dangerously.*
        Philip Spencer, severely.
        Michael O'Connor „
        Anthony Dolan   „
        John Gilbride   „
        John Lappin   „
        John Egan,   slightly.
        Gregory Connelly „
        Thomas Conroy   „
        Thomas Ferris,   severely.
        John Moore (3102) „
        James Burke,   slightly.
        Patrick Lynch   „

* These men died of their wounds.

224

P^{te.} William Mills, slightly.	P^{te.} James Lodge, slightly.
Martin Caggins ,,	Roger Sullivan ,,
Patrick Stock ,,	Thomas Tierney* ,,
Thomas Keating ,,	William Hackett ,,
Patrick McGuire ,,	John Brown* ,,
Michael Cox ,,	William Hamilton ,,
James German ,,	Connor Hogan ,,
Michael Connors ,,	James Weir ,,
Patrick Gallagher * ,,	John Daley ,,
Martin Noone ,,	John Mullen ,,
William Brett ,,	Patrick Sullivan ,,
James Bernard ,,	Edmund Price ,,
Patrick Joyce ,,	James Hayes ,,

The undermentioned men were returned among the killed, but it was found afterwards that they had been taken prisoners :—

P^{te.} William Nan.	P^{te.} J. Cavanagh.
John Looney.	John Mair.
Martin Petty.	

Attack on the " Quarries," 7th June, 1855.

KILLED.

Captain Corbett.	P^{te.} Thomas Kelly.
Wray.	Francis Cassidy.
Lieut. Webb.	Thomas Brereton.
Serg. John Haverty.	James Burke.
Corp. Michael Sherlock.	Owen McSorley.
P^{te.} James O'Donnell.	Bernard Hynes. ×
Richard Size.	John Fitzgerald.
Dennis Flemyng.	Anthony Murtagh.
Henry Johnstone.	Michael Whitstone.
Michael Ryan.	Thady Rourke.
Patrick O'Neill.	

WOUNDED.

Major Bayley, mortally.†	Col.-Serg. O'Shaughnessy
Captain Maynard, severely.	severely.
Lieut. Kenny ,,	Patrick Dwyer ,,
Grier, slightly.	Serg. John Savage, mortally.†

* These men died of their wounds. † Died the following morning.

Serg. M. Kelly, severely.
Corp. John Reilly, severely.†
    James Rush, slightly.
    Daniel Purcell, severely.
    Henry Caton.
Drum. Michael McCann, slightly.
P^{te} Patrick McMahon, mortally.*
    William Coyle, slightly.
    Timothy Nolan ,,
    James Maddigan, severely.
    V. McDonough   ,,
    Michael Cook, dangerously.
    Thomas Donlan, severely.
    George Barber, dangerously.
    William Ferguson, severely.
    Owen Sweeney   ,,
    George Monaghan ,,
    Thomas O'Brien, slightly.
    John Burke, severely.
    John Rutter   ,,
    Robert Clinton, dangerously.
    Owen McDonald, severely.
    Patrick Fogarty   ,,
    Martin Cassidy   ,,
    James Bradley   ,,

P^{te} Dennis Conway, severely.
    James Byrne*   ,,
    Michael Gleeson, slightly.
    Michael Gillan, severely.
    James Carson, slightly.
    Henry Connors, severely.
    John McMahon   ,,
    John Eckersley   ,,
    John Lilliman   ,,
    John Nowlan, slightly.
    John Campbell ,,
    Patrick Boyle, dangerously.
    Henry Purcell, severely.
    Timothy Sullivan ,,
    Thomas Keating ,,
    Martin Cunningham, slightly.
    George Graham, dangerously.
    Richard Walsh, slightly.
    Richard Reid, severely.
    John Connors, slightly.
    Patrick Higgins* ,,
    George Walker   ,,
    James Patten   ,,
    William Kelly.
    Thomas O'Neill.

Assault on the Redan, 8th September, 1855.

KILLED.

Capt. Grogan.
Serg. John Flaherty.
    Samuel Price.
Corp. Joseph Cullen.
P^{te} Thomas Fahey.
    Bartholomew O'Brien.
    Michael Myers.
    Edward Price.
    Thomas Conroy.
    Thomas Dunleavy.
    James O'Donnell.

P^{te} John O'Neill.
    Robert Whittaker.
    Patrick Sullivan.
    Thomas Dunne.
    Robert Quinn.
    Edward Ward.
    John Colgan.
    John King.
    John Barrett.
    George Kidd.
    Michael Caffory.

---

* These men died of their wounds.   † Blown up by a fougasse.

Pte. Patrick Filbling.
James McGough.
William Terrant.
Arthur Sealy.
John Griffin.
William Hayes.

Pte. Thomas Moore.
Edward O'Brien.
Henry Wright.
John Bourke.
Bernard McGuinness.

WOUNDED.

Lt.-Col. G. V. Maxwell, severely.
Capt. Mauleverer   „
Beresford   „
Lieut. Lambert   „
Hopton   „
Scott   „
Watson   „
Ens. Walker   „
Serg.-Major Cooney, severely.*
Col.-Serg. Gilmore, mortally.*
Serg. Thos. Prendible, severely.
(3125.)
Hugh Millan, slightly.
Patrick Mahon „
John James, severely.
Thomas Prendible, slightly.
(2848.)
Mich.Wrenn, dangerously.*
Joseph Grennan, severely.
Thomas Kilroy, slightly.
Corp. Patrick Connelly, lost an
arm.*
Patrick Dolan, severely.
James Condon   „
James Herlin   „
John Quill*   „
Daniel Hourigan, danger-
ously.*
Drummer Thomas Carey,
severely.
Martin Nee*   „
Pte. Thomas Kelly   „

Pte. John Nowlan, severely.
John Price   „
Patrick Shannon   „
Patrick Briggey   „
John Kenny   „
Michael Beglan   „
William Mills   „
John Farrell   „
Michael Murnick   „
John Higgins, slightly.
James McNamee, severely.
James McCormick, slightly.
Thomas Rielly   „
Tully Horan   „
John McDermott   „
James Canter, severely.
John Walsh*   „
Richard Rutledge „
Pat. McNamara „
John Nelly   „
Patrick O'Rourke, slightly.
John Kelcher, dangerously.
Henry Hawkins, severely.
Timothy Noon, slightly.
Patrick Gannon, severely.
Thomas Platt   „
James Quinn   „
Edward McAvenna, slightly.
William Brett   „
Michael Dowd, severely.
Patrick Connors   „
Timothy Sullivan   „

* These men died of their wounds.

P^{te.} John Scanlon, slightly.
John Burnside, severely.
George Matthew   ,,
John Coffee, slightly.
John Connolly, severely.
James Maddigan, slightly.
Patrick Graynan   ,,
Edward Jennings, severely.
William Whitehead, slightly.
John Connors, severely.*
  (2844.)
Daniel Quinn   ,,
Isaac Hallet, slightly.
Michael Cunniff, severely.
James Carney   ,,
Joseph Kelly, dangerously.
Michael Mulcahey, slightly.
John O'Brien, severely.
William Casey   ,,
Robert Stack   ,,
Michael Lawson   ,,
John Lyons   ,,
Wm. Ashworth*   ,,
John Holden   ,,
James Connell   ,,
John Coogan, slightly.
James Farrell   ,,   (2713.)
James Marmion   ,,
Arthur Neill, dangerously.
John Burke, slightly.
Thomas Reilly   ,,
Lawrence Farley, severely.
Francis Faulkner   ,,
James Patten   ,,
William Quinlan*   ,,
George Smith, slightly. .

P^{te.} William Brown, slightly.
Thos. Sullivan, dangerously.*
Andrew Gunning*   ,,
John Connors, severely.
  (2081).*
Michael Danaher, dangerously.
Edward Reilly, severely.*
George Bryan   ,,
Charles Mabe*   ,,
Richard Handley   ,,
Charles Clarke, slightly.
John Connors, severely.
William Dunmody ,,
Dominick Murray ,,
Henry Purcell   ,,
Thomas Corbett, slightly.
Christopher Doyle, severely.
John Gascoyne, slightly.
John Lee, severely.
George Smith ,,
Patrick Dunn ,,
Michael Rooney, dangerously.*
Thomas Cox, dangerously.
Samuel Geage, severely.
Michael Cummings ,,
Thomas Murphy, slightly.
Jas. McAllister, dangerously.
John Lewis*   ,,
Michael McKeon, severely.
James Cunningham   ,,
Timothy Moran*   ,,
Thomas McLoughlin* ,,
George Walker, slightly.
Patrick Keane, severely.*

* These men died of their wounds.

Appendix B

Names of Officers, &c., made Companions of the Order of the Bath, and awarded the Legion of Honour, Order of the Medjidié, the French and Sardinian War Medals, and Brevet-Promotion for their Services during the Crimean War.

COMPANIONS OF THE ORDER OF THE BATH.

Colonel H. Shirley.
Lieutenant-Colonel E. J. Jeffreys.
Lieutenant-Colonel G. V. Maxwell.

THE LEGION OF HONOUR.

Colonel H. Shirley, 4th Class.
Lieutenent-Colonel G. V. Maxwell, 5th Class.
Brevet-Lieutenant-Colonel E. H. Maxwell, 5th Class.
Brevet-Major N. Steevens   ,,
Captain G. R. Browne   ,,
Captain G. R. Beresford   ,,
Serjeant James Goggins[1]   ,,
Serjeant Joseph Grennan[2]   ,,

THE ORDER OF THE MEDJIDIÉ.

Colonel H. Shirley, 3rd Class.
Lieutenant-Colonel G. V. Maxwell, 4th Class.
Lieutenant-Colonel E. J. Jeffreys, 5th Class.

---

1. Sergeant James Goggins served throughout the campaign, and was conspicuous for his gallantry on several occasions, as well as for the coolness and judgment which he invariably displayed in the discharge of his duties during the siege. He is now (1878) staff-sergeant on the recruiting service in Ireland.
2. Sergeant Joseph Grennan served throughout the campaign, and was specially mentioned by Major Lord Alexander Russell, Rifle Brigade, for his brave conduct at the final assault on the Redan.

Lieutenant-Colonel K J.V. Browne, 5th Class.
Brevet-Lieutenant-Colonel E. H. Maxwell, 5th Class.
Major the Honourable J. J. Bourke   ,,
Brevet-Major J. H. Burke[3]   ,,
Brevet-Major E. G. Maynard, 5th Class.
Brevet-Major N. Steevens   ,,
Captain W. C. Pearson   ,,
Captain H. H. Day[4]   ,,
Lieutenant R.Vernor   ,,
Lieutenant E. A. Perceval   ,,
Assistant-Surgeon W. Harris   ,,
  Quartermaster T. Moore   ,,

THE FRENCH WAR MEDAL[5]

Sergeant-Major Stephen Cunningham:—

Took a very active part in the attack on the "Quarries" on the 7th June, 1855, and was recommended for a medal and 5*l.* on that occasion, but could not obtain it, the regiment having received the allotted number. Was noted at the Horse Guards.

Colour-sergeant Hubert Kelly:—

Very distinguished conduct on the 8th September, 1855, in going out of the advanced trench under a very heavy fire and bringing in the body of Colour-Sergeant Gilmore, who was lying mortally wounded some distance in front.

Colour-Sergeant Maurice Canty:—

Volunteered to form one of the attacking party ordered against "Egerton's Pit" on the 12th April, 1855, as also on several other occasions.

Sergeant John Myers:—

Commanded sharpshooters, and was conspicuous on the 17th October, 1854.

Drummer Richard Grannon:—

Gallant conduct at Inkermann.

---

3. Major Burke served on the staff of General Sir John Burgoyne throughout the campaign.

4. Captain Day was killed in action during the Indian Mutiny, 1857, before the issue of this decoration.

5. The statement of services is taken from a book entitled, *Medals of the British Army and How they were Won.*

Acting-Corporal Henry McKeon:—
Sharpshooter, and showed general gallant conduct in the trenches.

Private Michael Ryan:—
Distinguished himself on the 8th September, 1855, in bringing in his officer, Captain Beresford, who was severely wounded. Present and did duty during the whole campaign.

Private Bernard M'Namara:—
Was a sharpshooter at the beginning of the siege, and recommended for a medal for distinguished service in December, 1854, but did not receive it, as he was invalided to Scutari.

Private Thomas Handley:—
Distinguished himself about the night of the 14th August, 1855, when some young sentries were disposed to retire before a body of Russians, by forcing them back to their posts, and remaining out himself all night close to a Russian rifle-pit

Private Henry Spellacy:—
A sharpshooter; on the 22nd October, 1854, wounded and made a Russian officer prisoner; volunteered on all occasions.

THE SARDINIAN WAR MEDAL.[6]

Colonel Horatio Shirley, C.B.:—
Served the Eastern Campaign of 1854 and 1855; the battle of the Alma; siege of Sebastopol; was General Officer in the trenches at the attacks on the Quarries, 7th June, and on the Redan, 18th June, 1855; and commanded a brigade at the assault on the Redan, September 8th, 1855, when he was slightly wounded.

Lieutenant-Colonel George Vaughan Maxwell, C.B.:—
Served the Eastern Campaign of 1854 and 1855; the Battles of Alma and Inkermann; siege of Sebastopol; commanded the 88th Regiment at the assaults on the Redan, 18th June and 8th September, 1855, and was severely wounded at the last assault

Lieutenant-Colonel Edward John Vesey Brown .—
Served the Eastern Campaign of 1854 and 1855; the Battles of the Alma and Inkermann, and siege of Sebastopol.

Brevet-Major Thomas Gore:—
Served the Eastern Campaign of 1854 and 1855; the Battle of the Alma, and siege of Sebastopol

---

6. The statement of services is (with slight alteration) taken from a book entitled, *Medals of the British Army and How they were Won.*

Brevet-Major Edmund Gilling Maynard:—

For leading the men under his orders into the Russian works, called "the Quarries," in the most gallant manner on the 7th of June, 1855.

Captain John Edward Riley:—

For gallant conduct at Inkermann; he was most active in rallying his men when retreating; also was most active during the action as adjutant He likewise behaved exceedingly well on picket in the middle ravine in the beginning of October, 1854 when the enemy advanced upon him.

Lieutenant George Priestley:—

Was very conspicuous in the attack on the Redan, 8th September, 1855, leading the Grenadier Company in a dashing manner.

Private J. Sullivan:—

Displayed general activity and gallantry during the night of 7th June, 1855, in the attack on the Quarries.

Private W. Dunmody:—

This man, with only one other, answered to the call of Colonel G. V. Maxwell to rally round a gun when the regiment was repulsed at the beginning of the Battle of Inkermann. He served throughout the whole campaign, and was always conspicuous for his soldier-like conduct; he was at last severely wounded in the attavk on the Redan, 8th September, 1855.

OFFICERS WHO WERE AWARDED PROMOTION BY BREVET, FOR DISTINGUISHED CONDUCT IN THE FIELD DURING THE CAMPAIGN.

Major G.V. Maxwell, Bt.-Lt.-Colonel, 12th December, 1854.

Captain E. J.V. Brown, Bt.-Major, 12th December, 1854.

Captain J. H. Burke, Bt.-Major, 12th December, 1854.[7]

Major E. H. Maxwell, Bt-Lt.-Colonel, 2nd November, 1855.

Captain E. G. Maynard, Bt.-Major, 2nd November, 1855.

Captain N. Steevens, Bt.-Major, 2nd November, 1855.

Captain B. B. Mauleverer, Bt.-Major, 6th June, 1856.

Captain T. Gore, Bt.-Major, 6th June, 1856.

---

7. Major Burke served on the staff of General Sir John Burgoyne throughout the campaign.

Appendix C

*Return of the Number of Casualties in the 88th (Connaught Rangers), from their arrival in the East to the 30th April, 1856.**

Officers.

	No.	Names.
Killed in action	4	Captains Corbett, Wray, and Grogan ; Lieut. Webb.
Died of wounds	3	Major Bayley; Lieut. and Adjutant Maule ; and Lieut. Preston.
Died of disease	3	Major Norton; Bt.-Major Mackie ; Asst.-Surgeon Shegog.
Severely wounded	13	Lieut.-Colonel G. V. Maxwell ; Captains Maynard, Mauleverer, G. R. Browne, and Beresford ; Lieutenants Crosse, Baynes, Kenny, Lambert, Hopton, Scott, Watson, and Ensign Walker.
Slightly wounded	6	Colonel Shirley ; Lieut.-Colonel Jeffreys; Captain Steevens ; Lieut. and Adjutant Little; Lieut. Grier ; Quartermaster Moore.

Total casualities   29

Sergeants, Drummers, Rank and File.

	Sergts.	Drummers.	R. & F.	Total.
Killed in action	8	0	106	114
Died of wounds	3	1	41	45
Died of disease	7	0	174	181
Total	18	1	321	340

Sergeants, Drummers, Rank and File.

	Sergts.	Drummers.	R. & F.	Total.
Wounded severely	18	6	218	242
Wounded slightly	5	1	152	158
Invalided (not included in above)	2	1	40	43
Total . . .	25	8	410	443

Disposal of the Wounded and Invalided Men.

	Sergts.	Drummers.	R. & F.	Total.
Discharged	7	4	121	132
Recovered and returned to duty .	9	9	75	93
Remaining in hospital	2	1	27	30
Total . . .	18	14	223	255

Prisoners of War and Missing.

R. & F. Total.

Number who rejoined . . . . 4 }
Number of whom no account has been received . . 7* } 11

Officers, &c. who suffered Amputation.

	No.	Names.
Officers	2	Captain G. R. Browne, right arm. Lieut. and Adjt. Maule, left arm.
Sergeants	4	Serg.-Major, Cooney, a leg. Col.-Sergeant McNally ,, ,, ,, Glyn† ,, Sergeant J. J. Holmes ,,
Drummers	1	Michael McCann ,,
Rank and file	24	
	Total 31	

* Of these men, three turned up afterwards at Scutari—viz., Privates Maurice Shea, Daniel Bresnahan, and William Flower. Of the remaining four, the under-mentioned men absented themselves as follows :—
No. 2142, Pt. John Kelly, sharpshooter ; absent since 18 Oct. 1854.
,, 2106, ,, Michael Kelly; absent since 23 Dec., 1854 ; supposed to have deserted.
,, 2793, ,, Thomas Carroll, deserted off sentry in the trenches, 12 Jan. 1855.
† Sergeant Clyn suffered amputation twice, and died in Scutari Hospital.

Recapitulation of Casualties.

	Officers.	Sergts.	Drummers.	R. & F.	Total.
Killed in action, died of wounds and of disease	10	18	1	321	350
Wounded	19	23	7	370	419
Total . .	29	41	8	691	769

Return of Officers and Men who landed in the East, 1854-5-6.

	Officers.	Sergts.	Band, Drummers, &c.	R. & F.	Total.
Embarked, April, 1854 .	32	39	30	810	911
Reinforced since . . .	27	44	8	964	1043
Total . .	59	83	38	1794	1954

Appendix D

*Non-Commissioned Officers appointed to Commissions in the
Regiment during the Eastern Campaign.*

Sergeant-Major William Little, Ensign 10th August, 1854.*
Qrt.-Master-Sergeant John Frederick Grier, Ensign 5th Nov. 1854.
Colour-Sergeant Patrick Dwyer, Ensign 16th August, 1855.
Paymaster-Sergeant Edward Cape, Ensign 25th October, 1855.
Quart.-Master-Serg. William Evans, Quart.-Master 28th Dec. 1855.

---

* Ensign Little, as before mentioned, succeeded to the adjutancy of the regiment
on 15th November, 1854. After serving with the regiment through the campaign,
he was appointed adjutant of a depôt-battalion, in which he became a major ; he
was eventually promoted to an unattached lieutenant-colonelcy, in April, 1870, and
retired from the service in August, 1873.

LEONAUR

ALSO FROM LEONAUR

AVAILABLE IN SOFTCOVER OR HARDCOVER WITH DUST JACKET

THE RELUCTANT REBEL *by William G. Stevenson*—A young Kentuckian's experiences in the Confederate Infantry & Cavalry during the American Civil War..

BOOTS AND SADDLES *by Elizabeth B. Custer*—The experiences of General Custer's Wife on the Western Plains.

FANNIE BEERS' CIVIL WAR *by Fannie A. Beers*—A Confederate Lady's Experiences of Nursing During the Campaigns & Battles of the American Civil War.

LADY SALE'S AFGHANISTAN *by Florentia Sale*—An Indomitable Victorian Lady's Account of the Retreat from Kabul During the First Afghan War.

THE TWO WARS OF MRS DUBERLY *by Frances Isabella Duberly*—An Intrepid Victorian Lady's Experience of the Crimea and Indian Mutiny.

THE REBELLIOUS DUCHESS *by Paul F. S. Dermoncourt*—The Adventures of the Duchess of Berri and Her Attempt to Overthrow French Monarchy.

LADIES OF WATERLOO *by Charlotte A. Eaton, Magdalene de Lancey & Juana Smith*—The Experiences of Three Women During the Campaign of 1815: Waterloo Days by Charlotte A. Eaton, A Week at Waterloo by Magdalene de Lancey & Juana's Story by Juana Smith.

TWO YEARS BEFORE THE MAST *by Richard Henry Dana. Jr.*—The account of one young man's experiences serving on board a sailing brig—the Penelope—bound for California, between the years1834-36.

A SAILOR OF KING GEORGE *by Frederick Hoffman*—From Midshipman to Captain—Recollections of War at Sea in the Napoleonic Age 1793-1815.

LORDS OF THE SEA *by A. T. Mahan*—Great Captains of the Royal Navy During the Age of Sail.

COGGESHALL'S VOYAGES: VOLUME 1 *by George Coggeshall*—The Recollections of an American Schooner Captain.

COGGESHALL'S VOYAGES: VOLUME 2 *by George Coggeshall*—The Recollections of an American Schooner Captain.

TWILIGHT OF EMPIRE *by Sir Thomas Ussher & Sir George Cockburn*—Two accounts of Napoleon's Journeys in Exile to Elba and St. Helena: Narrative of Events by Sir Thomas Ussher & Napoleon's Last Voyage: Extract of a diary by Sir George Cockburn.

LEONAUR

ALSO FROM LEONAUR
AVAILABLE IN SOFTCOVER OR HARDCOVER WITH DUST JACKET

IRON TIMES WITH THE GUARDS *by An O. E. (G. P. A. Fildes)*—The Experiences of an Officer of the Coldstream Guards on the Western Front During the First World War.

THE GREAT WAR IN THE MIDDLE EAST: 1 *by W. T. Massey*—The Desert Campaigns & How Jerusalem Was Won---two classic accounts in one volume.

THE GREAT WAR IN THE MIDDLE EAST: 2 *by W. T. Massey*—Allenby's Final Triumph.

SMITH-DORRIEN *by Horace Smith-Dorrien*—Isandlwhana to the Great War.

1914 *by Sir John French*—The Early Campaigns of the Great War by the British Commander.

GRENADIER *by E. R. M. Fryer*—The Recollections of an Officer of the Grenadier Guards throughout the Great War on the Western Front.

BATTLE, CAPTURE & ESCAPE *by George Pearson*—The Experiences of a Canadian Light Infantryman During the Great War.

DIGGERS AT WAR *by R. Hugh Knyvett & G. P. Cuttriss*—"Over There" With the Australians by R. Hugh Knyvett and Over the Top With the Third Australian Division by G. P. Cuttriss. Accounts of Australians During the Great War in the Middle East, at Gallipoli and on the Western Front.

HEAVY FIGHTING BEFORE US *by George Brenton Laurie*—The Letters of an Officer of the Royal Irish Rifles on the Western Front During the Great War.

THE CAMELIERS *by Oliver Hogue*—A Classic Account of the Australians of the Imperial Camel Corps During the First World War in the Middle East.

RED DUST *by Donald Black*—A Classic Account of Australian Light Horsemen in Palestine During the First World War.

THE LEAN, BROWN MEN *by Angus Buchanan*—Experiences in East Africa During the Great War with the 25th Royal Fusiliers—the Legion of Frontiersmen.

THE NIGERIAN REGIMENT IN EAST AFRICA *by W. D. Downes*—On Campaign During the Great War 1916-1918.

THE 'DIE-HARDS' IN SIBERIA *by John Ward*—With the Middlesex Regiment Against the Bolsheviks 1918-19.

LEONAUR

ALSO FROM LEONAUR
AVAILABLE IN SOFTCOVER OR HARDCOVER WITH DUST JACKET

WINGED WARFARE *by William A. Bishop*—The Experiences of a Canadian 'Ace' of the R.F.C. During the First World War.

THE STORY OF THE LAFAYETTE ESCADRILLE *by George Thenault*—A famous fighter squadron in the First World War by its commander..

R.F.C.H.Q. *by Maurice Baring*—The command & organisation of the British Air Force during the First World War in Europe.

SIXTY SQUADRON R.A.F. *by A. J. L. Scott*—On the Western Front During the First World War.

THE STRUGGLE IN THE AIR *by Charles C. Turner*—The Air War Over Europe During the First World War.

WITH THE FLYING SQUADRON *by H. Rosher*—Letters of a Pilot of the Royal Naval Air Service During the First World War.

OVER THE WEST FRONT *by "Spin" & "Contact"* —Two Accounts of British Pilots During the First World War in Europe, Short Flights With the Cloud Cavalry by "Spin" and Cavalry of the Clouds by "Contact".

SKYFIGHTERS OF FRANCE *by Henry Farré*—An account of the French War in the Air during the First World War.

THE HIGH ACES *by Laurence la Tourette Driggs*—French, American, British, Italian & Belgian pilots of the First World War 1914-18.

PLANE TALES OF THE SKIES *by Wilfred Theodore Blake*—The experiences of pilots over the Western Front during the Great War.

IN THE CLOUDS ABOVE BAGHDAD *by J. E. Tennant*—Recollections of the R. F. C. in Mesopotamia during the First World War against the Turks.

THE SPIDER WEB *by P. I. X. (Theodore Douglas Hallam)*—Royal Navy Air Service Flying Boat Operations During the First World War by a Flight Commander

EAGLES OVER THE TRENCHES *by James R. McConnell & William B. Perry*—Two First Hand Accounts of the American Escadrille at War in the Air During World War 1-Flying For France: With the American Escadrille at Verdun and Our Pilots in the Air

KNIGHTS OF THE AIR *by Bennett A. Molter*—An American Pilot's View of the Aerial War of the French Squadrons During the First World War.

LEONAUR

ALSO FROM LEONAUR
AVAILABLE IN SOFTCOVER OR HARDCOVER WITH DUST JACKET

THE ART OF WAR *by Antoine Henri Jomini*—Strategy & Tactics From the Age of Horse & Musket

THE MILITARY RELIGIOUS ORDERS OF THE MIDDLE AGES *by F. C. Woodhouse*—The Knights Templar, Hospitaller and Others.

THE BENGAL NATIVE ARMY *by F. G. Cardew*—An Invaluable Reference Resource.

THE 7TH (QUEEN'S OWN) HUSSARS: Volume 4—1688-1914 *by C. R. B. Barrett*—Uniforms, Equipment, Weapons, Traditions, the Services of Notable Officers and Men & the Appendices to All Volumes—Volume 4: 1688-1914.

THE SWORD OF THE CROWN *by Eric W. Sheppard*—A History of the British Army to 1914.

THE 7TH (QUEEN'S OWN) HUSSARS: Volume 3—**1818-1914** *by C. R. B. Barrett*—On Campaign During the Canadian Rebellion, the Indian Mutiny, the Sudan, Matabeleland, Mashonaland and the Boer War Volume 3: 1818-1914.

THE CAMPAIGN OF WATERLOO *by Antoine Henri Jomini*—A Political & Military History from the French perspective.

THE AUXILIA OF THE ROMAN IMPERIAL ARMY *by G. L. Cheeseman.*

CAVALRY IN THE FRANCO-PRUSSIAN WAR *by Jean Jacques Théophile Bonie & Otto August Johannes Kaehler*—Actions of French Cavalry 1870 by Jean Jacques Théophile Bonie and Cavalry at Vionville & Mars-la-Tour by Otto August Johannes Kaehler.

NAPOLEON'S MEN AND METHODS *by Alexander L. Kielland*—The Rise and Fall of the Emperor and His Men Who Fought by His Side.

THE WOMAN IN BATTLE *by Loreta Janeta Velazquez*—Soldier, Spy and Secret Service Agent for the Confederancy During the American Civil War.

THE MILITARY SYSTEM OF THE ROMANS *by Albert Harkness.*

THE BATTLE OF ORISKANY 1777 *by Ellis H. Roberts*—The Conflict for the Mowhawk Valley During the American War of Independenc.

PERSONAL RECOLLECTIONS OF JOAN OF ARC *by Mark Twain.*